The B.B. KING *Companion*

The B.B. KING *Companion*

Five Decades of Commentary

Edited by
RICHARD KOSTELANETZ

Assistant editor
ANSON JOHN POPE

OMNIBUS PRESS
LONDON · NEW YORK · SYDNEY

Printed in the United States of America

Exclusive Distributors
Book Sales Limited,
8/9 Frith Street,
London W1V 5TZ, UK.

To the Music Trade Only:
Music Sales Limited,
8/9 Frith Street,
London W1V 5TZ, UK.

A catalogue record for this book is available from the British Library.

Visit Omnibus Press at http://www.musicsales.co.uk

This paper meets the requirements of ANSI/NISO Z39.48-1992 (Permanence of
Paper).

For Erika Luchterhand

Contents

PART THREE: LUCILLE TALKS BACK

PART FOUR: PAYING THE COST TO BE THE BOSS

Introduction—B.B. King:
The Bach of the Blues

RICHARD KOSTELANETZ

*I don't think there is a better blues guitarist in the world
than B.B. King.*
—ERIC CLAPTON, *in an interview in* Rolling Stone

*To play guitar with B.B. King would be like discussing
religion with Jesus.*
—MARTIN MULL, *interviewed by Tom Snyder (May 27, 1996)*

For over forty years now, B.B. King has been enthroned as the Master
Bluesman. Thanks to good health, sensible living, and the constitution of
a one-time prodigious cotton field hand, he continues to perform hundreds of times a year around the world; thanks to his own perfectionism,
no one has displaced him in his prominent position in the eyes of not only
blues connoisseurs but the larger public.

In the '40s and '50s, King was virtually unknown to the white community. Although he had his first hit record in 1949, and he had toured
continually since 1954, playing an unsurpassed 342 one-night stands in
1956, his audience was largely limited to what was then known as the
"Chitlin' Circuit." True, some whites had bought and treasured his
records, and some at times even ventured into black neighborhoods to
see him perform; but he had not yet played before an audience that was
predominantly white. Perhaps because he had not diluted his blues with

jazz or pop, he had never sung in a folk club, he had never been invited to a jazz festival, and he had never gone to Europe. In a 1950s interview, King claimed that he had never encountered racism in America, because he played only for black audiences, a telling remark in that as a performer he had no anticipation of stepping over the very real racial lines of the day.

This all changed, suddenly, with the growth of the blues audience in the '60s, first among acoustic folk musicians and then in the form of blues-rock, as performed by primarily British bands such as John Mayall's Bluesbreakers, briefly featuring guitarist Eric Clapton. Clapton made no secret of his love for King, and some white audiences began wondering what the "real thing" sounded like. Early in 1967, King received an invitation from a familiar San Francisco hall. "We used to play the Fillmore before Bill Graham bought it," he recalled in 1989. "I was booked out there by the agency. When I got there, I didn't know that it had changed. It used to be about 90 to 95 percent black. This time it seemed to be 98 percent white, so I thought maybe we had gone to the wrong place. I knew we were liked by some whites, but I didn't know that our popularity had reached the position where we could play an audience where we'd have mostly whites and go over. Bill carried me into the same old dressing room we used to go to, and I was very nervous—very, very nervous. I was kind of frightened, because I was considering how I would go over, whether the people would like me this time.

"Bill Graham introduced me himself. He said, 'Now, ladies and gentlemen,' shortly, just like that, 'I bring you the chairman of the board, B.B. King.' That was the first time I heard that. And at that time, when everybody stood up, it was the first standing ovation I ever had in my life. And I cried, because I'd never had it happen before. It was very touching to me. Everybody was honoring me so much I was hoping I really deserved it. It's a feeling I can't describe to you. It's almost like going to another country where people don't understand what you are trying to say and maybe you might need to call for an emergency of some kind, and you can't make anybody understand. Well, I felt lost. It is kind of like looking at a baby that's crying, and you want to help it but you don't know how to."

That concert was such a success that King was booked into the Fillmore East, which he played in early March 1968, and a month later at a private concert, in tandem with Janis Joplin, in Greenwich Village that I attended. A few days after the assassination of another King, Martin Luther, Jr., it was a performance to remember. A rounded, middle-aged black man of average height, with a broad smile, advanced to the middle of the small stage. His hair was processed high on his head in a "conk" style which resembled a prosthetic crown. Behind him were five musicians: a drummer, an organist, a bassist, a trumpeter, and a saxophonist.

King only briefly acknowledged the terrible loss that had occurred by the assassination; instead, he took a deep breath, closed his eyes, and plucked a riff that made his audience gasp in awe. No one they had ever heard before could play guitar like that, and no one has done so since. The notes were clear and crisply played, in a bouncing sequence; and they were played more slowly than most electric guitarists would, the fingers on King's left hand bending each note for its particular resonance. It was truly beautiful; it was sublime. After a few more runs, he began to sing "Every Night I Got the Blues" in a voice that was neither sweet nor harsh. Its one distinction was that his lyrics were enunciated with unusual clarity—more clearly than most of the blues singers or even rock singers whom we had already heard.

Since those career-turning concerts, B.B. King has played in colleges both white and black, in Central Park, in open-air festivals, at Radio City Music Hall, at nightclubs both fancy and plain and on national television. He has traveled around the world and played even in Africa and Asia. The Moscow news service, Tass, reported that over one hundred thousand people attended his concerts in a month-long tour of Russia early in 1979. Over the past three decades, he has traveled beyond the Chitlin' Circuit without, in certain respects, ever leaving it.

I saw King in Manhattan again in 1979, as the top act on a golden bill that also included Bobby Blue Bland and Muddy Waters, two friends and colleagues for over two decades. Even though tickets cost an average of ten dollars apiece, they sold out a large Manhattan theater for two shows on a Friday night and then sold out Symphony Hall in Newark the following night—all thirty-four hundred seats. He had enlarged his backup group, so that it now had, in addition to the bassist and the keyboard man, a rhythm guitarist and six horn players, all led by a conductor-arranger whom King introduced as "Mister Owens, Mister *Calvin* Owens." It is now called the B.B. King Orchestra.

His audiences at these concerts consisted largely of middle-aged blacks, elegantly attired, complemented by a few younger whites, informally dressed. It was apparent that most of them had seen B.B. King perform before. He had only to pluck an opening riff before the audience cheered its recognition of the song to follow. He rocked from side to side as he played, his eyebrows arching high and his face going through grimaces and smiles as he executed spectacular crystalline runs; and then he pulled the guitar way down to his right hip while he sang into a microphone across his left shoulder.

On both evenings, near the end of his set, he promised a brand-new song, "one I just wrote. I'm sure most of you have never heard it before. I'm almost scared to try it." After an opening phrase on his guitar, the audience knew that he would again sing his masterpiece, "The Thrill Is Gone." Even in the wake of Bland and Waters, I sensed that everyone knew this man was still the King of the Blues.

We met in his Newark dressing room, just before his set. Unlike performers who prefer to keep to themselves before they go onstage, King was affable and relaxed. He wore gold-rimmed glasses, bifocals; since he takes them off only when he goes onstage (because they slide down his nose as he plays), most of his fans would recognize him on the street less by his face than by his left-hand ring of diamonds set into the letters "B.B." He spoke slowly and somewhat formally, in great control of what he was saying, only his elongated vowels betraying his Mississippi origins.

Even though he had been interviewed hundreds of times before, he evidently liked doing it again, much as he enjoyed playing his guitar night after night. Ever hospitable, he offered his guests fried chicken from a large tin and canned liquids from his portable cooler, and he asked his valet to keep other guests away from the door until we were done. He is the kind of engaging man most of us would like to befriend, because he is so cordial, considerate, and aristocratic. In a business full of instability, he has remarkable loyalties—at that time, the same record company for eighteen years, the same business manager for a dozen years, and an arranger who worked with him back in the 1950s.

As American royalty, this King arose from a lowly birth—on September 16, 1925, in the countryside between Itta Bena and Indianola, Mississippi, a few miles west of Greenwood—notorious Greenwood, right in the heart of the Mississippi delta region. His mother left his father when he was four, taking her only child, then named Riley B. King, back to her own hometown, Kilmichael, in the Mississippi hills east of Greenwood. When she died five years later, young King inherited her plantation hut and lived alone amidst an extended family. "I stayed there mostly because that was home to me, instead of living with a relative here, a relative there. Some of them I didn't like anyway. That's one thing about those little places. It's kind of like a little village, a little area where everybody knows everybody. Everybody else in the area was my mom and everybody my dad. You had guardians all around you. You couldn't play hooky from school, like the city kid does," he remembered, "because if you were supposed to go to school and you didn't go, it would get out that you didn't. Anybody could chastise you about it, anybody. You had no way out, really. Usually most of the people in the area knew you and liked you—white, black and what-have-you."

It was here that he learned singing in the church and guitar from a minister uncle, and before long he was regularly performing in a gospel quartet. When school wasn't in session, he worked twelve hours a day in the fields, mostly walking farm implements behind a mule. "My education ended in the tenth grade. I didn't finish high school."

During World War II, farm workers were excused from military service if they stayed on the farms and if they were paid more than the $5.15 a month that King had previously received as a hired hand. For the first time in his life, he had enough money to break the economic stranglehold that would otherwise have kept him on the plantation. He could afford to take public buses to the Mississippi cities—Jackson, Greenville, even Hattiesburg in the south—where he played the blues on street corners, "making more money on a weekend than I could in a week." At the end of the war, he moved north to Memphis and lived for a while with a cousin, the bluesman Bukka White. (King's mother's mother and White's mother were sisters.) "There was a lot I had to learn when I moved to the city. I'm still learning."

His first professional break was a ten-minute daily program on a local radio station. He played the blues and wrote jingles advertising Peptikon Tonic. This show was so popular that it was expanded to fifteen minutes and moved to lunchtime, and King was given an additional hour-long disc jockey program, which had yet a second hour on Saturday. He also formed a trio that included on piano a young man named Johnny Alexander, Jr., who was later known as Johnny Ace. Their first hit was "Three O'Clock Blues" (1949). Before long, Riley King was known as Blues Boy King, or B.B. for short and just plain B to his friends.

Meanwhile, he was beginning to tour outside Memphis, taping his radio program in advance of his absence; by 1954, he decided to make touring his principal activity. "I noticed that my popularity and income would be better if I started moving about. I'd been to New York by then, and a lot of the major cities, and I came over pretty well." In his book, *Urban Blues* (1966), Charles Keil reprints an itinerary for late November 1962 that includes, on eight successive nights: "Rhythm Club, Baton Rouge, LA; Stardust Club, Longview, TX; High School, West Helena, AR; Fairgrounds Night Club, Muskogee, OK; Stevens, Jackson, MS; Club Handy, Memphis, TN; Madison Night Spot, Bessemer, AL; Club Ebony, Indianola, MS." Every day King and the band drove, and every night they played the blues.

Even in 1979, he was still performing at least three hundred nights a year. A full sixteen weeks of each year were spent in extended residencies in Nevada hotels, and this is one of the reasons why King had lately moved his permanent residence from 10 West Sixty-sixth Street, off Central Park in Manhattan, to Las Vegas. However, if you ask him where his home is, he'll point to the floor of his dressing room and say, "Here." Behind him were stacks of unanswered letters; beside him was a bag with his composing notebook and a portable tape recorder. The night after the performance would be spent in a chartered bus journeying from Newark to Buffalo.

King himself is self-taught. Had he actually been drafted into World War II, he would have qualified for the postwar GI bill and thus could have gone to music school at government expense. That he did not get such education is more of a regret to him than one might think; for, before any discussion of art turns technical, he will tell you that the principal tragedy of his professional life is that he does not have a musical education. "Wouldn't it be a sad thing," he said, while looking at the floor, "if a person could speak but could not write down what he'd want to say and pass it on to someone else?" To compensate, King took correspondence courses. However, he still does not consider himself sufficiently adept. He says that he can hear a printed score in his head "slowly, but I read, I've been reading, trying to, since the late fifties, but I cannot write down what I want, the way I want. That is sad, very, very sad. Any person who doesn't get educated to the point that he can write down what he wants to say is sad. In my case, musically, it's awful; it's terrible."

King has literally devoted his adult life to performing, and there is no other subject he would rather talk about. Sooner than boast of his competence as a singer or a guitarist, he will tell you, "I'm supposed to be the entertainer—the guy who goes out there to make the audience feel good, to make them enjoy what I have to present. I think I know my job pretty well. You get out, and you work hard as you can. You try to play as many tunes as you can with as much care in doing it as possible. You can't satisfy all the people. You know you're not going to; you know that everybody isn't going to like it. Some people want you just to get up there and sing and play. Others want you to move.

"Let's say we'll split the audience into four groups. One group wants to hear only the old songs, all the hits you've made; but you've made albums that had tunes on them that weren't hits. Another group wants to hear those hits, too, but they're open-minded and want to hear what else you have. Then you've got another group that comes to hear somebody else that is along with you, another act in the show, and they want to hear things that are moving. And you want to keep them too. Then you have another group that doesn't want to hear any of the older stuff you've done. They want to hear something that's happening. All right. You're thinking about the whole audience. When people come out to hear you with someone else, I fix my program so I'll have something that will make them remember B.B. King. I can make friends. That is what I think of when I'm onstage—an entertainer trying to make friends. And I think I've done pretty good through the years."

Even as he sings, King listens to his audience, partly to hear which songs go over best. He is prepared to change his program in midconcert to win its allegiance. "I'm concerned about them. Those are the people that caused me to be on the stage, and they can take you off the stage. It's kind of like in any business. Are you listening to them, pro or con? Each audience is kind of like, excuse the word, a lady. They have a right to change their mind, and they do. You have to be alert enough to tell that if you're not going very well in this direction, change it, abruptly. There are times when you imagine you have long rubber arms and can envelop the audience and make them move, or not move, with you." When King talks about live performing, he speaks with the authority of someone who has performed three hundred days a year, often with two or three shows a day, for over forty years—*for at least twenty thousand audiences.*

I heard B.B. King perform again ten years later, in 1990. At that time it took me a few months to catch up with the singer-guitarist after getting an assignment to profile him. He had toured Europe and then the West Coast and Texas, checked into a Las Vegas hospital for a diabetes attack, and went to Memphis first for a recording session and again to receive an honorary doctorate from Rhoads College. Just before I saw him in Westbury, Long Island, he had performed on successive days in Birmingham, AL; St. Louis, MO; Kansas City, MO; East Lansing, MI; Toronto, Canada; Rochester, NY; Wilkes-Barre, PA; Sparta, NJ; Devon, PA; with only one night off. At the Westbury Music Fair, he followed his longtime associates, Bobby Blue Bland and Millie Jackson. Though seats were empty for their acts, by the time King strode onto the revolving stage, accompanied by not one but two middle-aged, bespectacled bodyguards, the house was full.

He addressed an audience of nearly two thousand as though we were his friends, as though he had already shaken our hands. After witty introductions of his seven-man, uniformly attired band, led by "my nephew Walter King," he played on his guitar a few riffs that emphasized the extended, emphatic vibrato that is uniquely his, his face contorting through every flourish (in another visible trademark). So familiar were most of his songs to his audience that a cheer arose whenever he began to play; at the end of each number came hearty applause.

In deference to his age, and news reports of a recent hospitalization, his nephew pushed forward a simple chair that was at first refused and then accepted, with no loss of the extraordinary vocal projection that is another B.B. King trademark. Every move the group made looked as though it were spontaneous, though you knew each had been performed a hundred times before. The climax of his set was an extended, patiently articulated narrative about a wayward man who comes home at 5 a.m. to find his wife leaving him, and around that tale he introduced passages from several favorite songs, including perhaps the most familiar of all, "The Thrill Is Gone."

When that was done, he asked coyly, "Could you stand just a little bit more?" As the audience cheered, a tall thickly built middle-aged black lady rushed onstage modestly to plant a shy kiss on King's cheek; a shorter, slighter, bespectacled, younger woman did likewise to his lead trumpeter. Since this last move happened behind King's back (and he can't see too well without his glasses anyway), Walter whispered in his ear, prompting King to ask her for a quarter, which, less successful with his joke than he hoped, he reduced to "twenty cents." He launched into another familiar song, "Sweet Sixteen," before staging a collapse into his chair. Two band members rushed forward to pull him back to the audience's cheers, each having by now become an accomplice to the other's artifice; but the move also reminded everyone, including himself, that when B.B. King dies it will probably be onstage.

As he took his concluding bows, the audience rose to applaud, if only to reaffirm their affection. Ever the generous potentate, King began distributing souvenir guitar picks to everyone in front of him, giving people something to remember him by, as he would say, or simply making friends. When he went up the aisle, his bodyguards beside him, he accepted kisses and shook hands with every man, woman, and child seeking his attention; it would be several minutes before he had moved out of reach. Not even Duke Ellington was quite so popular, but he was only a duke.

In the intervening ten years King had gotten heavier, especially in his belly, now looking more like a president-for-life in an underdeveloped country; his hair has specks of gray. Whenever he began to boogie to the music, he would suddenly stop, covering his eyes as though he were ashamed for his body. Whereas the other musicians were once his age, now they are noticeably younger, including a show-stealing trumpeter who snaps his mop of kinky hair from side to side whenever his instrument is at rest. (The fact that King allows a back-up musician to do this reveals great generosity, not to mention self-confidence.)

The audience was basically the same as before, consisting mostly of his loyal fans, which is to say middle-class, middle-aged blacks who have seen him many times before. They came dressed in silks and suits, often with ties, much as they would to a wedding; and they were prepared to compare the current show with the previous ones. Like every legend, King has set standards against which, alas, he must continually compete. At twenty-five bucks a ticket, respect didn't come cheap.

Even though he has also been making records for over forty years—a few dozen albums and scores of singles—King has yet to make a disc as superlative as his live performances. Records can capture his guitar playing, which remains inimitable, so that anyone turning on the radio, say, can usually tell after a few plucked notes that the guitar they hear is his. However, some of the awe is lost when you cannot see the expressions on his face and the agility of his fingers; some of the communication is lost when the audience doesn't respond with you. King has not yet learned to compensate, as, say, the Beatles did, by exploiting the radical possibilities of recording technology. Most of his recordings are unedited transcriptions of his live performances. The best of these is probably a disc he made thirty years ago, before the B.B. boom—*Live at the Regal* (a Chicago blues palace).

In *Listen to the Blues* (1973), Bruce Cook observes, "As booze [is] to bluesmen, so heroin is to the jazzmen, so amphetamines to country and westerners," and in blues songs there are far more references to alcohol than to any other drugs. But King eschews all stimulants, not on religious grounds but for practical reasons: "If you spin around many times you can't stand straight. I know that, because I've been drunk. I'm not trying to be a preacher or a priest. After the show, a man can do what he wants to do in his own room. I can see a man drinking because drinking is socially acceptable. I'm not against guys smoking grass, if I don't see them. I don't think smoking grass is any worse than smoking cigarettes, but it's not socially acceptable. But onstage, no drinking, no smoking, no drugs, no pills, no booze, no nothing else. I'll fire a man if I catch him using them."

Charles Keil quotes one Chicago disc jockey in the mid-1960s, introducing him as "the president of the Amalgamated Blues Association, Incorporated!" while another referred to King as "the boss hoss—like Sea Biscuit, he never lost a race!" By the time Bill Graham introduced him to white audiences, he was known to be the living master of an acknowledged tradition. As an artist, he has been less of an inventor than a perfectionist, less of a mixer of musics than an extender, who has brought a particular style to its unsurpassed culmination. He is the blues singer who has no egregious faults, other than the absence of them (which some think betrays the funky origins of the blues). B.B. King is not a Stravinsky or a Charles Ives—a volatile, fecund innovator—but a daily working, prolific master, like Johann Sebastian Bach. Indeed, he is the Bach of the Blues.

* * *

This book collects much of the best literature written about King and sometimes with him. If only because King is so articulate, not only about his art but his life, not only about technical matters but about his feelings, he invariably moves to the forefront of the articles about him. However, his talk resembles his music. If he is always performing the same song in different ways, so the details of his early life, for instance, always seem to differ slightly, whether told by him or by others quoting him. This autobiographical repetition, always with variations and new nuances, is one theme of this book. Another is that, in print or on disc, King always sounds like himself. Ranging from the first known article in a Memphis weekly newspaper to a recent memoir by his principal biographer, from record liner notes to an elaborate chapter of an unpublished doctoral thesis, this book is a genuine companion: useful, intelligent, communicative.

As in all of the volumes in the *Companion* series, this book draws on articles, interviews, and reviews written over a long period of time. Other than silently correcting obvious typographical errors, they are presented as they originally appeared. Thus, names of songs, dates, etc., may vary from article to article (or even within single articles themselves!). Because of the historic interest of many of these pieces, we have decided to "let them stand" as they originally were.

I'm grateful to Anson John Pope for his assistance, to the guitarist Ethan Fiks for some early help, to Sheldon Harris and Dave Booth for their clippings, to Richard Carlin for commissioning this book, to his colleagues for shepherding it into print, and to the authors, editors, and publishers who permitted me to reprint their texts here.

Richard Kostelanatz
NEW YORK, NEW YORK, MARCH 1997

PART ONE

Every Day
I Have th
Blues

B.B. KING: GUITAR STRUMMER REALIZES AMBITION TO CUT ORIGINAL PLATTERS (1994)

COLIN ESCOTT

Colin Escott, a specialist on blues, rockabilly, and early country, originally wrote this essay for the music-collector's journal, *Goldmine;* another version appeared as the booklet accompanying a fat CD box of King's classic songs. It is the best comprehensive introduction to the man and his art.

"We don't play rock and roll. Our music is blues, straight from the Delta. I believe we'll make it on that."
—**B.B. King, 1957**

B.B. King has been the most fortunate and unusual of bluesmen: a success on his own terms, and in his own time. He remains perhaps the best-known blues musician, respected and loved by both the intransigent blues fan to whom anyone successful is instantly suspect, and the casual listener to whom he represents their entire understanding of "blues."

A reputation like that is not easily come by. It's partly the result of B.B.'s forty years on the road, and his proselytizing zeal for the music he loves. He has come to a theater near you, and he has put on a great show. His is the hardest music to fake because—at its core—it's pure feeling. Certainly, there's a dash of theater in his presentation, but the blues according to B.B. King still deals with the nuts and bolts of everyday life. He must have played "Three O'Clock Blues" ten thousand times, but even now—resplendent in his three piece suit—he can still make you believe he's walking the back streets crying.

Throughout his career he has used his catholic taste to constantly rejuvenate his music. The Blues is a narrow furrow, lending itself to ossification. Bluesmen are renowned for developing a style, then putting on blinkers. B.B. King has managed to keep his music evolving, but has never lost sight of his core musical values. Even in the company of U2, he is still confidently and identifiably himself.

Over the course of B.B. King's lifetime, the blues has moved out of the mainstream of black music and into the mainstream of popular music, an achievement that—in great measure—is his achievement. Since the 1960s, the blues has been slowly co-opted by white audiences, but B.B. has retained at least a toehold in the black community while playing to college audiences, the supper club crowd, the festival circuit and—at last count— 57 foreign markets from Tasmania to Russia.

Now, some two thousand miles west of Itta Bena, in a townhouse in Las Vegas, Riley King mulls over his achievements. Latterly a non-smoker, almost vegetarian, and almost a non-drinker, he seems curiously ascetic in a city founded upon excess. His surroundings, like himself, are unfailingly modest, but just in case you think that he has not received his just rewards on this earth, there is a late model Rolls-Royce in the garage. The king of cars for the king of the blues.

The Pep-Ti-Kon Boy

To say B.B. King was born poor says everything and nothing. He was born in the poorest state, Mississippi, into the poorest social group—black farm laborers, and he grew up during the Great Depression. But there were few, even among white farm owners, to whom young Riley King could compare himself, and feel that he had been dealt a bad hand.

Itta Bena, Mississippi, where Riley B. King was born on September 16, 1925, isn't near anywhere, except other small towns like Inverness (where Howlin' Wolf was born), Rolling Fork (where Muddy Waters was born), Richland (where Elmore James was born) . . . and so on. Not that they would have grown up knowing each other because "near" in today's terms doesn't apply to Mississippi in the '30s and '40s when rural blacks counted themselves privileged if they had a mule to ride.

When B.B. was four years old, his parents separated, and he grew up in the care of his maternal grandparents in Kilmichael, Mississippi. His mother died when he was nine, and, in 1940, B.B. moved in with his father's new family in Lexington, Mississippi. He stayed there two years before returning to Kilmichael, and subsequently, Indianola. He wrecked a tractor on the Barrett farm near Indianola in 1946, and decided that his future might be brighter in Memphis. When he tallies his years in the music business, he usually starts counting at 1946.

Once settled in Memphis, B.B. searched out bluesman Bukka White, a distant relative on his mother's side. He hung around with White for a few months and they worked a day job together at a tank construction company before B.B. got homesick and returned to Mississippi. In the latter part of 1947, with a spell in a gospel group and a parallel career as a streetcorner bluesman under his belt, he left again with a small stake, determined to stay the course in Memphis. "I thought I would be popular as a gospel musician," he said, "and I begged [the other] guys to leave the plantation because I thought we were pretty good. They would always say 'Next year.' I had started to sing on the streetcorners and play. I would play what someone would ask me to. They'd ask me to play a gospel song, which I'd be glad to, and they would compliment me highly. People would ask me to play and sing a blues, and they'd give me a tip, sometimes even a beer. On Saturday evening I would do this, and many times I would make more playing than I would [on the plantation] in the whole week."

B.B. may not have known it, but he couldn't have chosen a better time to arrive in Memphis. In 1948 a floundering hillbilly and pop station, WDIA, decided to change format and orient itself toward the black community. It wasn't a new experiment in the South, but it *was* a new experiment in Memphis. At that time, radio was a mixture of live performances and records. Live performers were paid by their sponsor rather than the station, and used their spot (usually fifteen minutes) to announce their personal appearances. WDIA was immediately successful in its new suit of clothes, and its achievement was partially emulated across the river in West Memphis, Arkansas, by KWEM, which began to devote part of its broadcast day to the blues.

"I went to KWEM and asked if I could sing on the radio and that's how I came to know Sonny Boy Williamson,"[1] recalled B.B. "I had heard Sonny Boy on the radio from Helena, Arkansas, and by the time I got to Memphis he had moved to West Memphis, and I started to go over there and play the blues. It happened that he had two jobs one night and he arranged for me to fill one of them. So I went out to the 16th St. Grill. The lady's name was Miss Annie. She paid me twelve dollars that night, which was more than I had ever had in my life. Miss Annie said she would hire

---

1. The "Sonny Boy Williamson" to whom King refers is Rice Miller, the Chess recording artist; not the original Sonny Boy Williamson who had died in 1948.

me six days a week if I got a radio spot where I could advertise her place. So I went over to WDIA and got a job there."

The story goes that B.B. arrived at WDIA in a rainstorm, soaked to the skin, carrying his guitar wrapped in newspaper. The program director, Nat D. Williams, asked him what he wanted, and B.B. said he wanted to get on the air and make a record. The WDIA staff auditioned him, liked what they heard, and put him on the air. B.B. went back to Mississippi, collected his wife, Martha, together with their few belongings, and moved to Memphis.

The owners of WDIA had a stake in a patented cure-all, Pep-Ti-Kon. "If you feel run down, tired, achy, painy, can't sleep, are nervous, can't eat, have indigestion and bloating gas, you are guaranteed satisfaction," B.B. would call over the air. "Get Pep-ti-Kon today and see if you don't say, 'Man, I'm really living.'" "Man, I'm really smashed" would have been closer to the mark; the major ingredient was alcohol.

As early as 1948, Riley B. King was known as "B.B." or "Bee-Bee," which had always been thought to stand for "Blues Boy" or "Beale Street Blues Boy." An article in Memphis's black newspaper, *Tri-State Defender*, dated March 29, 1952, though, suggests another derivation. It gave a run-down of what was then a very short career, and went on to say: "Riley King, whose public had christened him 'Singing Black Boy,' [is] producing a popular radio show of his own. His public donated nickname was short-ened to 'B.B.' King and under this title the slim guitar strummer from Itta Bena realized his ambition to cut original platters."

The first original platters that B.B. recorded were for Bullet Records in Nashville. WDIA pulled a few strings to get its budding star two releases in July and November 1949. The sides were cut in the WDIA studio. The first release celebrated "Miss Martha King," and showed that B.B. had already mastered the rudiments of T-Bone Walker's guitar style, but unlike Walker, who had a dry, insinuating vocal style, B.B. sang full-throated, like Roy Brown in training.

If Bullet had an option on B.B.'s services, it wasn't exercised, and it wasn't until the following year that he got a chance to cut more origi-nal platters. Modern Records had been formed out on the West Coast by Jules, Saul, and Joe Bihari. Some said they were brothers, but there wasn't much family resemblance and it's probably safer to say that they were cousins. Jules looked after what would be termed A&R (artists & repertoire) in today's parlance, and he did what record men had been doing since the '20s: he packed his bag and hit the road. He schmoozed with dee-jays, gave them a little encouragement to play Modern

Records, collected outstanding debts, and sniffed around to see if there was anyone worth signing.

When Bihari came to Memphis early in 1950, he discovered that there was a studio in town. This was a godsend; without a purpose-built recording studio he had to record at radio stations or set up portable equipment in hotel rooms. The new Memphis Recording Service was owned and operated by Sam Phillips, later the founder of Sun Records.

Jules Bihari heard about B.B. King from Ike Turner, signed him to his new RPM label, and took him to Phillips' studio. Phillips recorded B.B. for approximately a year—from mid-1950 until June 1951. Five singles were drawn from the titles he supplied. B.B.'s sound was nowhere near as distinctive as it became. His voice was thinner, as indeed he was, and his guitar playing had yet to take on the drama and poise that would become his trademarks. The promise was undeniable, although in hindsight the records said more about the way Phillips' thoughts were heading than B.B.'s. "She's Dynamite," the fourth single, was a cover of a fast-breaking Tampa Red song. In contrast to the mannered restraint of Tampa Red's original, there was a barely contained explosiveness in B.B.'s version that pointed unerringly into the future. Sam Phillips' future, that is.

In June 1951, Phillips recorded the epochal "Rocket 88" with Ike Turner's band, featuring Jackie Brenston. He pitched the master to Chess Records, and it went on to become the second biggest selling R&B record of the year. The Biharis felt they had been double-crossed, and they severed ties with Phillips, hiring Turner (who had already split from Brenston) to record their artists in makeshift studios around Memphis. In late 1951, B.B. rerecorded Lowell Fulson's 1948 hit, "Three O'Clock Blues," at the black YMCA. It spent the early months of 1952 on the R&B charts, peaking at number one in February.

B.B. King had arrived. Ever conscious of security, he tried to juggle his WDIA commitments with touring, but by 1955 he had opted to put a full-time band together and hit the road. He has been there ever since.

Every Day I Have the Blues

By the mid-'50s, B.B. King's reputation was well-established, and his records were selling consistently, but something strange and unprecedented was happening to black music. If a song was catchy, well-produced, and not too overtly "black," it stood a chance of crossing over into the new rock 'n' roll market. Fats Domino and Chuck Berry became masters of making black music for white kids. B.B. King did not. His music was adult in content, raw in execution, and lacked the catchy little hooks so beloved of Top 40 radio. Few, even among blues musicians, were playing with the aggression and white-knuckle tension that were B.B.'s trademarks. Occasionally, the Biharis would force-feed him a song like "Bim, Bam, Boom," and today those novelties are the only records from his long career that will not play.

While Fats, Chuck, and others were mastering the two-and-a-half minute pop playlet, B.B. King was screaming the cuckold's blues and hollering thinly veiled threats over a backdrop of riffing horns and his own blistering guitar. The cost of being true to himself was that he was grounded in the so-called Chitlin' Circuit, which was not really an established circuit as much as an ever-changing number of lounges, roadhouses, and theaters that catered to an almost exclusively black clientele.

"We don't play for white people," said B.B. in 1957. "Of course, a few whites come to hear us on one night stands but they are so few we never run into segregation problems. I'm not saying we won't play for whites, because I don't know what the future holds. Records are funny. You aim them for the colored market, then suddenly the white folks like them, then wham, you've got whites at your dances. That's what happened to Fats Domino, (but) we don't play rock and roll. Our music is blues, straight from the Delta. I believe we'll make it on that."

When B.B. strayed from the blues, it was toward supper club ballads. He was recording with strings a decade before "The Thrill Is Gone," and he cut entire albums of big band era songs by Ellington and Basie after the Biharis got a deal on the arrangements. Although only a year or two older than Chuck Berry or Fats Domino, B.B. neither rocked nor rolled. He says he simply didn't relate to it.

In 1958, B.B.'s contract with the Biharis expired, and he began playing a cat-and-mouse game with them. In an attempt to squeeze out a little front money, he solicited offers from other labels and actually got as far as cutting a session for Chess Records before the Biharis panicked, paid up, and brought him back to the fold for another term.

By the end of his contract with RPM (then known as Kent Records), there were several compelling reasons to leave and stay gone. The Biharis' royalty rates were lower than the major labels were paying, and they appended a cryptonym ("Taub," "Ling," or "Josea") to most songs that King wrote which ensured that they got fifty percent of the composer's share of the publishing royalties in addition to one hundred percent of the publisher's share. They also marketed their albums on the Crown label for 99 cents, which meant that the royalties (calculated as percentage of list price) were lower than if they were on regular priced LPs, which then sold for $3.98 or $4.98. B.B. had to juggle economic reality against personal loyalty toward the Biharis, especially Jules. "Jules was my man," he said. "He was like a casino owner. As long as you're doing what you're supposed to do, there was no limit to what he would do for you . . . He knew about black music. He was a beautiful person. He was just there for you. Saul was more like a lawyer, and Joe was a good guy, but Jules, I love him." The bottom line was that B.B. needed a label with more clout in the marketplace, so he went shopping.

ABC

B.B. King signed with ABC-Paramount Records, as it was then called, in 1961 for a term beginning the following year. Formed in 1956, the label had enjoyed steady success in the pop market with Paul Anka, Steve Lawrence, and others. Their track record with black music was spotty until they signed Ray Charles away from Atlantic Records in 1960. Almost immediately, Brother Ray found the land where white and black music meet, and he became ABC's best-selling artist. After that, it was inevitable that ABC, under the tutelage of Sam Clark, would try to replicate his achievement. When B.B. King and Fats Domino became available, Clark whipped out his checkbook. In fact, it was Fats Domino who suggested to B.B. that he try his luck at ABC. As a token of faith, ABC gave B.B. an upfront guarantee of $25,000—probably more money than he had seen from the Biharis in several years.

ABC made a few subtle changes to B.B. King's approach. They didn't force the Ray Charles formula on him, but they framed his vocals against a larger orchestral backdrop. The arranger and *de facto* producer was usually Johnny Pate. "We would sit and discuss what we were gonna do," says B.B., "with a board of people and map it out. It was businesslike." Brass (as opposed to reed instruments) featured heavily in Pate's orchestral voicings. The sound was fuller, but the essential character of B.B.'s music remained intact. Most of his singles sold between fifty and a hundred thousand copies, and ABC was obviously unwilling to jeopardize those sales with left-field experiments.

Chart success during B.B.'s first years with ABC is difficult to measure because *Billboard* magazine suspended its R&B chart between November 1963 and January 1965. During that time, B.B. saw his first Hot 100 entry, "How Blue Can You Get," which spent two weeks in the listings, peaking at 97.

The first sign of a change in direction came with "Help The Poor" from the pen of veteran black songwriter, Charlie Singleton ("Don't Forbid Me," "Trying To Get To You," etc.). B.B. fronted some Latin percussion and a female chorus (a *black* female chorus, thank you). The most surprising omission was the guitar; the only guitar to be heard was probably not B.B.'s, and it was buried way back in the mix. The result was a modest chart showing, two weeks in the Hot 100 peaking at 98, but it served notice that B.B. King's music was subject to change.

It was Johnny Pate who had the idea of recording B.B. King on his home turf: a black nightspot. To that point, live albums were predominantly the preserve of jazz musicians who weren't after the call-and-response between themselves and the audience so much as the ambience of a live date. B.B.'s *Live at the Regal,* recorded in Chicago on November 21, 1964, captured the last flowering of blues as quintessentially black music. B.B. himself admits that the Regal was one of the few venues where he could still expect such a response. The album later gave his newfound white followers their first taste of "church"—the two-way channeling of energy between performer and audience.

Sid

"We have mostly Negro adults at our gigs," B.B. was still saying in 1966, "but I've noticed in the last year or so I've had a lot [more] of the white kids come than ever before." It was a statement that disguised the larger truth that blues was no longer the voice of the neighborhood. Instead, it became the voice of white middle class kids—many of them overseas. The catalysts, as B.B. acknowledges, were musicians like Mike Bloomfield, Elvin Bishop, Al Kooper, the Rolling Stones, and Eric Clapton. An earlier generation of white acolytes had listened to Big Bill Broonzy spin little homilies about life on the plantation (which Broonzy, the most urban and urbane of singers, had learned for the occasion); now the kids were sitting in their bedrooms with a Harmony guitar and a stack of B.B. King albums.

In 1966 and 1967, this attention began to be reflected in a little press from unaccustomed sources. B.B. was the centerpiece of *The Urban Blues,* a groundbreaking book by Charles Keil—part history and part polemic. Keil was one of the first to state the case for R&B in the same way that writers had been making a case for country blues for years. B.B. and his contemporaries, once written off as crassly commercial, were now acknowledged as keepers of the flame.

In 1967 B.B. took on a new manager, Sidney Seidenberg. At the time, Seidenberg was a music business accountant, and insists that he never wanted to be a manager. His relationship with B.B. began when he took over the books in 1966, and then—at B.B.'s insistence—became his temporary manager the following year. The relationship was made permanent in 1968. It was no easy task; the specialist press coverage and first glimmer of overseas interest were doing nothing to alleviate B.B.'s most pressing problem, that of meeting his payroll. "He had no market," says Seidenberg. "Blues wasn't even considered good enough for the R&B spots."

The state of B.B.'s thinking can be gauged from an interview he gave to Stanley Dance in 1966. "A lot of the younger Negroes," he said, "don't want to be associated with the blues. [They] are trying very hard to raise [their] standards . . and when they're approached with the blues, [they] figure in a lot of cases, this downs [them]." Seidenberg saw it as his task to open up new markets to replace the old ones. "One of the things I did as an accountant," he said, "is plan, and I told B.B. about five year plans, and goal-setting, which is how we still work today. Right from the start I tried to work on new things for him to broaden his career and stretch his talent."

Sam Clark at ABC was high on Seidenberg's list of people to visit. He renegotiated the contract, selling ABC on the first five year plan with its stated intention of breaking B.B. outside the R&B market. Seidenberg gives credit to ABC for staking B.B. to a bigger contract, recognizing that he was looking to invest the money in B.B.'s career and not treat it as a capital gain.

Coincidence or not, B.B. was beginning to see some of his biggest hits in years. The record that set the pace was "Don't Answer The Door," originally a 1965 hit for its writer, Jimmy Johnson. B.B. covered it the following year. He brought an edge, verging on paranoia, to his reading of the song. It was the defiant plaint of the poor joe on the night shift wondering if it's open house at his house while he's gone. Even if you're sick, he tells his woman, "I don't want the doctor at my house/I want you to suffer 'til I get home."

Sensing a groundswell of interest in the blues among the rock audience, ABC launched its Bluesway label; B.B. was its linchpin. In 1968 and 1970 he gave the label its only major hits with "Paying The Cost To Be The Boss" and the magnificent "The Thrill Is Gone." Rising to number 15 on the pop charts, "The Thrill Is Gone" became B.B.'s biggest hit to date. It had been adapted with elegance and taste by B.B., his producer Bill

Szymczyk, and arranger Bert de Coteaux from an old Roy Hawkins blues that dated back to 1951.

"I had been carrying that song around for seven or eight years," says B.B. "We had tried it many times but it would never come out like I wanted it. That night, it just seemed right. We were in the studio from ten o'clock until 2:30, 3:00 in the morning, and we'd done 'The Thrill' and a couple of others. Funny thing was, Bill Szymczyk didn't like it at first. Anyway, we finished it and went home. About five in the morning, Bill calls me and says, 'B., I listened to the three songs. Have you listened?' I said, 'Yeah.' I told him I thought it was good. He says, 'I've got this idea to put strings on "Thrill,"' and I said, 'Fine.' About two weeks later, he got Bert de Coteaux to put strings on it, and it really did enhance it."

Szymczyk, who later made his mark (not to mention his fortune) with the Eagles, had only been working in production for two years, starting inauspiciously with Harvey Brooks' *How To Play Electric Bass*. Inevitably, his idea of using strings on B.B.'s sessions appalled purists, but purists exist to be appalled. The Academy of Recording Arts and Sciences shared the popular view that "The Thrill Is Gone" was a magnificent record, and handed B.B. his first Grammy for the trophy room.

The success of "The Thrill Is Gone" gave Seidenberg the leverage he needed to pitch B.B. to the supper club bookers in Vegas, and open up the lounge market. "They have a lot of rooms in Vegas that need a lot of talent," he says, "and we got in there by promising to work for very little money on the basis of, 'Give us a chance, if we do good—keep us.' One of our earliest shots came when Sinatra was working the main room at Caesar's and we were working the lounge. Sinatra's people had to okay it, which they did because they all liked B.B."

B.B.'s entry into the lounges meant that within the space of two years his music had been introduced across the broad spectrum of white venues, from hippie palaces like the Fillmores to the supper clubs. Seidenberg was tapping into the large closet blues audience that wouldn't have gone to see B.B. at the Regal—even if they'd known he was playing there. The result was that, as 1969 closed, Seidenberg stated that B.B. had played to more people that year than during all other years of his career combined. The million-plus who—strictly speaking—hadn't paid to see B.B. when he toured with the Rolling Stones bolstered the grand total, but the turnaround in his career was still undeniable. The following year, he became the first bluesman to appear on *The Tonight Show*, and then, in October 1970 over 70 million people saw him when he guested on *The Ed Sullivan Show*. The blues had arrived on prime time; it had only taken fifty years.

The upsurge in interest from the white rock market coincided with the birth of in-depth rock journalism. Interviewers came to call; they asked B.B. to analyze his style and elaborate upon his influences. Forcing an intuitive musician to explain what he does can be counterproductive, but B.B. proved himself as eloquent with words as with the guitar. His list of influences changed from interview to interview but T-Bone Walker, Django Reinhardt, Lonnie Johnson, and Charlie Christian were usually there. Significantly, even the two bluesmen had a jazzy slant to their work.

As LPs became more than a collection of singles and single-length filler, B.B. had an opportunity to stretch beyond his accustomed one or two chorus solos. He changed the architecture of his solos, now that there was room for them to build. He usually started with a little five-note signature, followed by some delicate, oblique phrases that betrayed his debt to Lester Young. Like Lester Young, B.B. loved sliding into notes, insisting that his brief experience playing the clarinet had given him a taste for "glissing." He also claims not to trust his ears, preferring to hit below a note, then slide up into it.

Another shortcoming that B.B. made into a virtue was his inability to master the slide. Instead, he developed his trademark perpendicular-to-the-neck vibrato. He says it was his interpretation of Elmore James' and Bukka White's slide guitar, but the trilling effect is closer to Django Reinhardt's vibrato. "For about thirty-two or thirty-three years I've been trying to do it, and now they tell me I'm doing a little better," he told *Guitar Player* with dry understatement. In truth, he had it down as early as 1953; on "Please Love Me," cut in Texas that year, he comes on like Elmore James from Hell.

The significant difference between B.B. King and his (mostly white) disciples is that he had long ago mastered the concept that less can be more when it comes to the number of notes in a solo. "If it's done well with less, then use that," he says. "If you need more, you try to put it in there. When I first started school, I stuttered and stammered so bad, my teacher would slow me down and say, 'We got time—take your time.' I think the same thing started with my guitar." Over the years, B.B. has become a master of dynamics, tension and tone, using relatively few judiciously placed notes for the maximum emotional impact, much like his heroes Lester Young and Johnny Hodges.

One late '60s trend that mercifully passed him by was the temptation to be socially significant. "Help the Poor," for instance, has no social relevance whatsoever. "Help the poor, baby. Help poor me," he sang with his usual feel for a good punch line. So, while other bluesmen fell prey to the perceived need to be topical, B.B. rarely strayed from the blues' traditional terrain. Through the riots, the Vietnam war, the advent of feminism, and other social upheavals of the late '60s and early '70s, B.B. King kept to his home turf: male-female relationships at the nuts-and-bolts level: "You must be crazy, woman, you just gotta be out of your mind/As long as I'm footin' the bills, I'm paying the cost to be the boss."

Indianola to London

By 1970 Bluesway had been discontinued, and B.B. was back on ABC. The challenge he has faced over the last 20-plus years has been that of bringing sufficient variety to his music so that every album doesn't sound the same; at the same time, he mustn't alienate his core audience or over-reach. Essentially, it's an impossible challenge. Some albums, like the countrified *Love Me Tender,* cry out to be remaindered; others are sustained, often sadly under-regarded masterpieces.

As the years rolled on, ABC (absorbed into MCA in 1979) assigned different producers to try to introduce some variety to the basic mix. In a parallel move, Sid Seidenberg tried to broaden the audience by booking round-the-world junkets. B.B. became a tireless ambassador for the blues much as Louis Armstrong had been for traditional jazz two decades earlier. After years of negotiations, they even cracked the Soviet Union; only mainland China now remains elusive.

Just as specialist blues critics have been poised to write him off, B.B. has tended to return spectacularly to form. *Lucille Talks Back* was one example, and it saw B.B. himself in the producer's chair for a change. "When it comes to a blues album, I think I'm qualified to say what's good, and what isn't," he remarked drily at the time. There was another sweet return to basics on the *Blues 'n' Jazz* set, produced by Sid Seidenberg.

B.B. has the sales figures in front of him, so he must know better than anybody that blues (or any ethnic music for that matter) needs to be assimilated in some way with pop music if sales are to be incremented in tens of thousands or hundreds of thousands. Examples from *Graceland* to John Lee Hooker's recent deification are legion. B.B. had occasion to discover what hitching his wagon to a pop star can do for his bottom line when he dueted with U2. "Sid said, 'Do you know about U2?'" said B.B. "I said, 'Yeah,' and he said, 'Well, you're gonna be in Dublin,' and he was thinking that twenty years ago I toured with the Rolling Stones. When we got [there], they were in the audience, and I didn't know it. After the show they came back, and we talked about half-an-hour. When they got ready to leave, I said to Bono, 'You know sometime when you're writing, would you write one for me?' He smiled and said, 'Yeah.' About a year later, Sid called and said that Bono had written a song for me. He said they were gonna be playing Fort Worth, and could I open the show for them too. Then I found out that he had wrote the song not for me, but us to sing together. Anyway, we rehearsed it, and that night I came back for the finale and he and I sang 'When Love Comes To Town.' Forty thousand people stood up. Forty thousand people!"

It's a pity that B.B. needs an affiliation with U2—or anyone—to get his music heard, but B.B., who should have the most resentment, has the least. He knows that it's one way of resolving a problem endemic to marginalized music. The usual blight of the bluesman's career is acclaim without success. Knowing that a bunch of critics in Europe think you're one of the greatest living examples of something-or-other doesn't put gas in your tank. B.B. King has found both success and acclaim, perhaps not in equal measure—but certainly more equally proportioned than many of his contemporaries.

The willingness to undertake collaborations with U2 and others stems in part from commercial considerations, and in part from B.B.'s desire to grow and evolve as a performer. He wishes he had studied music formally, and he's rare among bluesmen in that he is an avid record collector. He comes back from tours with a bag full of CDs—complete Tampa Red on some obscure Belgian label, a Roy Milton reissue, a B.B. King reissue that he doesn't have, and new stuff that looks interesting.

It was well over twenty-five years ago that *Hit Parader* did its first feature on B.B. King, closing by asking the question: Who will fill his shoes when he's gone? It seems to be a question that won't need answering for a while. B.B. is crowding 70, but shows no sign of letting up. His stamina is protean.

These days, there are black blues revivalists. Not very many to be sure, but a few. Even so, none of them will grow up hearing all B.B. King heard and seeing all he saw. You may see him on television or in a supper club, and the presentation may be slick, but the music is still informed by the Delta, its roadhouse joints with chickenwire to protect the singers, its Whites Only hotels, and 500 mile jumps between gigs on gravel roads. That is the stuff of history. That is what you hear when B.B. King comes to town. It won't come again.

THE SOPHISTICATED TRADITION: URBAN STYLES, THE SECOND MOVE TOWARDS AMERICA AND THE DEVELOPMENT OF SOUL (1972)

RICHARD MIDDLETON

An early analysis of the urban blues tradition, placing B.B. King within the context of his peers. Although the language is a little academic and dated, this still gives one of the best overviews of the variety of blues styles: from Kansas City jazz to Chicago electric blues to R&B.

Urban blues are associated particularly with the second move towards the American mainstream, which was connected with the Second World War. But they were then already part of a pre-existing tradition. So just as they coexisted with modern city styles during the move of the forties, as we have seen, so the tradition which formed them—sophisticated as it is—coexisted with the earlier city blues of the late twenties and the thirties. However, this does not contradict the idea of a cultural retreat in the thirties and thus that of a dialectical pattern of blues development. For city blues are associated with the ghettos of the big cities, particularly those in the North (and especially Chicago). The urban tradition, on the other hand, is associated with Southern cities, and cities, moreover, in particular parts of the South. It existed only in special locations and under special conditions. Thus pre–World War Two coexistence was one of time only. The urban traditions involved—the most important of which are those of the South-West and of Texas—developed independently of the general development of blues at the time, and they became widely accepted only in the early forties when a change in general mood made their widespread adoption possible. They do not therefore affect my picture of the overall shape of blues development.

The special nature of the urban blues context in the twenties and thirties is clearest in the South-West: Kansas City and the Territories. This was still a frontier area, and as such it was characterised by an unusual optimism, hope and sense of vast possibilities among both Negroes and whites, and also by an equally universal gusto of life-style. Both Kansas and Oklahoma became States after the Civil War. The simultaneous settling by whites and blacks, and the absence of any tradition of slavery or racial conflict, resulted in a relatively relaxed and flexible system of race relations. As a result the main characteristics of the music are hope, energy and relaxation. In contrast to the city styles developing at the same time over the bulk of the country, there is relatively little trace of bitterness, hysteria and neurosis.

Kansas City blues can be instructively compared with Classic blues. There are three principal areas of similarity. Like Classic blues, K.C. blues are closely connected with jazz (as is usual with sophisticated blues styles). Indeed, they are as much jazz as blues; the two traditions are one. The singers worked with the big jazz bands typical of the area (Jimmy Rushing with Walter Page, Benny Moten and Count Basie, Joe Turner with Pete Johnson, for example), and the music these bands played was in any case grounded in the blues. K.C. blues *are* the jazz of the South-West. Many stylistic facts follow from this. Among them is our second point of similarity between K.C. and Classic blues: the use of popular material, particularly ballads, which is then realised in typical jazz (and sophisticated blues) manner. Rushing, for example, often sang ballads (he started as a ballad singer), and there is a certain romantic lyricism in his vocal style. But any hint of sentimentality is controlled, the fantasy brought down to earth and made real, by the particularity and blueness of his impeccable phrasing, by the finesse, discipline and precise articulation of the band, and by the tension between the two. The optimism of frontier life is expressed but nevertheless realistically understood. The use of popular material makes possible a structural subtlety (introductions, codas, etc.) which again is derived from jazz. The third area of similarity with Classic blues is the sense of balance in the music. K.C. blues balances black and white, group and individual, and hope and reality in a way which suggests a kind of 'natural' synthesis: a position not unusually weighted by external factors in either direction.

There are differences, however. These are twofold, and they define the reason why K.C. blues were able to succeed and develop into the predominant sophisticated style in blues history, while Classic blues failed and died. The first difference is symbolised by the fact that though Jimmy Rushing was influenced by Bessie Smith, he was also strongly influenced by his cousin, Wesley Manning, who was a boogie-woogie pianist. In other words sophistication (and Rushing had a comparatively Westernised upbringing, singing in church choirs, glee clubs and operatic societies, and even learning to read music) is combined with the physical security of corporeal rhythm. Pete Johnson, whose band usually backed Joe Turner, was a well-known boogie pianist in his own right (and a comparatively primitive one); and probably the most widely known K.C. style is the 'good-time', strongly boogie-influenced, swinging style of the more physical numbers. Unlike early city blues, K.C. sophistication is thus aware of the more primitive and physical aspects of the Negro's existence. The second difference is connected with this. The K.C. community, like that of Classic blues, is basically jazz-like: a collection of complementing individuals, whose jazz-style solo choruses and shorter responses and obbligati play the same role as the instrumental contributions in Classic blues. However, the K.C. big band, unlike the Classic small group, introduces group as well as personal statement. Its ostinati are sophisticated—they are harmonically conditioned in shape, for example—but in tribalising function they are identical with the ostinati of later city blues. The combination of individual and group statement—together also with the other characteristics I have mentioned: jazz influence, the use and realisation of popular material, the sense of balance and the combination of sophistication and 'blackness'—has remained typical of all urban styles.

The K.C. blues community was noteworthy for its strength and solidity. Ralph Ellison has written of how, as a boy in Oklahoma, he looked on the blues world as a third institution alongside school and church. It was an establishment. Already there was something about it of the secular church typical of later urban blues.[1] As a community it seems to have been more stable and more relaxed than the ghetto community of which city blues sing. And the result of this is a strong framework of convention and taste, which is manifested in the expertise and discipline of K.C. blues, particularly the band's subtle shading of dynamics, and its balance and control of chording. The music is expressive, but 'dirty' effects are stereotyped and formalised. The combinations of tribal solidarity and sophisticated taste, and of 'dirtiness' and refinement, are others which have become typical of urban blues as a whole.

Similar refinement appears in K.C. vocal style. Rushing, for instance, was a lyricist. His combination of power and lyricism—which again is characteristic of urban styles—creates what might be called a lyrical shout, which is intense in feeling and rich in tone but 'musical' in delivery and carefully finished off with a favourite conventional phrase-ending. The characteristic relaxation of the style results in the beginnings of after-the-beat phrasing, which is to permeate later urban singing. This technique pulls out the melodic phrase, hanging on to it after the beat has gone, and, in effect, accepting the tension that is created. It contrasts strongly with the nervousness and aggressiveness typical of before-or-on-the-beat city-style phrasing.

Of course, this 'musical' approach is not characteristic of every K.C. singer to the same extent. The two great partnerships differ here, in fact, and thereby point to the variety within urban blues, which matches that within country and city blues. Thus Rushing and Basie are the more 'musical,' the closer to jazz; Turner and Johnson are the less sophisticated, the nearer to blues tradition. The one partnership is more tasteful; the other is 'dirtier.' Turner is more of a shouter, more direct and more immediately physical, and Johnson's band is the more boogie-influenced; Rushing is the more lyrical, and Basie's band is the more subtle. The influence of the two singers is interesting. Both had a considerable amount, but Turner's was the more widespread and the longer-lasting, Rushing's the narrower. Rushing influenced mainly blues and jazz musicians; Turner's influence extended to white Pop music, especially Rock 'n' Roll. In view of the slightly more primitive nature of his style, Turner's greater success in, and influence on, the music associated with the move towards the mainstream in the forties is significant. The network of connections taking in the commercial discovery of boogie in 1938 (after its 'obscurity' in the ghetto), its influence on Turner's music and *his* influence on the sophisticated singers of the early forties tells us a considerable amount about the nature of this move, as well as the character of K.C. blues.

The other important urban tradition belongs to Texas. The urban Texas style is related to that of rural Texas in the same way as city style is related to that of the Delta. In both cases the latent character of the country form is realised. Its implications and needs are fulfilled. In Texas it is as if the rural style had been waiting for its natural setting, environmental and musical: waiting, that is to say, for the tension, alienation and sophistication of urban life and for the comforting, communalising function of a band. In urban Texas blues there is also considerable influence from K.C. blues—the Texas singers usually used a small, five, six or seven piece band and transferred characteristics of big band K.C. style into that context—and in the Texas blues of the thirties and forties the two traditions are not always easy to disentangle.

So the rather clean, formalised timbres and the light, beautifully balanced textures of urban Texas blues probably stem from the K.C. style, though they could equally be a natural development from the urbanity of country Texas blues. The same applies to the self-disciplined treatment of boogie rhythms—as in K.C. blues and the Texas country style, these never threaten to replace conscious effort totally by mind-destroying physical orgy—though the typical jazz-influenced instrumental solos and melodic style must stem from K.C. blues. The Texan vocal is derived from its rural forbear. It is a sophisticated, relatively 'musical' treatment of the holler, light in tone, relaxed in phrasing (with touches of after-the-beat phrasing and of melisma) and controlled in delivery. And yet its character bears comparison to the 'lyrical shout' of K.C. blues too. There can be no doubt about the derivation of the guitar style, however. This is a development of country Texas style, the backing of a band freeing the guitarist to make his chords even lighter and more infrequent than in the country, and to concentrate even more on single-string solo work, which is even more complex and virtuosic. In fast songs these solos are usually in a consistently dancing, corporeal-triplet rhythm, while in slow songs the influence of the rhythmically complex melodic style of jazz results in the development of the suggestions of a-metrical arabesque found in Texas country blues into a complicated, short-note, around-the-beat, across-the-barline technique. These two styles have remained the basic styles of all urban guitarists.

Clearly urban Texas blues display a similar cultural orientation to that of K.C. blues. But they bring a special feeling and emphasis, and a particular technique, and these are produced more within the narrower limits of a purely blues tradition. Partly this involves a clearer acknowledgement of the neurosis bound up in city life, which contrasts with and complements the good-time optimism of the South-Western tradition. There is still the typically Texan relationship between the intensity of feeling and suffering, and the discipline of artistry and professional expertise, but now the feeling discernible is that much more jumpy and nervous than in the country. The other great difference between the urban and rural styles, of course, is the novel communalising power of boogie rhythm, supporting band and tribalising (though relatively refined) ostinato. And in this the urban Texas and K.C. traditions are at one.

The urban Texas style, then, itself displays the influence of K.C. blues, and is thus the first sign of a synthesis of the two traditions. The man most associated with this synthesis was Louis Jordan. He it was who adapted K.C. style to the small band (usually piano, bass, guitar, drums, trumpet and sax), which was adopted by the best-known Texas singers, like T-Bone Walker; and it must have been chiefly through this adaptation that K.C. influence was mediated to such singers. On to this framework Jordan grafted the influence of the Texan vocal, guitar and spirit, and the resulting synthesis set the trend for the sophisticated blues of the early forties. It reflected the sophistication involved in the second move towards the American mainstream, and also the changed, 'blacker' basis of this sophistication. With it Jordan himself achieved enormous and inter-racial success (cf. Bessie Smith in the twenties), and also influenced the other popular blues singers of the time. Now mostly forgotten, these comprised a host of names, quite apart from Jordan, Joe Turner and T-Bone Walker: Wynonie Harris, Sonny Parker, 'Bull Moose' Jackson, Amos Milburn, Lowell Fulson, and so on.

Obviously the music of these singers, and the movement it reflected, can be compared in some respects to the early city blues and the first movement towards the mainstream. Louis Jordan, for instance, was an entertainer as well as a bluesman, and as such may be compared to singers like Papa Charlie Jackson. Like Jackson, Jordan saw no reason to draw a line between the Negro and wider America; he refuses to keep the ghetto in its place. He exploits the styles of sophisticated blues for entertainment, laughing at the boogie, refining the blues shout, parodying the solidarity of call-and-response and at the same time bringing them into the context of the mainstream of American life. He is strongly rooted in Negro culture, but he is sufficiently at home in a wider setting to be able to laugh at it and utilise it as entertainment. Once again there seems no reason for not regarding black and white as one, the Negro as an American. It is important to remember the changes which have taken place, however. As we have seen, the most important of these are, first, an increase in physical emphasis, boogie rhythms, 'dirtiness', and so on; and second, the introduction of techniques with communal, even tribal implications: supporting bands, and in particular their ostinati and riffs. And these changes are considerable. If the Negro appears once again as an American, then, he is now an American with a very strong, particular background of his own. And this stance has remained typical of all urban blues.

It is this stance which is the basis of what we may term the modern urban style. This developed out of the synthesis of the early forties and emerged, primarily in the hands of the great B.B. King, in the early fifties, after the post-war dominance of modern city blues. From there it grew gradually into Soul. This development took place primarily in Memphis, which is to urban blues what Chicago has been to city styles. The move of the forties did not die: it developed. Musically its sophistication was retained, while its 'blacker' aspects were intensified. The mover was thus more and more on the Negro's terms. The psychological revolution of these years, growing towards Soul, results in a new kind of cultural synthesis, a new kind of psychosocial position and a new self-confidence and relaxation. Culturally the Negro is, as it were, standing still, conscious of his heritage, and beckoning America towards him. And the resulting culture is more and more taking on the appearance of a new establishment, a new subversive mainstream. So the self-confidence, relaxation, cultural stance and characteristic ritual of the urban traditions are developed in the new context and crystallise gradually into the Soul revolution.

The growth of Soul out of urban blues is imperceptible. So, for example, the change in lyrics from the traditional stress on failure, helplessness, aggressiveness and tension to an emphasis on help, success, love, satisfaction and solidarity, a change which is typical of Soul, begins in modern urban blues. The ghetto is accepted, but the need for, and possibility of, change is emphasised. Urban blues appear more and more to have the function formerly reserved for the church: the creation of emotional satisfaction, relaxation and solidarity, though in a harsher, more secular world. The increasing influence of church music and liturgical technique points the development. The blues community is becoming a secular church. This development coexists with the continuing appeal of city styles, but the importance of such styles has gradually diminished. They are increasingly regarded as old fashioned, and associated with subservience and bad times. The new Negroes are no longer subservient, no longer in the ghetto (psychologically speaking). Their singers have 'been through' the ghetto experience and the urban abyss—the urban blues, unlike previous sophisticated styles, 'take note' of the cultural isolation, the suffering and the 'dirtiness' involved—but they are coming out into a recreated mainstream.

Probably the most important development in modern urban blues is the development of the singer's priestly persona and quasi-liturgical performance-ritual. Charles Keil has shown that the modern urban singer is the archetypal secular priest. His picture of B.B. King is of a man completely devoted, priest-like, to his people and to his function among them: a representative, who offers his personal experience, his role and his skill in the solution of their problems. He is himself—and his individuality is very important—but more than himself.[2] This conception of aura, transferred to Pop, has become known as an image. The links between the urban singer and the preacher are close. Some men have been both; many have been involved in both worlds.[3] 'Both give public expression to deeply felt private emotions; both promote catharsis—the bluesman through dance, the preacher through trance; both increase feelings of solidarity, boost morale, strengthen the consensus.'[4] The change in lyric-type which was mentioned is thus not surprising. The quasi-liturgical techniques used by urban singers have also developed. An urban blues concert is a carefully structured affair. Keil's description of a Bobby Bland performance makes this clear.[5] Bland typically runs from analysis and pleas for help through solutions, through love, praise and satisfaction, to final solidarity, using drama, mime and choreography on the way. He starts from the situation given by the Negro's everyday life; he ends with a recreated situation (nowhere is the blues' social role more important, obvious and successful), which is characterised by solidarity, 'good feeling' and what the urban blues community knows as 'mellowness'. Community is created out of the atomised fragments of city life.

Despite the synthetic nature of the urban style of the early forties, and thence of the modern urban style, there can still be discerned in the work of the first modern singers a divergence of stylistic emphasis corresponding to the distinction between the two principal urban traditions. A liking for light textures and timbres, a Texas-style vocal and a casual, entertaining spirit implies a tendency towards the Texan side of the urban synthesis. Adherence to richer textures, big band riffs and lyrical, romantic vocals, on the other hand, bespeaks a tendency to the K.C. side. This is particularly interesting because when the influence of urban blues produced Rock 'n' Roll, these two aspects can still be made out. The chief stylistic distinction in Rock 'n' Roll thus dates back to the birth of the different styles of urban blues.* It is interesting, further, since it is in modern urban blues that, for the first time in blues history, commercialisation becomes of real importance; and the precise result of commercialisation—dilution of the character of the style—is bound up with the stylistic distinction within urban blues, so that the 'natural' development in Texas-orientated music is towards an empty, facile triviality and in K.C.-orientated music it is towards sentimentality and the unrealised escapist ballad. The character of the style produces its own particular type of commercialisation; and this process, which can be found in modern urban blues to some extent, was carried into Rock 'n' Roll too, where it often had such unfortunate effects.

Unsynthesised stylistic traditions become more difficult to find in the mature modern urban style; and in the work of its greatest figure, B.B. King, they disappear. The breadth and character of King's stylistic synthesis are apparent from the influences he himself acknowledges: Blind Lemon Jefferson, Leroy Carr, Lonnie Johnson, Samuel H. McQueen of the Fairfield Four Gospel Quartet, and Gene Autry (on his singing); T-Bone Walker, Elmore James, Django Reinhardt and Charlie Christian (on his guitar playing). These influences seem to show, first, King's basically sophisticated position, which, as the name of Elmore James suggests, is nevertheless aware of the 'dirtiness' of the ghetto; and second, the way the mature modern urban style, though built on the old sophisticated tradi-

---

*By this time, of course, the two urban traditions are no longer associated simply with their places of origin. From the early forties on, their influence is found in urban blues from all parts of the country. When they are referred to in the future, therefore—in this chapter and in that on Rock 'n' Roll—it is the style and its influence, not the source, which is meant.

tions, starts to take on the wider awareness—particularly of church music, jazz and popular music—characteristic of Soul.

Indeed, at the core of King's style is a grafting of a wider awareness onto a synthesising acceptance of the urban traditions. Vocally he adds to Rushing's lyricism, Turner's shout and Walker's relaxed sophistication a rich intensity of tone, a fervour and a rhetorical delivery derived from the church (the preacher as well as the music); a much more developed and subtle behind-the-beat phrasing; and (often quite complex) melismata, which originated in Gospel singing. The effect is to increase the opposition to the beat, the boogie bounce and the communalising riff, and to add an intensified awareness of personal experience and suffering. To a basis made up of group support and physical strength is added the knowledge that good times are not all and the group not everything. Set against and complementing this basis is King's personal vision. The result, paradoxically, is not tension but relaxation, 'good feeling' and 'mellowness'. King is in personal control, and in fact the spirit of the music stems from the first signs of the individual's *mastery* of experience, which is typified by the singer-hero's command, and which is characteristic of Soul. King's dominating persona, the rhetorical yet lyrical sweep of his vocals and his relaxed phrasing all display the new self-confidence of the individual, brought about by the post-war psychological revolution.

Not surprisingly the importance—at least the overt importance—of communalising techniques like ostinato decreases in King's music. Ostinati are still important, but they are now more subtly worked into a more varied, heterogeneous and individualised whole (modern urban blues and Soul usually use a big band, so making this variety possible). Similarly, boogie rhythms still provide the basis of physical strength so essential to all blues in the towns, but they are now increasingly subtly absorbed into the general rhythmic flow, the importance of the body being complemented by more spiritual aspects of experience. Ghetto simplicity is broadening into a culturally more interesting panorama. In both cases the increased variety characteristic of King is symptomatic of the wider awareness increasingly typical of urban blues as a whole. And the result, from the point of view of social implications, is midway between the tribalistic unity of city blues and the individualism of Classic blues, appreciating and appropriating characteristics of both, and promoting a synthesis which is more complex than the first and more workable than the second.

For similar reasons the importance of solo work in King's music is high. The traditional, jazz-influenced solo style of urban blues absorbs the impact of the complex melodic style of modern jazz, together with its spiritual implications, so that King's guitar, for instance—the most important and characteristic soloist involved—develops out of the Texas-derived guitar style of urban tradition a short-note, around-the-beat technique of an unprecedented complexity. King often uses this style even in songs which are fast and basically corporeal in rhythm. Its religious implications are apt for the music of a secular church, and they match the similar vocal techniques of melisma and off-beat phrasing, which are derived from Gospel music. In fact, the purely personal spiritual release into 'timelessness' suggested by the beat-and-metre-destroying arabesque of this solo style complements the more primitive religious vision of the group, created by call-and-response and ostinato.

An emphasis on release, relaxation, mellowness, satisfaction, mastery, and so on should not blind us to the problems of urban life, which indeed remain the raw material for urban blues, just as for all other town styles. As I said, urban blues starts from the experience of the ghetto, and certainly King does not neglect the suffering involved. However, this experience is now but a starting-point. Urban blues' growing ability to deal with it is real—as real as the fact that their increasingly predominant function is the creation out of it of solidarity and satisfaction; and the increasing importance of the solution song-type, which is to become so characteristic of Soul, cannot be denied. Indeed, the growth of urban blues into Soul is imperceptible, as we have seen, and, though King is fundamentally the classic modern urban blues singer, the occasional appearance in his work of an ecstatic spirit and of harmonic and antiphonal structures typical of Soul may serve to confirm this.*

Soul is the blues of the Negro revolution. The objection that it is not blues because it admits so-called non-blues elements is invalid. Fundamental cultural and social changes necessitate fundamental musical changes. Were blues not to change in order to reflect the developments of recent years, it is a fact then that it would cease to be blues. And, as we shall shortly see, it is just the field-widening changes accomplished in Soul music which do reflect the Negro revolution. Similarly, the objection that Soul is not blues

---

*This section was written before King, in the last couple of years, began to move very noticeably towards Soul and to extend his audience to whites as well as blacks. He seems now to be aiming at the same kind of position as Ray Charles and Aretha Franklin. See below.

because it becomes at times commercialised is irrelevant. Increased commercial pressures are again a result of the cultural changes of recent years, and in any case they do not alter the basic question, which is whether good blues have been created within the Soul category, and to which the answer is, yes.

As one would expect, Soul fulfils those developments in modern urban blues which have been identified as pointing towards it. The background to this fulfilment may be summarised once again as, historically, the Negro movement, unique in character, of the early and middle fifties, and the changes connected with this, and, culturally and psychologically, the growth of the philosophy of soul, together with all its effects. Underlying it is the fact that what in the forties was culturally and psychologically new and strange has become accepted and established.

Musically, the most obvious result is the addition of the influence of jazz, Gospel music and popular music to urban blues style. The growth of a wider awareness which we noted in modern urban blues is thus consummated. The simultaneous popularity of 'hard bop' jazz, a back-to-the-roots style influenced by Gospel and blues, and of Gospel itself makes it clear that what is involved is the growth of blues into a wider musical movement. So the implications of jazz, Gospel and popular music are added to those of blues: jazz, the Afro-European music of black-and-white America; Gospel, the ecstatic music of the Negro church and black solidarity; and popular music, the expression of the white mainstream and the American Dream. The development in Soul of such techniques as jazz-like treatment of popular ballads and Gospel-like lyricism and fervour falls into place. And it is clear that one important result is the fusion of the myths of the American Dream and the Promised Land, for the influence of popular music demonstrates the wider, all-American appeal and relevance of Soul, through which blues begins to leave its specific origins and emerge into the mainstream of American culture, while the influence of Gospel makes clear the extent of the recreation of this mainstream by the Africa-derived religious and communal forms of the Negro folk. Soul brings into being a community which is both secular church and new mainstream. And its novel amalgam of cultural elements, its unique relating of black and white, primitive and sophisticated, must be ascribed to this fact. These developments bring other results too. One is the possibility of commercialisation (an unfortunate donation from popular music). Another is the development of a cultural synthesis (rather than a clash), as the self-acceptance, self-assurance and relaxation of the soul philosophy leave behind the old destructive tension of the blues experience, release its creative potential and make possible the solution of the traditional cultural problems. The absorption of other styles and materials, which both part-constitutes and is symptomatic of this solution, symbolises on a wider scale the change in blues itself from clash to synthesis; and it may be a most significant example and forerunner of the cultural pluralism which is surely the only possible solution to the cultural clash and tension characteristic of our world in general.

The formative process of Soul's synthesis of different musical traditions can be examined in the music of Ray Charles, the first great Soul singer, the setter of most trends and the embodiment of the confusion of category endemic in Soul. Charles is known as a Pop singer, a jazz singer and pianist, a blues singer and a Gospel singer. He *is* all of these. He learned blues and Gospel during his youth in the South, and learned jazz and popular music after moving to Seattle. During the mid-fifties he began to put these elements together and became a Soul singer.

Charles sings many popular ballads; these are the expression of his Americanness. But, in line with jazz and sophisticated blues tradition, he realises their hope and fantasy through interpretations based on personal experience, and phrasing inseparable from the particular occasion, individual and feeling. His phrasing is considerably influenced by jazz and Gospel music, the balance of the two varying from song to song. Using the painful knowledge of reality which jazz has acquired and the eternal Now of ecstatic fulfillment which Gospel gives, Charles is capable of turning the most trivial utterance of Tin Pan Alley into a moving profession of faith in the ultimate achievement of the American Dream. Not always though: the dangers of commercialism and sentimentality are not always avoided. Charles also sings urban blues, which are strictly within the tradition—and which come from any point in the tradition, from Kansas City through the Rock 'n' Roll-like styles of the early forties to the classic style of modern urban blues. And he sings jazz standards in true jazz fashion, usually backed by a jazz-playing big band and his own piano, which in style takes us back to Kansas City and Count Basie but also outwards to modernists like Horace Silver and Milt Jackson. Jazz instrumentals are another facet of his repertoire.

The diversity of influence is clear, then. Charles takes material from differing musical traditions and adapts it for the situation in which he is working. But he also begins to mutate and create material himself, combining different influences to form a new style which is recognisably that of Soul. His method is often the juxtapositive one natural to the early formative stages of a radical development. Thus sections in urban blues style are combined with sections whose use of vocal response, ostinato, drone, ecstatic vocal style, fervent shouts, etc., shows their derivation from Gospel music. Such Gospel sections can be combined with sections in a 'popular' style; or 'popular' and blues sections can be juxtaposed. The amount of juxtaposition varies from song to song, and also a better integrated approach to materials gradually increases in importance. Sometimes sections flow into each other rather than remain totally separate; sometimes a vocal of unified style continues throughout a song despite changes of sections; sometimes an ostinato continues throughout in the same way. Each song works out its own more-or-less integrated coalescence. But in all, the effects and functions of the particular constituent elements are what one would expect: jazz and popular components contribute hope, the American Dream and the realisation of these; Gospel contributes the Promised Land, ecstasy, liturgy and solution; blues contributes the problems which need solving.

In some songs Charles achieves what is obviously the goal: an autonomous, identifiable Soul style. These are his best-known songs—*Hallelujah I Love Her So, I Gotta Woman* and so on—and, while all his songs are concerned with love, it is significant that *these* love-songs are the principal examples in his work of the solution- and satisfaction-types so characteristic of soul music. New spirit and new style are intimately connected. Problems are now easily surmounted; stylistic confusion is over. The result is a perfectly integrated style influenced by blues, jazz, popular and Gospel music but belonging to no category except its own, and a 'mellow', ecstatically erotic mood which has become so typical of so much Soul.

A similar development has occurred in the case of Aretha Franklin, the greatest female Soul singer. Like Charles, she comes to Soul from partly outside blues tradition; like him, she develops a Soul music by juxtaposing various styles and influences; and like him, she gradually achieves an integrated Soul style. Unlike him, however, the centre of her musical experience is Gospel music, learned in her father's Detroit church, and in her case the juxtapositive process takes the form of the incorporation of Gospel influence into blues and ballad, together with an increasing awareness of jazz technique.

At first the genres are discernible. Blues are transformed by Gospel-derived vocal technique—shouts, humming, ecstatic tone, melismatic, rhythmically-very-subversive phrasing; by the use within the blues harmonic structure of the Gospel technique of 'harmonic ostinato', in which a harmonic cell is repeated over and over again; and by the resulting mood of exaltation and ecstasy, which may be described as the fulfilment of that perfect balance of the physical and the spiritual found previously in B.B. King. The love-theme, which in blues is usually touched with suggestions of failure, hesitation and suffering, is transformed into a declaration of success and faith, and the erotic mood created—fervently spiritual yet sensuous—is typical of Soul. Ballads are treated similarly. Their fantasy and sentimentality are realised in traditional fashion but they are transformed by the predominant influence of Gospel technique in order to produce the now-familiar ecstasy, which in this context usually results in a lighter, sweeter sensuousness, again typical of much Soul music.

There are obvious reasons to compare Aretha Franklin and Bessie Smith. In persona, power, talent, cultural stance and approach to popular material the two women are similar. The three chief differences illuminate the revolutionary nature of Soul. First, a maternal persona, which the growing self-confidence of the Negro male and his opportunity to identify with the lady-killing King, Charles or Bobby Bland makes redundant, is replaced by a purely erotic one. Second, neurosis is increasingly replaced by relaxation. Third, and underlying this, there is a change in community and musical structure, which has become more solid, more dependable and more tribal in orientation; the influence of the church, with its associations with black solidarity, is connected with this.

These differences fertilise Aretha's evolvement of an autonomous, integrated Soul style. As with Ray Charles, a style which can only be called Soul is created, and the significance of genre falls away. Influences are still discernible but they have coalesced into something new. As with Charles, typical Soul song-types appear, paralleling the growth of specifically Soul structural and stylistic characteristics, which speak of blues and popular tradition but become autonomous and identifiable in nature. For example, songs of self-assurance may be paralleled by the growth of the intimate and close-knit call-and-response typical of Soul, and in particular by the use of vocal group response—often an ostinato—which is derived from Gospel music. Or the appearance of songs of achievement, pleasure and satisfaction may be accompanied by the use of a characteristic fade-out technique, in which an ever-repeated call-and-response motif over an ostinato or drone gives the new feelings and relationships permanence.

The other great singer I have mentioned, Bobby Bland, can take over here. A one-time, self-confessed disciple of B.B. King, Bland has developed directly out of the urban blues tradition. He has treated Soul as an expansion of its blues component, and from the beginning his development has been an integrated, not a juxtapositive one. Not surprisingly, it is in his work that Soul reaches its first real maturity. Bland still sings urban blues, retaining and renewing his obligation to his roots, but the bulk of his songs can be fully understood only in the context of Soul culture.

Often much of their significance comes from their function and their setting within a Soul concert. Bland sings all recognised song-types: 'priest-songs', which announce the people's representative and hero, his character and dependability; 'problem-songs', 'scolding-songs' and 'reality-songs', which analyse the troubles of life but which musically also provide solutions through ritual, group support and catharsis; 'solution-songs', which deal with the need for love, help and solidarity, and again create these through ritual; 'praise-' and 'satisfaction-songs', which celebrate love and pleasure in the ecstatic style we have already met in the songs of Ray Charles and Aretha Franklin; and 'solidarity-songs', which dramatise, formalise and ritually enact the solidarity and togetherness created. This order is the one that would be followed in a concert: from problem to solution. All the songs deal, as usual, with the sexual relationship. In Soul this is treated not only for itself but also as a microcosm of the relationships within the community as a whole, and as a symbol, with which the audience can identify. In particular, identification is with one side of the relationship set up between Bland and his female vocal group. Cementing of this relationship, which is what the concert is designed to achieve, represents the cementing of relationships within the audience and the drawing together of the whole community.

Bland's musical style is archetypal. His forms are expert and varied, in the urban blues tradition, and his use of climax is striking. His structures can be one of three types: a development (harmonically) of the 12-bar blues; a ballad; or a 'harmonic ostinato'. Or they can combine aspects of two or all of these. The 'harmonic ostinato' is particularly interesting since it is a symptom of the cultural stance of Soul in general. It is an ostinato—and therefore time-destroying and tribal in implication—but also harmonic, not melodic. It is thus a sophisticated-primitive unity. The harmonic cell chosen is often IV-I: 'Amen', over which the singer-preacher delivers his message.

The response-techniques in Bland's songs are varied, comprising individual and group response, personal statement and (melodic as well as harmonic) ostinato, as is traditional in urban blues. But vocal response is especially important, in particular that of a female group. His group is the Bland-Dolls; Ray Charles has a similar group known as the Raelets.

The importance of this vocal group, as we have seen, lies in the way it can focus attention on the sexual relationship, and in the way this relationship can then be dramatised in order to represent other and wider relationships. Vocal response thus has a psycho-social and a socio-ritualistic function. The relationships it creates are varied. It can be straightforward, dramatic question-and-answer or call-and-response. It can consist of a harmonic ostinato by the vocal group (and in this case by the band as well—or instead), which is simply expanded and elaborated lyrically at the same time by Bland. Here melody grows out of ostinato. To the urban tradition of solo and group statement is thus added the innovation of the simultaneity and interdependence of the two. The result is a kind of sophisticated heterophony: two simultaneous versions of the same statement, but one harmonic (though an ostinato), the other melodic and growing out of the harmony. This is another sophisticated-primitive ambivalence, of course, and its implication—typical of Soul—is the total interdependence of individual and group, and the undesirability of the total *in*dependence of either party. Yet another response-relationship can consist of a vocal group ostinato, together with a *changing* solo. This slightly varies the always intimate relationship of individual and community.

Bland's vocal is formed out of urban blues traditions, jazz tradition and Gospel techniques, and these fuse into a 'hot', fervent, ecstatic whole, which is rhythmically and melodically complex and subversive, relaxed and subtle in phrasing, and beautifully controlled in flow and climax. Its basis varies. This can be a 'lyrical shout', a ballad tune, an ecstatic incantation. But the treatment turns it without fail into Soul: into a sophisticated yet 'black', integrated unity. The band is similarly varied in texture and technique, as is traditional in urban blues, and in Bland's songs it is 'soulful', rich and heavy, adding to the fervour of the music.

Now Bobby Bland, together with Ray Charles and Aretha Franklin, has achieved a great deal of success among a white audience, as well as a black one. We have seen that Soul is culturally ambivalent; it seems to be so in audience too. For the first time a blues style which makes no concessions to white taste and values is popular among whites at the same time as it serves the needs of Negroes. Both groups enjoy the same songs. This is surely connected with the way Soul appears to be relaxing the tension of the blues tradition, destroying the premises of the culture-continuum and creating a genuinely bi-cultural synthesis. The significance of such developments, especially for a study of the relationship between blues and white Pop music, is undeniable. And so the whole question of the white position with regard to the blues is raised.

1. Ellison: *Shadow and Act.*

2. Keil: *Urban Blues* pp. 96–113.

3. Ibid. pp. 143–8.

4. Ibid. p.164.

5. Ibid. pp. 118–142.

Suggested Listening

Jimmy Rushing: Blues I Love to Sing: Ace of Hearts AH 119.
Joe Turner: Jumpin' the Blues: Arhoolie 2004.
T-Bone Walker: The Blues of T-Bone Walker: Music for Pleasure. MFP 1034.
Louis Jordan: Let the Good Times Roll: Coral CP 59.
B.B. King: several records available.
Ray Charles: several records available.
Aretha Franklin: several records available.
Bobby Bland: Call on Me: Vocalion VA-P 8034.

"FROM ITTA BENA TO FAME" (1952)
JIM ROBERTS

This early article on King is reprinted from the *Tri-State Defender,* published in Memphis, Tennessee, in 1952. This is one of the first known articles on King, and it's not surprising it appeared in a Memphis newspaper catering to that city's black population.

On September 16, 1925, the world took little note of the fact that Riley King was born in the small Delta town of Itta Bena, Miss. But less than 25 years later anyone who was a regular patron of the corner juke box knew the guitar playing, blues-singing B.B. King!

Today surveys conducted by the journals of show business place the quiet spoken, unassuming Itta Bena guitar player at the top of the ladder in terms of popularity and nation-wide record sales!

Orphaned at 3 years of age by parental separation and death, little Riley King began to impress friends with his singing at an early age while being shifted around from relative to relative. He became the tenor soloist in a youthful quartet and while living with a God-fearing uncle who raised him strictly within the church, young King made friends with the pastor who regularly treated his congregation to guitar music.

The minister's shiny guitar became a source of great fascination for young Riley, and the cleric, hoping the boy might someday become a minister himself, frequently let the youngster pick out tunes on the instrument. Through constant practice and devotion, Riley finally mastered the shining guitar and won new friends in playing and singing with a young people's quartet at the Church of God in Christ.

Coming face to face with troubles of the world at 11 years of age, Riley King went to work for a neighboring farmer at $2.50 a week, including room and board. One of his earliest thrills was the purchasing of his own $3.00 guitar, made possible through carefully hoarded pennies. Riley was still singing every Sunday in the church when his long-missing father located him and took him to Lexington, Miss.

In Lexington, Riley attended the Saints Industrial School and Ambrose Vocational School until becoming dissatisfied with his new family arrangement. And so, one day Riley King ran away from Lexington, traveling to Indianola, Miss.

Next came a 6-year stint at a tractor driver, blended in with continual singing and strumming on the precious guitar. Discovering that his informal audiences were always sincerely fond of his musical expressions, Riley decided that the time had come to make the music pay off.

A transfer truck brought him to Memphis, the home of the blues, the mecca of W.C. Handy and the Beale Street Immortals. Then began a new era for Riley King, the ambitious guitarist. It was a grim, disillusioning and uncertain period of singing and playing in public parks and on street corners. His audience was the people, he played the music their hearts and lives know, he played anywhere and anytime they would ask him.

Having a solid religious background, Riley at first resisted the requests of many for the singing of blues themes. However, those who desired the blues paid more for them and so the practical Riley sang blue tunes as well as religious songs.

Hearing Riley play and sing one day on the streets of West Memphis, Ark, the famed Sonny Boy Williams took him aside and whispered, "If you stop street singing, I'll make a man out of you. Come on down to the radio station where I work and I'll put you on my program!"

Riley King jumped at the chance. And his public jumped at his music. Small jobs in cheap night spots were thrown his way. But the guitar player from Mississippi wanted to make records and do a radio show of his own.

Acting on a tip, Riley searched out the veteran Memphis showman, Robert Henry. He found the friend of struggling artists one wet and dreary afternoon in Memphis and soaking wet with drenched guitar, Riley sought his help.

Shortly thereafter, Riley King, whose public had christened him the "singing black boy" from Mississippi, was producing a popular radio show of his own. His public donated nick-name was shortened to "B.B. King." Under this title, the slim guitar-strummer from Itta Bena realized his ambition to cut original platters.

In swift succession followed a 10 months disc jockey stint and the birth of such tunes as "Miss Martha King," "B.B. Boogie," "My Baby's Gone" and others. Then, out of the blue came "3 O'Clock In The Morning!"

After a sluggish start, the new tune spread like wildfire across the nations' juke box circuit, finally becoming the "most played" disc and the hit blues tune of the year.

Today, the Itta Bena, Miss, school boy, farm hand, tractor driver, singer and guitar player is traveling throughout the Mid-South on a successful "Star-billing" tour, under the management of his Good Samaritan, Robert Henry.

Like others before him, B.B. King walked through Beale Street mists and found a winner.

INTERVIEW (1967)
STANLEY DANCE

This early interview was conducted by British-born jazz critic, Stanley Dance. Another interview done around this same time and often cited in these pages appeared in Charles Keil's pioneering chapter, "B.B. King Backstage" in his book *Urban Blues* (1966), which remains in print.

I was born on a plantation right out from Indianola, not too far from Itta Bena. Most of my boyhood was spent around there. My father and mother separated when I was about four, and my mother carried me up in the hills of Mississippi. She passed when I was about nine, and I spent a lot of time alone then, because my father didn't know where I was.

I worked for the white people my mother had worked for. I lived by myself, but they fed me and let me go to school. The school was a one-room building, with one teacher and about eighty-six kids, and that was where I got most of my elementary education. I had to walk five miles each way—ten miles a day. I didn't think much about it then, but now I wonder how I did it. I used to milk ten cows in the morning and ten cows at night. These people I worked for didn't have much money, but I got about $15 a month. Now, believe me, it was one of the happiest parts of my life, because there, then, they were just simple people. Today, I find, people are different. You've got to be at a certain level to be recognized, but then, whoever you were, you were that particular person.

I had a mule and a plough when I was twelve, and we used to plough six months out of the year. On the plantation, we always worked five-and-a-half days a week, usually six, and often six-and-a-half. I once tried to figure out how far I must have traveled in ten years of ploughing, six of them behind a mule. I never heard of a vacation until I left the plantation. Kids work in the South when they are not at school. We would go to school in December and January, when it was cold, but when it stopped raining we would begin working. They plant the cotton in the middle of March and when it comes up in April the kids have to start hoeing. They lay it by when it is stronger than grass, and it opens around October 5th.

When my father found me, I was fourteen. He had married again and had other children. I would rather have stayed where I had been living, where I had more freedom and went to school, but he took me back to the Delta where I was born.

My uncle there was married to a lady whose brother was a sanctified preacher. The preacher used to play guitar in the church, and afterwards he would usually go back to my uncle's to visit his sister, and I would always go along, too, because I liked to fool with his guitar. I liked it so much that I later asked my boss if he would get a guitar for me that a friend of his had, and take it out of my wages. He did that, and I never forget that red guitar with a round hole in it. It cost $8.

That was how my musical career began, but there were no teachers of music through there that I never heard about. Four of us boys got a little quartet together, but I wasn't interested in blues then. I always thought I might be able to get somewhere in the spiritual field. The Golden Gate Quartet were our idols, and we'd hear them on the radio. I learned by just watching and listening to that preacher play. I kept fooling with the guitar and I learned three chords. It seemed as though I could sing almost anything with those three chords, like 1, 4 and 5.

Then I began to run into different guys who were playing guitar, and I'd ask them things. I met Robert Junior Lockwood and Sonny Boy Williamson, and it was Sonny Boy who later gave me my first break. The work scene was fairly plentiful. They'd play the plantation halls and joints where a lot of gambling went on. The men who ran them would hire any name that would bring the people in. Those that danced went into the dancehall part, and those that wanted to gamble went in the other. A guy who could draw could easily get a guarantee of two or three hundred dollars, because the man who had the joint could probably make that much at the door, plus his gambling. Sometimes they'd have a trio, and sometimes it might be Sonny Boy alone—and you'd be surprised how they'd dance to just him and his harmonica.

A lot of times, when guys like Sonny Boy came to Indianola, I wouldn't have any money, but I'd try to slip in. I'd have to walk there, and we lived eight miles out of town. You might be lucky enough to get a ride *to* town, but you'd have to walk back that night. Johnny Jones had a nightclub there, and he was really the guy who kept the Negro neighborhood alive by steadily bringing people in, like Louis Jordan, who was real popular during this period, around 1939. So was Charles Brown. Johnny Jones was a very nice fellow, and he knew the guys on the plantations didn't have any money during the week, but he would often let us in and we would pay him off when we came in Saturday.

Then came the war. The plantation owners controlled the local boards down there. If you were a good worker, you didn't stay in the army. I think they thought the home front was just as important. I was inducted into the army, did my basic training and everything at Camp Shelby, went to Fort Benning in Georgia, and was sent back to the farm from there. I'd been sworn in and passed in everything, but I was a good tractor driver. The only thing was, I couldn't leave the plantation until the war was over. If you left, you had to go back in the army. Sometimes I wish I had served my full term, because then I would have been able to study music. But it didn't happen, and then I got married.

It was a funny thing, but it was when I went in the army that I started singing blues. A lot of fellows seemed to get religious and sing spirituals when they got in there, but me, I didn't. When I got home I realized a lot of fellows were making a living singing the blues, but my people were very religious and I was afraid to sing the blues around the house. My aunt—I did the spiritual album for her a few years ago—would get angry with anyone singing the blues. I would have to do that away from the house, but I found later on that people seemed to like my singing and playing.

So I would work all the week and sometimes on a Saturday I would have $8 or $10. I would take this money and buy me a ticket to the nearest little town—me and the guitar. I would go to this little town and stand on the corners and play. The people seemed to like it and they would tip me a nickel, a dime or a quarter. That sort of thing is still done in the South. Sometimes on a Saturday I'd visit three or four towns, sometimes as far away as forty miles from where I lived, and sometimes I'd come home with maybe $25 or $30. So I found I made more in that one day than I had in the whole week. The money was nice, but that wasn't all of it to me. I wanted to do it, and it made me feel good that they enjoyed listening to me.

Later on, the war was over, and I went to Memphis and got a job. It was about 130 miles north, but to me that was like going to Europe. I had never been out of Mississippi except when I was in the army, but I had heard of Memphis and W.C. Handy, and I wanted to see what it looked like. Two of us hitch-hiked from Indianola to Memphis, and I found my cousin, Bukka White, who was living there.

Sonny Boy Williamson had a radio show every day in West Memphis, right across the river in Arkansas. So one day I went over there. He had Robert Junior Lockwood playing guitar with him, Willie Love playing piano, and a drummer. This was the second Sonny Boy, the one whose biggest record was *Eyesight to the Blind,* and not the original Sonny Boy who made the Bluebird records. He was about twenty-five years older than me, and maybe even older than the original Sonny Boy.

They remembered me from Indianola and I asked him if he'd let me do a song. He said yes, but he'd have to hear it before they put it on the air over this station, KWEM. He liked it, put it on the air, and told the people to call up if they liked it. And they did. Fate had it that he had two jobs this particular night, so then he said, "Look, boy, I've got a job, and if the lady will take you I'm going to let you play it while I work somewhere else. And you better *play,* or you're going to answer to me!"

He called the lady and she said okay. The 16th Street Grill was one of those joints I was talking about, with dancing, and gambling on the side. Gambling was legal. It was wide open there, and sometimes the sheriff or the police would come by. It was the same on the plantations, but there the boss man would only call the sheriff if someone got hurt real bad, and on some of those plantations there would be a thousand families.

Well, the lady agreed to pay me $12 a night, five nights a week, and my room and board. She said I could keep the job if I got on the radio daily. This was more money than I'd ever had before in my life, although

I was a very good cottonpicker. I've picked almost 500 pounds of cotton in a day, which is a lot of cotton. I was really a very good farmhand, I'm proud to say. I remember that nowadays whenever I have a big hit, remember when I earned thirty-five cents for picking a hundred pounds of cotton. A good cottonpicker would usually work from around nine in the morning to six in the afternoon.

So then it happened that I couldn't get on the same station Sonny Boy Williamson was on, but they had just opened the first radio station—WDIA—with Negro personnel in Memphis. (It was white owned.) I went over there and walked into the station with my little guitar on my back. I saw a man called Nat Williams—he was a professor, but he was working as a disc jockey then—and he asked what he could do for me. "I want to make a record," I said. I don't know what made me say that, because I didn't go there to make a record, but to get on the air. He called Mr. Ferguson, the general manager. He asked me my name and I told him, Riley B. King.

"Do you play that thing you have on your back?"

"Yes."

So when I started playing and singing for him, he liked it, and it gave him an idea.

They'd just got a new product called Pepticon, which was going to be competition for Hadacol, a tonic that had been big. He called the program director and he said, "We've got ten minutes open, from 3:30 to 3:40, with nothing set. Let's put him in there." So I sang a couple of songs. They didn't pay me, but I could advertise where I was playing, and that was my objective in the first place. After that, they would bring me on every day as the Pepticon Boy, and later this got so big that they had to give me more time.

I got me a little trio with Johnny Ace on piano and Earl Forrest on drums, and on the two nights I had off from the lady's place I would go out and do one-nighters. Even before I got the trio, I could earn $25 by myself. I didn't know what to do with all this money, and I messed it up. I started drinking and gambling a little bit. Guys would give me stories, too, and I was very generous. I don't regret that.

When one of the disc jockeys left the station, they made a disc jockey out of me, and they said I'd have to get a new name. The product that sponsored me was selling so well, and I was on the air for them fifteen minutes a day for about $50 a week. It got so popular that on the Saturday the salesmen would take me to the little towns outside Memphis, and we'd have a big truckload of the stuff, and I'd sit there singing, and they'd get rid of any amount of this tonic that was supposed to be good for tired blood. One of the salesmen said they would listen to me because they could see I had an honest face!

The first name they gave me on the station was *The Boy from Beale Street,* and then it got to be *The Beale Street Blues Boy.* The people got hip and started calling me "B.B.," and that was how the name B.B. King came about. I did very well and got very popular, so when another disc jockey left they gave me his show, too, and I ended up with two hours and fifteen minutes a day. I used to sing along with the records once in a while, and record companies that put out blues began to get interested. I was still doing one-nighters with the trio around the city, sometimes a hundred miles away, but never so far away that I couldn't be back in Memphis by morning.

They didn't like horns too much in the beginning, because you couldn't get anybody who could play blues the way they wanted it, but then I began to run into guys who are now very big in the jazz field, like George Coleman, who was with Miles Davis, Herman Green, who was with Lionel Hampton, was with me for a time, and so was George Joyner, the bassist. I got Phineas Newborn his first union card, and he, his brother Calvin, who plays guitar, and his old man, who plays drums, were all on my first record date. Booker Little, and fellows like that worked with me, too.

We worked together, but they didn't always like it, because my timing was so bad. My beat was all right—I'd keep that—but I might play thirteen or fourteen bars on a twelve-bar blues! Counting the bars—that was out! These guys would hate that, because they had studied, but all my musical knowledge was what I'd got from records. I tried to play it right, but I ended up playing it my way. The one thing they did like was that I paid well. I could afford to pay them $20 or $25, and if I made more I paid more. They liked that so much that they would be running to get the job, even if they hated what happened to the bars. There wasn't that much work then, and by my being on the radio so much it made mine the most popular band in the city. Another reason those musicians liked working for me was because they could go out, be back, and go to school next morning. I was a young man then myself, about twenty-two.

The radio station leased cars for me and was really very nice. I was there three-and-a-half years, but it could have been a lifetime job. They gave me leave of absence, but they'd find a place for me today if I wanted to go back and go to work. We called it the *Mother Station of the Negroes,* because there was nothing like it before. It had been a hillbilly station, but after these people bought it they programmed nothing but Negro music, and I think it was the only station of that kind. The Spirit of Memphis group was doing pretty good when I first came to Memphis in 1947, but they weren't as popular as they became later, and I think this station helped their popularity.

Beale Street isn't what it used to be, and it was really Beale *Avenue*, not Beale Street. It's about a quarter-mile long, ten or twelve blocks, from the River to the East. I remember when Handy's Park used to be like a circus. Beale Street runs along its south side, Third Street on the west, and Hernando on the east. There used to be parties, jug bands, and everything going on there, something different in each corner, but the crowd usually ended up with the blues singers. It wasn't like a theater with the names up outside. There you had to be *heard*, and whenever a fellow got to feeling good, there all the people would go. But it got to be so noisy that the all-white police ran the cats out. They were attracting so much attention that they were tying up traffic on Third Street, which is a main thoroughfare. They still tried, and some days good policemen would let them carry on a while. Another park they used to settle in was Church Park, in the Negro part.

When I came there, Beale Street had already changed some, and there weren't so many places to play as they claim there used to be. They still had some of the familiar places like the One Minute Café, where winos and people like that could get a coke and a hotdog for a dime when they got hungry. Or they could get a nickel's worth of chili, and stuff like that. Then they had two or three theaters, but it wasn't like it was in Handy's day, which I've heard about from oldtimers, when there were many, many clubs, where you could go and gamble and everything. I guess it's the same with Harlem, but the first time I came to New York was in 1952. Memphis seemed nice to me, and a big change coming there from Mississippi, just as it was later going to Chicago and New York. But Memphis is a nice place to live. It's called *The Gateway to the South* because all the main highways heading to the South come through the city, and there's a famous bridge across the Mississippi there.

I was never in any kind of trouble (touch wood!), so everybody respected me. I didn't have much education, but I always tried to be a gentleman. The Newborns tried to help me, and later on I found out how important it was to study, and I began buying books.

This was when I really began to fight for the blues. I refused to go as rock-'n'-roll as some people did. The things people used to say about those I thought of as the greats in the business, the blues singers, used to hurt me. They spoke of them as though they were all illiterate and dirty. The blues had made me a better living than any I had ever had, so this was when I really put my fight on. A few whites gave me the blah-blah about blues singers, but mostly it was Negro people, and that was why it hurt. To be honest, I believe they felt they were trying to lift the standards of the Negro, and that they just didn't want to be associated with the blues, because it was something still back *there*.

To me, it wasn't like that. If Nat Cole could sing in nightclubs and be a great, popular singer; if Frank Sinatra could sing his songs and be a great person; if Mahalia Jackson could sing spirituals and be great—why couldn't I be a blues singer and be great? Then there were so many people who wanted to play like me, and sing like me, that I wanted to bring it up to a level where they could be proud.

I only made tenth grade in school, but I've read a lot of books. Some years ago I studied the Schillinger system and it helped me a lot. And although I had no formal training, I have asked the musicians around me a lot of questions.

Before I left Kent and went to ABC, I made an album of instrumentals. It wasn't just like I wanted it, and a lot of times I was afraid to make suggestions in case they didn't turn out too well. And when I had faith and confidence, I don't think the record people had. I often got the impression that they didn't understand traditional blues, but were thinking of it in terms of rock-'n'-roll. The blues are almost sacred to some people, but others don't understand, and when I can't make them understand it makes me feel bad, because they mean so much to me. It's something like a kid being whipped for something he didn't do. He has no defense and he just has to take it. That's how it is with me and the blues sometimes.

I know blues records well, because that's how I've made my living for seventeen years. There are different types. Some are dirty. They put a label on them and they have dirty lyrics. Others don't. If you study the blues, and stay broadminded in your study, you'll find there are many different classes. I remember when Louis Jordan was so successful. They just described him as a rhythm-and-blues entertainer, but the man was so talented—'way ahead, in my opinion, of everybody else who was supposed to be in that class. He was a great showman. When it came to doing something on stage before an audience, he was tremendous. Then there are people like Joe Turner and Memphis Slim who are great, too, but quite different. People wonder what makes the difference.

I'd like to go to Europe, but at present I'm a little bit afraid. When a lot of Negroes here say they don't like the blues, I often wonder how people in Europe would go for it. I don't have any showmanship. I want people to accept me, shall I say, for what I get out of what I have. Not on how I look, but for my ability in doing what I'm doing. Some people expect you to jump around. Some Negroes say, "I don't like blues, but I like you." I used to try and argue with them, but now I won't. I just won't say anything. Maybe the next time I meet them they'll say, "Funny thing, but I like blues, too."

MY TEN FAVORITES (1979)
B.B. KING, AS TOLD TO JIM CROCKETT

> Like all professionals, King knows the tradition in which he works, gladly identifying his most important predecessors and distinguishing among them. Even though he mentions his masters again in this book, note how the figures in his pantheon, as well as his remarks about them, are always different. Whereas most of his models were black bluesmen who performed solo or with minimal backup, some, like Charlie Christian and Alonzo "Lonnie" Johnson, performed mostly in jazz ensembles. A few were white—Chet Atkins, the country guitarist/producer who is acknowledged at the beginning of this interview, and Django Reinhardt, a Belgian gypsy, who is mentioned at its end and then again later in the book.

B.B. King is easily the best known blues guitarist in the world. He has walked away with *GP*'s guitar poll in that category every year since it started. His five consecutive wins made B.B. the first member of *Guitar Player Magazine's* Gallery Of The Greats.

But not only is B.B. a great performer, he is also a serious blues and jazz scholar whose personal library of rare recordings exceeds 20,000 discs. And when he goes on the road, B.B. is never without at least thirty or forty cassettes, each carefully indexed in a notebook, which span such musicians as Django Reinhardt, Oscar Peterson, Barney Kessel, Bill Jennings, Big Joe Williams, George Benson, Louis Jordan, Kenny Burrell, Ben Webster, Billie Holiday, Andre Previn, Ray Charles, Johnny Moore, Coleman Hawkins, Eddie Vinson, Etta James, and many, many more, including little known artists whose work is represented by only a handful of 78's.

B.B. King knows every nuance, every break, every chord change on his tapes, and his conversation about them is frequently punctuated with, "Now listen to this! Watch this slur coming up. Man, that's right out of Blind Lemon's version. Here, let me play his other tape."

The world of guitar is, to B.B., an ever expanding one, one that grows with each unexpected discovery. It isn't limited to blues or any other style—and neither is his own scope.

One of B.B.'s greatest joys is turning people on to those guitar greats whom time has passed by. He likes nothing better than to watch a listener's face light up upon that first hearing of Robert Nighthawk, Earl Hooker, or Elmore James.

And ask B.B. who his own favorite guitarists are, and he'll say, "Well, there are so many, it's hard to know where to start." But, in almost rapid sequence he'll cite T-Bone Walker, Blind Lemon Jefferson, Lonnie Johnson, Django, Charlie Christian, Johnny Moore, Saunders King, Bill Jennings, Big Joe Williams, Lightnin' Hopkins, Chet Atkins, George Benson, Elmore James, Bukka White, Earl Hooker, Robert Nighthawk, Muddy Waters, Wes Montgomery, Tal Farlow, Barney Kessel, Herb Ellis, Lloyd Ellis, and Kenny Burrell. And that's just for starters.

—*Editor*

* * *

I have had so many favorite guitar players over the years, that it's hard to just narrow it all down to ten. And I've been influenced by other musicians, too, people like alto player Louis Jordan, trumpeter Cootie Williams, Johnny Hodges, Bobby Hackett, Cleanhead Vinson. I'm a mixture of many people. Like if you listen to Louis Jordan's phrasing, you'll hear B.B. King. When you hear men like these play a melody it's so beautiful! They may never put anything else in it, but if they were playing about a bird, you could see it flying.

But back to guitar players. I'm as much a jazz fan as I am a blues fan. I like country and western music, too. Chet Atkins, to me, is a master guitarist. But among my very favorites are these ten men: T-Bone Walker, Blind Lemon Jefferson, Johnny Moore, Bill Jennings, Big Joe Williams, Lightnin' Hopkins, Charlie Christian, Earl Hooker, Robert Nighthawk and Lloyd Ellis.

T-Bone Walker, for instance, has a touch that nobody has been able to duplicate. I've listened to Alexis Korner, Big Bill Broonzy, and others—all possess a certain touch and tone settings that are different. And when I hear T-Bone play, his tone setting is like no one else's. He has a strange way of holding his guitar, slanting it away from him instead of having it lay flat against his stomach. It's almost like he were playing a steel guitar, but he curls his left arm underneath and reaches his fingers up over the top.

And he seems to kind of scrape his pick across the strings—how he's able to hit specific strings I just don't know. And that touch he gets! I've tried my best to get that sound, especially in the late Forties and early Fifties. I came pretty close, but never quite got it. I can still hear T-Bone in my mind today, from that first record I heard, "Stormy Monday," around '43 or '44. He was the first electric guitar player I heard on records. He made me so that I knew I just *had* to go out and get an electric guitar.

The first electric guitar player I heard in person, though, was a sanctified preacher named Archie Fair in the hills of Mississippi. He was my uncle's brother-in-law. I must have been about 7 or 8. He'd visit my uncle, and when it was time for the adults to go in the kitchen for dinner (the kiddies ate later, if we were lucky), he'd lay his guitar on the bed and I'd crawl up and play with it. One day he caught me and decided to show me a few chords—C, F, and G. Even today I still use those same three chords a lot, and use that I-IV-V progression in many of my songs.

T-Bone used to use a lot of horns, too—trumpet, alto, tenor, and baritone. They made a beautiful sound, like shouting in the sanctified churches, in just the right places. He had a good rhythm section, too. And to me T-Bone seemed to lay right in between there somewhere. That was the best sound I ever heard.

Blind Lemon Jefferson played acoustic guitar, and just solo, but he played the same kind of thing. His way of execution left you with the *feeling* that you could hear someone else backing him up. And he had a special way of phrasing, too, that I don't hear from many people today. Anyone can play 64 notes in a bar, but to place just one or two in that same bar in just the right place, or maybe even let one go by, then double up on it in the next bar—that's something special. Blind Lemon was my idol.

Johnny Moore was Oscar Moore's brother. When Oscar was with Nat Cole, Johnny played in a similar trio with Charles Brown who played piano and sang. This was in the Forties. When Charles decided to go on his own, Oscar left Nat and joined Johnny as a duo. Then they got another singer/pianist. After a couple of years Oscar and Johnny split up; Oscar stopped traveling while Johnny rejoined Charles Brown. I remember seeing Oscar and Johnny playing together in Los Angeles—it was like meeting gods!

Johnny used a big Super 400. He used to like to put in quite a few chord changes when he was playing—things like big, fat 9th chords. They were really modern changes, but they always fit what he was doing. He would slide into his chords sometimes, giving a good, bluesy feeling to a ballad. I think people will start talking a lot more about Johnny Moore in the future.

Bill Jennings used to play in Louis Jordan's band [Tympany Five]. I first heard him on "Ain't That Just Like A Woman." Later, Louis featured him on tunes like "Salt Pork, West Virginia." I and a lot of other guitar players have lifted things from him. Billy Butler is another guy who listened to him. His rhythm was so even and so driving. You know, once you start a beat to going real good, keep it. That's what he did so well. So many guys back then were so good that if you listen to those old recordings today, they're still good.

Big Joe Williams is another great one. His playing with Sonny Joe Williamson was beautiful. Tunes like "Baby Please Don't Go" were really setting a pace.

Lightnin' Hopkins was another one like that, another style setter. Blues guitarists have to all come through players like these two. In the same way, lady singers have to come through Bessie Smith and, later, Dinah Washington—these two covered everything. So did Big Joe and Lightnin'.

Charlie Christian was amazing. I first heard him around 1941 or 42. There were 10¢ vending machines then, like juke boxes but with pictures. You put in a dime or quarter and you could see the most popular people of the day. That's how I first saw Duke Ellington, Louis Armstrong, Count Basie, and Louis Jordan. And that's how I saw Charlie Christian. I was still in Indianola, Mississippi, at the time.

To me, Charlie Christian was a master at diminished chords. A master at new ideas, too. And he was kind of like a governor on a tractor (I used to be a tractor driver). If a tractor is bogging down in the mud, the governor will kick in and give it an extra boost. Christian was the same way—when the band would hit the bridge, he would keep the whole thing flying and get it really taking off. Barney Kessel plays a lot like him, but with ideas that are more of today.

Charlie didn't fluff notes much, either. A lot of us slide into notes because we aren't sure. Like if you want to hit a Bb, you hit a B and slide down into it, or hit an A and slide up. But Charlie Christian *knew.* He was so sure. It really bugs me when someone plays a little flat or a little sharp. All notes that you play in my band have to relate to the actual pitch. Like if the pitch of C were one inch wide, you could play at the outer edge of that inch or at the inner edge; but if you get even a tiny bit outside that inch it bothers me. I always play right in the center—I may slide up or down, but I always land in that center.

Earl Hooker was the best slide guitarist I ever heard. To me he is the greatest. He always *knew* exactly what he was doing. For instance, take a truck driver (I used to drive trucks, too)—you tell him to park next to the curb, and he knows *exactly* where to put the rig. That's how Earl Hooker played.

Robert Nighthawk was Earl's teacher. Robert Nighthawk was one of the greatest slide players I ever heard, certainly among the best. I can hear his playing in Earl Hooker. I was influenced somewhat by Robert, but only by his slide work. Earl Hooker, though, could get me both ways.

Lloyd Ellis is something *else*, man. He still lives in Las Vegas. Been playing with Red Norvo the past two or three years. The things he does are unbelievable. Wes Montgomery carried his own chords as he soloed. That's sort of what Lloyd does, but with rhythm. Lloyd, Red, and Monk Montgomery [Wes' bass playing brother] had a drumless trio, but Lloyd's rhythm playing was so full that you'd swear you heard a drummer in there, too.

* * *

That's ten, but I could go on indefinitely. There's my cousin, Bukka White, a marvelous guitar player; Wes Montgomery was one of my favorite guitarists, too, and a good personal friend; Barney Kessel is another great player and friend, and so is Kenny Burrell: I never met Tal Farlow, but I love his playing so much that I feel we've known each other for years; Herb Ellis is another great one, and so is Muddy Waters—especially in his early slide work; and Django Reinhardt can't be omitted, either, particularly some of his rare recordings with just a regular rhythm section.

It's nice to think back to all the wonderful guitar players, but there are a lot of great ones coming up every day, and their playing will influence me too, just as I hope that my playing will, in some small way, influence others.

PART TWO

How Blue Can You Get?

This interview appeared just after B.B. King broke through to the white, rock audience. Many of the issues raised by the interview are typical of the peace-and-love era, and B.B.'s answers give a unique glimpse of his thinking at the time. This interview was originally printed in *Changes,* a magazine published by Sue Graham Mingus, then the wife of the jazz bassist Charles Mingus. It was the first extensive interview with King of which I am aware. The author's unusual name, unfamiliar to both Ms. Mingus and myself, does not appear in any index of writers' names or any national data base and thus may be a pseudonym.

T.F.—I was checking out some of your old sides like "Blues For Me," "Easy Listening Blues," "The Soul of B.B. King," "A Heart Full of Blues," and quite a few years after these sides were released I read somewhere that you were looking for a band that could echo the combination of your voice and guitar. Have you found the band yet?

B.B. King—I'm still working on that . . . what I really wanted was the arrangement along with the guitar. The guitar is an extension of my voice . . . of me, so I want the band to be equally so; which is what I'm working on now, and it seems to be coming that way. My reason for saying that, is that a lot of times I get arrangers to write. I'm not a very good arranger myself, but I want the arrangers who do write and arrange for me to be able to write the sounds around my voice to where

49

it would sound just like me singing . . . in other words, if you didn't hear me singing, you'll still hear it through the band.

T.F.—I think "Easy Listening Blues" is unique, in terms of the total sound, and the way it was arranged with the organ, piano, tenor, interwoven into your guitar playing.

B.B. King—*That was my own little arranging, but that still isn't what I really want.*

T.F.—In many ways though that was a masterpiece of arranging, and blues sound-wise that record opened up and implied so many possibilities. Do you have plans to do another instrumental album like that?

B.B. King—*I've got plans to do another one. I'm not sure just yet what, and how, I'm going to do it. I've got some ideas on it . . . yes, but I'm not sure just what we are going to do yet . . . I'm not sure, but I do have plans to do one.*

T.F.—How do you compare that phase of your career to this present one, musically?

B.B. King—*Well, we cut that album about 12 years ago, and of course with what is going on now . . . you've got soul music, hard rock, and then now I notice that a lot of the jazz musicians are beginning to somewhat integrate their sounds into the soul, rock, and with the bluesy feeling. So I would think now, that had we done that now, what we did then, it would be a better seller than it was at that time. That's what I believe now, even though you've got so many talented people that are recording today, and they keep coming up with so many beautiful things till it's sort of hard to say man . . . it's really hard, but I do believe truly believe, that had we done that today, what we did then, I think that it would be more appreciated now.*

T.F.—You kept a pretty tight band together for a long time, and I see that the only member of that band still with you is Sonny Freeman . . .

B.B. King—*I have a couple of men that were in my big band that are back with me now . . . my tenor player, Louis Hubert who used to play baritone in my big band, and the trumpet player John Browning, are*

*back with me. They are a couple of the fellows who were with me dur-
ing the big band time, and of course what I'm carrying with me now is
six musicians. I don't think that I'll ever get it any larger . . . maybe one
man, maybe two men. I thought in terms of getting a second guitar and
a baritone and maybe another trumpet. I thought in terms of that
because the big sound is what a lot of people want.*

T.F.—Yes, those records are very rhythmic and danceable, and are a
blend of big band blues with swing. Is it the economics of the business
that now dictates the size of your band, or you want a different sound
now?

B.B. King—*Well, one thing I've always been concerned with is a good
sound. Now I used to also think in terms of dances, because that was
mostly all we played was dances, but in the last year and a half we've
been doing quite a few concerts. We've been playing a lot of the colleges, and mostly concerts everyplace we go. We haven't played many
dances in the last year and a half, and so my mind is kind of left trying
to really play for people to dance, but trying to play for people to listen
and to know me. I want them to really understand me and try to understand what I'm doing on stage, because what I'm doing on the stage
most of the time isn't just trying to show off my artistry in a way of
speaking, but to let the people know how I feel . . . , but to play the
best that I can, yes. But my playing now, this is the funny thing. I'm not
so concerned about the proper rules or rudiments in music now. I'm
interested more in playing what I feel at that particular time. Now
whether that is right, as far as the rules of music are concerned, beautiful, but if it's not right, still beautiful because it's what I feel.*

T.F.—Beautiful, because I always believe one can play all wrong, and it
will still come out right. In terms of your approach to the guitar, we
have T-Bone Walker, B.B. King and . . .

B.B. King—*T-Bone is the boss.*

T.F.—Both of you have moulded the guitar into a very distinct voice
within the Blues. Do you feel that the Blues has to be extended, and
how do you see the logical extension of the guitar?

B.B. King—*I look at that in one way and I think in terms of culture. I
think that each race of people have a certain something that's very dear*

to them, and music happens to be one of them, and I feel that the Blues music being performed by T-Bone Walker and B.B. King and a lot of the other brothers is superbly done, and I don't think that anybody can really do any better right now. But I do think that by listening to other music and other races play music, I think that it's a thing in which a lot can be learned. In other words, I can learn from you and you can learn from me and we learn from others. But in the end I think what we are doing has to advance.

T.F.—From within you.

B.B. King—Yes, right . . . because I think you are influenced. You know, the world is sort of funny man . . . you may not be able to understand a guy's language, but you still can hear his music.

T.F.—Yes, it's all based on sound.

B.B. King—Yes, you can feel that. Personally I call T-Bone Walker the Boss of the Blues Guitar, because he's had a sound for many many years that nobody . . . nobody but nobody, has really been able to copy completely. Nobody. But he has kept that . . . now I've tried to advance on mine because I still hear a sound that I haven't been able to play, and I don't know about him and a lot of the other guys, but you see I like music. I play Blues, but not only because I like Blues only, but I play Blues because I think I can play Blues better than I can play anything else. But I dig music . . . I dig Jazz, I dig Spirituals, I just dig Music . . . I dig Music, period. But you know, if I tried to play shall we say jazz, well I'll make a little parable like this . . . they say, it's better to be a big hog in a little pond than to be a little pig in the river, so I feel that I'm best suited where I am, that is in the Blues, because people say that I am a leader in what I'm doing, and I feel like, that I am.

T.F.—When the shout form of Blues with big Swing bands, and singers like Jimmy Rushing . . .

B.B. King—He's the Boss on that style of singing.

T.F.—Did the trumpet and saxophone riffs influence your guitar style?

B.B. King—Yes, I've been moved by different riffs and especially in that

Basie band. I tell you another man that has always killed me too playing, you know like if a guy sings a chorus and then plays it . . . Louis Jordan is a master on that. There have been many many people that I've listened to over the years and if I was going to try and say who influenced me more other than just the guitar itself it would be hard to say, because I've listened to so many great people man, so many . . . like a minute ago when you mentioned Jimmy Rushing, as far as I'm concerned Jimmy Rushing and Big Joe Turner, when it comes to just flat-foot singing . . . Blues, you just don't beat them. In other words, I usually do them like I do Charlie Parker . . . set them aside and then talk about everybody else. The same goes with Jimmy Witherspoon . . . great Blues singer, man. You see quite a few of the Blues singers like myself, never really went out and tried to, shall we say, do too many pop numbers. We would stay within this little thing. We'd do the Blues, and maybe a little bit of an extension that would lead just a little bit beyond the regular Blues, but never to go really into the pop field . . . only when I did a few ballads, yes, I did a few things with big bands, but at the time when I was doing the things with the big band . . . I'm talking about within the last decade, you know, there were pretty things but in a lot of cases they were too pretty, you see. So it really didn't say anything. They were too pretty to be B.B. King, so it didn't say nothing. To me a lot of it is good, but I guess I brought more to them than anybody else. Now, in time somebody might go back and pick them up and do what I've done, and that is, check them out, and see why. Somebody might do that, but I think I've already checked it out and found out why, because it was just too pretty, too perfect to be B.B. King.

T.F.—Yes, like the ballads "My Reward," and "Don't Cry," with strings on "Blues For Me." As you keep evolving do you find that it's more important to say, change the meaning of your songs by changing the lyrics or you just change the music?

B.B. King—I think I have to refer back to Duke Ellington on that. I notice that all of the things that he has done over the years, he still does them, but he'll modify the sound, you dig. So I think that has a lot to do with it, because if you've got a song, for instance like "Everyday I Have the Blues," which is a standard as far as I'm concerned . . . it was written by Memphis Slim, and has been done many ways. It's just like "Stardust" or "Body and Soul," or many of the good standard tunes. It's been done many times, but many different ways and the words are *there. It's just like a Law Book . . . it's there, the case is there, it's on record . . . you know what I mean. So what you do later is you just go back and you say, well, like the trend of change, people have it . . . the times change, but people have it . . . they are here. So what you do is do something that is going to tell the people of this generation the same story that you told the people of the other generations, but in the same language though. You've got to get the language. When I say language I mean the rhythm pattern of what is being played today, or the beats that are being put down today, and then you are able to get the people of today to understand the story that you are trying to tell of today, which is the same story that you told ten years ago, but on the level of what the people were listening to at that time. That's what I think.*

T.F.—That's very interesting. Say, take young black people who as they change feel that the images that held true for them no longer apply for them now. How do you bridge the gap, and remind them or make them see these images and other things that went down for what they really are?

B.B. King—*I try and make them look in the mirror . . . I try and make them look at themselves. I think in terms of things like this . . . in each generation or each decade, you had the young people that came along with their ideas at that particular time. Now, I can't say, I'm a parent myself, and I can't say with the exception of this, that the kids today are any more progressive or aggressive today than they were when I was a kid, but you work according to the tools that you have to work with.*

    Everybody is always looking, trying to invent, trying to find, and that's been happening ever since I've known anything about this world, and from history I've found that it didn't just happen this decade or when I was a kid, but all the way back you've had great people, great leaders. You've had people from the time of slavery, even when we first got here . . . you've always had somebody that wanted to make, shall we say, do something to try and make things better for us. You've always had that and you will always have it . . . you'll have somebody always that wants to look upwards, and then you'll have somebody that will say, I don't give a damn, and stay right where they are. Now, I certainly would like to say this, I was listening to some things, you know, like today, Black is popular . . . everybody uses the word Black, and appreciate being called Black, but I remember listen-

ing to Blind Lemon, a little blindman from Texas, singing about his Brownskin Woman and all that, you dig what I mean. That was way back, that was before I was born, so I've got a history on what I'm talking about. Then I remember a guy called Robert Nighthawk singing about "My Sweet Black Angel," you dig what I mean. Now, regardless of what anybody might say, whether they want to look over or want to omit it, or shall we say, take themselves away from it . . . I'm talking about Blues, or the way of life of the Blackmen that have lived the things that we sing about . . . I think that anytime that a person wants to omit what has happened, and just wants to do it like we do dirty clothes, kick them in the closet and close the door and say, oh it's all clean in there, knowing that it isn't something is wrong with his mind. And I don't think that the people today are really, shall we say, that short-sighted. I really don't think they are. So I think what is beginning to happen, because I notice now, through our travels, I'm beginning to see more young Black people coming around now, than I've seen in quite some time talking about Blues, you dig what I mean. Because everybody has usually been with whatever is happening today, you know, and a lot of people seem to stumble or step over what happened yesterday, or what is really reality. A lot of people over the years, I don't mean just now man, or in the sixties, but I'm talking about the fifties, you see, when I was young and was starting to sing the Blues, I then was singing to older people, not young people then, you dig . . . so you've had a few of the people all along that really face reality as it is, and you've got more now, beginning to say, well like, "Hey you know, I'm Black, I'm a Black person" or "I'm a Negro," or if it's in another race, you've got a lot of the whites, young whites now will say, "Hey you know like I may dig being somebody else, I might like to be somebody else, but I'm me," so hey, I've got me . . . let me do what I can with me, and this is what a lot of the young Black brothers are starting to do now. I noticed that, a few days ago I was in Medford, Mass. and I think I saw more young Blacks there, at this particular concert, than I've seen in quite some time. So I think it's been an advance . . . you begin to see more and more each time. Like we play the Fillmore East here and I see quite a few, and I notice even in the movement . . . one thing I'm a little sad about, is that I haven't been seeing too many young Black people in the Blues area . . . I mean playing Blues, but I notice that they are not ashamed of them like they once were. It used to be I'd be out on a big show, a big Rock'n'Roll Show . . . you know, you'll have big people like James Brown, Jackie

Wilson, people like that, and a lot of the young Black kids would
come up and say well, like eh, you B.B. King, and I'd say Yeh, and
they'd say, Well, I don't like the Blues you know, and I didn't ask
them if they liked them or not, you see. But what they didn't realize
was that my band was playing the show, my band was playing behind
the stars that they liked, you dig . . . so I must have known something
about it, or my band wouldn't have been playing it. But now I notice
that quite a few times the kids would come up to me and I've had a
few of them say, hey, you know I don't really dig the Blues, but I dig
you. But they don't know, I am Blues. But I'm thinking though, I
really believe this. I believe that people now are beginning to be proud
of themselves, and proud of what they have to offer. It's just like if I
go to a place man, to a union meeting, or to any type of business
meeting and I see big Black men sitting up there, that are holding
office up there, that knocks me out . . . you know, that gives me some-
thing to look forward to, I may never be a big businessman or a good
businessman, but at least I look up there, and see some of the cats
that are, and I see them now, more so, and it's happening more and
more, in all phases of whatever is happening.

T.F.—Right now though there are lots of very good Black Blues musicians that are not being nationally exposed. Do you think that the fact
that it took you so long to get nationally exposed has something to do
with why we don't see or hear about young Black Blues musicians coming up?

B.B. King—*Well that had a lot to do with it, because had it (the Blues)*
been exploited like the other types of music, we would have been
heard of. But by its not being a popular thing, nobody cared about it.
It was almost like a bad taste in the mouth, almost like using profan-
ity . . . if you said Blues, it was almost like a guy was illiterate com-
pletely, he didn't know anything, and this was the lowest form of
music, and that anybody could play it, which is so far from being
right. And I guess a lot of the people, especially young people, thought
of it as a low form of music, something that didn't require any skill or
anything of that sort, so they just bypassed it. But what has happened,
what has caused us to be heard, and I'll be honest and tell you the
truth, what has really happened is that you've had a lot of the white
young groups now that have started to play the Blues, and of course
some of them do . . . some of them play it, very well. They themselves

started to play it and being heard on the radio, and the people weren't ashamed to play theirs, and this opened the doors for us . . . for the guys, that have really been slaving with it for years and years, eating sardines and pork and beans, trying to live. Now it's something like I read, where somebody mentioned that unless certain people put their stamp of approval on certain things, well, it never would be known . . . I believe it was Stokely Carmichael or Rap Brown or one of them, in one of the books I read, where they said, unless it was approved as good by whites, that a lot of the blacks would never accept it. Now, this I read, and it seems to be just about true, and I'll tell you why, because I remember Ray Charles. I knew Ray man, years back . . . I remember when Ray was working with Lowell Fulson and many many people, and Ray hadn't just become a genius . . . Ray has been a genius ever since I've known about Ray Charles . . . a musician, superb, a singer, great, he's Ray Charles, you know. But until say eight or ten years ago when he started getting write-ups and they said well, like this is the genius, then that's when we said Yeah, yeah, that's the genius, you know. So what has happened, because now, in one way I have to say it this way . . . we don't have the means of really exploiting anything like it should be, because we don't own the radio stations or the television stations or the newspapers or the many media to really get it all over. We don't have these facilities to compete, so naturally it has to be coming in from the other side, but what has been, is that it's been a help, I think. Like the days of Boogie Woogie, we had a lot of giants in the Boogie Woogie field that started it, Mead Lux Lewis and many others, so when the white people accepted it was when they had somebody in that field that was very good too, you dig, and so this opens the doors though for the other guys where they can be heard too, and some of them get to be really in demand afterwards. The same thing happened with Rock'n'Roll. Now I was a disc jockey when Fats Domino started, same with Chuck Berry, Little Richard, and all these guys . . . I was a disc jockey at that time . . . I was playing, but I still was a disc jockey and I used to play their records on the radio station where I worked, until Elvis Presley came out, there wasn't too much happening as to where the guys could really make good. When Elvis Presley came out, then Fats Domino went up, Little Richard went up, Chuck Berry went up and all of them began to be giants at that time. And it was the same thing with a lot of the groups like the Dominos, the Drifters, I could go on and name quite a few others, but until the Hill Toppers and many of the other groups, the Ames Brothers and many others, opened the doors, they didn't let them in. So *it's been the same way here with the blues . . . until some of the English groups came over and started being played up all around, well like the Blues guys like B.B. King, Muddy Waters, and quite a few others . . . well, the only one that was being played was Jimmy Reed, and they called him a folk singer.*

T.F.—I've seen you perform mainly for Black audiences at places like the Twenty Grand in Detroit, the Regal Theatre in Chicago, and the Apollo Theatre in Harlem. In many ways, as you quite rightly pointed out Black people do not yet have the means to really make it worthwhile or comfortable for their great musicians, Blues musicians especially to get what they deserve in return for the amount of beauty they've given them, but at the same time for a very long time and up until quite recently the major support Blues has had, has been from Black people.

B.B. King—*This is true, quite true.*

T.F.—Now that more people all over the world are hip to the Blues, and are listening to them, do you think that it will become more and more difficult economically for say young Black people to be able to see the great Blues musicians perform live?

B.B. King—*Well, I don't think that it would really be more difficult in a way of speaking, with the exception of this . . . we as entertainers, or you as a writer, want to be known world-wide. If I had been just doing this, just to amuse myself, I would have stayed in Mississippi. But that wasn't what I wanted . . . I wanted to be creative, I wanted the world to know . . . I wanted you to know, I wanted him to know, them to know, I wanted everybody to know. So another thing one has to look at is this . . . I'm not doing it by myself. I have a group with me, that has to be paid . . . they don't do nothing for nothing, you know what I mean. So they've got to be paid, so in order for them to be paid I have to be paid. Then in order to let the world know what we want, it brings in many things like publicity, like management, like booking agencies, and many, many phases, because as you may know, what is happening in a lot of ways is politics. So here I am, the guy that is out there, trying to sing my Blues, but the only way I'm going to be able to make a television show, or anything else, or maybe get into pictures, is got to be* done through the agencies and through the management and everybody else, and they are going to talk politics before you get in there. So in that case, in a way, it might make it a little hard, in some ways, but, I think of it like this. When I see Ray Charles or Lou Rawls or Sammy Davis Jr. or some of the other people that I know, that are capable of entertaining people, capable of really creating things, it makes me happy and I feel good when I hear that Ray is going into the Copacabana, or when Sam Cooke or James Brown, or any of the people that I know deserve going there, it makes me happy to know that they are going in there. But now let's think of it in terms of the older people that are around you, that have to be paid. If I played some of the places that I used to play, well, nobody would get paid really.

T.F.—That's true.

B.B. King—*Because a lot of the places couldn't afford to pay what we would need to survive. This is what I'm talking about. Because as you grow, it's just like a child, when you are small you can get a suit for eight dollars, ten or twelve dollars, when you grow up to become a man, one suit, for the same person, will cost you three hundred dollars sometimes, if you want a good one. What I'm saying is that as you grow, it takes things to help you to grow . . . it's just like nourishment or food. As one grows he needs more . . . he has to have more to survive. Like I've run into a lot of places where the people come up and say, wow, I remember B.B. King . . . I remember when I paid a quarter to see him. Well this is true, but what they don't know is that I remember the time when I would have paid somebody to listen, if I had the money, you know. So this happens. But in time the operation gets to be like now, in the last two years we've been to Europe a couple of times. I was looking once where, just taking my group over there and back cost $14,000 . . . $14,000. Two or three years back, if I had made $14,000 in one year I would have been, oh man, if I can make it today, clear, $14,000, I would be happy. But they paid that to fly me and my group over there to do engagements. So you can imagine what it costs people now to go from here to there. For instance I'm supposed to be somewhere tonight. I've got to get my band over there, my equipment and all that has to get over there, then you've got to buy equipment, then you got to have some way for your group to travel because they've got to make it . . . they've got to make the job.*

T.F.—That's a change from your old band bus.

B.B. King—*Well, somebody stole that. These are the type things and a lot of the people when they don't think realistically, a lot of times they'll think small. They'll say, OK, here is a guy here, I know a time when we could get him for $150, now he wants $1,000 . . . why? But they don't think about the fact that there was a time when I could buy a can of sardines for a nickel and now they want a quarter for it or twenty-nine cents, plus tax, so everything goes up. Everything does. And the people that are working with you, sure, if you could live the same way that I used to live, oh man, it would be fine. Because people knew me. I could stay at this house or stay at this house, and a lot of times people would feed me free, and it was the same way with the band. A lot of times when I used to have a band, after we get off, sometimes we'd play for the rest of the night at the same place, just jamming and having fun. Cats don't do that now. Now, you'll find that once in a while people will want to jam, but not that way. The way we used to do, man, is like we'd be playing at a club and we get off at one or say two o'clock, well heck, we'd stay there until maybe sunrise next morning, because other musicians come in and we stay there and enjoy ourselves . . . cats have a few drinks, maybe get some food, a hamburger usually was what it was, or a couple of hotdogs and we'd be there . . . beer or some liquor, you know, but that doesn't happen like that anymore, because nowadays the people who pay to get you there, they'll be pleading to bring you in there, and as soon as the dance is over they'll say, Get up man, we've got to close the door, we've got to do this. They put you out.*

T.F.—I notice that a lot of people give the white Blues musicians credit for having brought about a mass interest in the Blues, and that in their interviews they say that B.B. King is the Boss, and also that they learned a lot from you and so many other Black Blues musicians. I wonder why say if you play at the Fillmore with some of these groups, you don't top the bill?

B.B. King—*I have topped the bill there.*

T.F.—Financially as well as name-wise?

B.B. King—*That happened too, but it doesn't happen as often as we think it should happen. But it is beginning to happen more. I think that goes back to the same thing I was telling you about a while ago. You have to become supersupersupersuper before you can really get that.*

T.F.—Like this new young white generation is supposed to be hip, and going by what they say they are supposed to be more aware than their parents, and they claim that they are trying to correct all the wrongs their parents did and all that . . . and in some cases we know that they do have some power, like in the music industry, since the record companies know that the groups will sell records for them, they allow the groups to decide what tunes to record, and now some of these white blues musicians have become producers and overseer the records now being made by the black musicians who are supposed to have companies, do you feel that there has been an outgoing trueness from the white blues musicians whose very presence today is due to people like you, Bukka White, Big Joe Williams, Robert Johnson and many, many others who really created the music. Do you feel that eventually they'd feel and say, we'll do right, we know what is right and push for what's right?

B.B. King—I think that as long as you have a world you're gonna have some people that are in it for themselves, and themselves only . . . You've got that and I believe that as long as you have a world you gonna have some of those people. But now, it seems like they are getting fewer . . . fewer, of those people that think of themselves only. It seems like to me that, that is happening . . . not fast enough though, but it seems like it is happening. But you've got some of the guys, for instance like Jimi Hendrix, and well, who else . . . Jimi Hendrix is one of the few people, then Taj Mahal, that are beginning, it seems like, to command their spot among the rest of the people as far as, shall we say, finance and billing are concerned.

T.F.—I read in *Jazz & Pop* magazine that during their last tour the Rolling Stones were getting $29,000 a night against a percentage of the door, and they were paying Ike & Tina Turner $1,200 a night to be on the bill with them.

B.B. King—Well, I have to think of that in terms of this . . . I've worked on package shows where there were all blacks on it, and I remember when I was getting with my band $1,000 a day, with thirteen people . . . that was what I was getting then. I had thirteen men to pay off, plus myself . . . thirteen men in the band, and of course there was the utility man, the drivers, and people like that. And I was out a long time before a lot of the people I was on the show with, and I'm sure they'd heard me before then, and I was getting I'll repeat $1,000 and I know that two or three of the people were singles. When I say singles, I mean just one person.

T.F.—Backed by the House band?

B.B. King—No, my band was backing them, and they were getting three and four times the amount that I was getting with the percentage. So that's nothing new, and a few of these, if I would mention their names, which I won't, have praised me for being one of the leaders, so I think of that somewhat in the same way that I think of the Stones tour. I was on that tour too. It did a lot for me . . . not financially. It did a lot for me as far as publicity is concerned, because a lot of people heard me . . . seen and heard me, that had never heard me, and never would have heard me, had I not been on that tour . . . so it did a lot for me like that . . . I've known Ike for a long time, I don't know Tina that well, but I know Ike . . . I've known Ike since he was a kid, and knowing Ike as I do, he wouldn't have worked for that. But whatever he got, it wasn't nothing like the Stones were getting. I know that. But I have to say this though, in another way. Each group that gets big has a manager and this manager is usually going to say yes and no . . . yes to yes and no to no. What I mean by that is that, it's what he thinks will help them, that he'll take. What he doesn't think is going to help them, he won't take. And in a lot of cases, the reflection goes back to the group, in a way of speaking, but you hardly ever find one of the managers who is the same age as the group.

T.F.—Now that you have been relieved of the many functions you performed when you had your big band, and have a team and A&R men etc., has this given you more time to create musically?

B.B. King—I think it's just like in Television . . . you can go to a TV studio and you'll find many people doing many things, but then you've got the director there, that coordinates them all. Take a person like me for instance, when I'm thinking, I'm thinking only of me and the guitar, in other words, what I can get out of that. I may hear an arrangement, that sounds fine to me, but if I've got a good arranger, well to him it is *a different story. He hears things that I don't hear. Same thing with an A&R man in the studio. He'll be able to bring out things . . . what he thinks, in terms of being commercial. Me, I'm thinking of creating something.*

T.F.—Is there ever a clash?

B.B. King—*Yes, there's usually a clash from time to time, unless you've got a very understanding person with you. Usually with my producer now I'll talk with him and I would say, Hey, I've got something that sounds like this, and I'll like to do it. He may not be too enthusiastic over the sound of it, but he won't fight me about doing it, but what he'll do is say, well look, what else have you got? So what they normally would do is wind up cutting what you want. . . .*

B.B. KING (1971)
MICHAEL LYDON

Michael Lydon is a near-contemporary of mine and was among the first rock critics to write an extended profile of King, first in *The New York Times Magazine* (October 27, 1968) and then in his book *Rock Folk* (1974). Lydon traveled with King and thus gives an intimate picture of life on the road.

At the end of 1969 B.B. King played the Fillmore, three years after Bill Graham first booked him and presented his blues to the young white rock fans. In those years, particularly the third, he had become prosperous and famous. Dozens of magazines had interviewed him, he had appeared on all the late night television panel shows, his albums were best sellers, and his singles were even edging into the charts. A year before when he played San Francisco he had stayed at the Oakland Holiday Inn; after the Fillmore he had done Oakland's black Club Showcase. This time he was at the Mark Hopkins, and his next date was a concert in the Hollywood Bowl. The chitlin' circuit wasn't behind him forever ("I still want to play for the people who were so loyal to me," he said), but the need to do that endless grind was over. He had made it, and was on his way to becoming what he is now, the true king, the Duke Ellington of the Blues.

He was playing and singing better than ever before, his control tighter and his emotional range wider. Where he might once have fallen back on surefire routines, he was experimenting. A year before he had said how he envied the melodic inventiveness of Charley Byrd and Kenny Burrell. "I just don't know where they get all those little notes, then string 'em together in pretty tunes," he said. "Oh man, I'd like to play like that." At the Fillmore he was still playing blues, but opening up their structure to a new lyricism. His singing could be no more rich than it always had been, but now it had a flamboyant zest that made him seem to sparkle in the spotlight. Most extraordinary, his processed hair, which virtually no black entertainer over thirty is ever seen without, was gone. He looked younger, and when he smiled, he looked like a ten-year-old at a carnival. Every crowd gave him long standing ovations.

"Yes, I'm liking success, all of it," he said one night in the dressing room. "My music is getting out, and I'm not having to worry where the next dollar is coming from no more. I'm not rich, understand, but farther from the edge than ever before."

A year before I had traveled with B.B. in the deep South; there and then the edge was a lot closer.

A cool night breeze blew outside, across the Mississippi and the cane fields that press against the town of Port Allen, Louisiana. Inside the Club Streamline, a bare cinder-block box crowded with chipped, linoleum-topped cafeteria tables, it was noisy, stifling, and rank with sweat. B.B. King was an hour late. He was coming from Mobile, where he had played the night before, and the customers—field workers in collarless shirts, city dudes from Baton Rouge on the other side of the river, orange-haired beauticians, oil refinery workers with their wives—were grumbling. "We want B.B.," shouted a lady with a heavy sprinkling of gold teeth.

"'Deed we do," answered someone, but Sonny Freeman and the Unusuals, King's six-piece touring band, kept rolling through "Eleanore Rigby." Then from a side door B.B.'s valet carried in a big red guitar, plugged it into a waiting amplifier, and left it gleaming on a chair in the dim yellow light.

"Lucille is here; B.B. can't be far behind," said the gold-toothed lady.

The tenor sax man took the mike. "Ladies and gentlemen, it's show time, and we're *happy* to pre*sent* the *start* of the *show*, the King of the *Blues*, Mr. B.B. *King.*" A wave of clapping washed back to the bar, and a heavyset man in a shiny maroon suit stepped lightly to the stage and picked up the guitar. The band started "Every Day I Have the Blues," and B.B. King, eyes screwed shut and body bent forward, hit a quick chord.

From that instant the very molecules of the air seemed alive; King and his guitar were a magic source of energy from which came fine glistening notes that drew the whole club into their tremulous, hesitant intensity. "Put the hurt on me," a man yelled. Women jumped up and stood twisting their hips, heads bowed, hands held high in witness. "Evra day, evra day I have the blues," B.B. sang, rocking back and forth, both fists clenched beside his head, and the shouting went on.

"Thank you, ladies and gentlemen," King said smoothly when he finished, the band riffing gently behind him. "So sorry I'm late, but we're so glad to have you with us and we hope to he'p you have a good time. If you like the blues, I think you will. Are you ready to get in the alley?"

A deafening roar said yes. He hit a high note that bent flat as it faded, then another, then another, the crowd erupted, and he was off again. For an hour he played the blues, rough and smooth, exultant and downhearted, blues that are fresh every time: "Rock Me, Baby," "Three O'Clock Blues," "Don't Answer the Door," and his classic "Sweet Little Angel." . . .

But at the break B.B. wasn't so happy. Splashing his thick neck with Fabergé Brut and touching up his roughly processed hair with Ultra Sheen, both proffered by Wilson, his valet, he moaned about his gas pains.

He's been going to a doctor for his stomach, he told the knot of hangers-on gathered around his dressing-room chair like retainers at a friendly throne, but that doctor hadn't meant nothing but misery.

"'No fried or fatty foods,' he says, 'no salad dressing, no liquor, and no women.' I told him, I said, 'Doc, those first things maybe, even liquor, but the last, forget it.' And he said to me, 'B., you can *say* forget it, but the pills I'm givin' you for your stomach, they gonna *make* you forget it.'"

He paused to get a chuckle of appreciation from the admirers. It came, and B.B. smiled too. "I'm not through yet, lemme go on.

"Now I didn't believe that doctor that some pill was gonna make *me* forget it, and for three weeks it didn't, I was goin' just like always. And this morning, I was with a sweet gal I been trying to make for fifteen years. She finally said the time was right, so there we was, trying to get something done before I had to get up and drive all the way here, and, you know what? Wouldn't do a thing! Not a blame thing," and he slapped his thigh, laughter bubbling out of him. "I played with it, *she* played with it, but it just lay there like a hound," and he held his index finger out, limply crooked. Everyone backstage broke up with B.B., and he sat there basking in his own joke, his grin wide and loose.

He went back on stage, chuckling, this time in a light green suit, purple turtleneck, and gold pendant. It was one o'clock, late for working people on a weekday night, and the club was emptying. But King played on, oblivious of the tables deserted but for bottles and overturned glasses. "Look at him, man," said Elmore Morris, King's entr'act singer for eleven years. "The greatest. It's the depth he gets to—he knows what they are and how to get to 'em. A mean man or small man couldn't do that; takes a real man like B. to penetrate like he does."

Born Riley B. ("I never knew what that B. was for.") King in Itta Bena, Mississippi, he became Riley King, the Blues Boy from Beale Street, when he got his first radio job in Memphis in 1948; in time that got shortened to Blues Boy King and then to B.B. "It still means Blues Boy," he says. "That's what I am. It's too late to change." Now forty-four, he looks his age but not a day older; there is no stoop in his stance, no gray in his hair, and no tiredness in his bright eyes and lively mouth. His face most often has a calmly mournful quality but can break up in laughter and suddenly have an impishness that just as suddenly disappears. At times, particularly in his Cadillac, he looks like a sober Negro doctor, exuding quiet success, but even then you see in his eyes that he is a bluesman, a man for whom the blues are his sorrow, his power, his essence. "I always start my show with 'Every Day I Have the Blues,'" he says simply, "because it's true."

The blues—"American music," says B.B.—are hard to define. "If you have to ask, you'll never know," some say, others adding more aggressively, "If you ain't got 'em, don't mess with 'em." The passion expressed in blues is, however strong, so subtle that great debates have always raged over which musicians and fans could really (or *really* really) play or feel them. Purists believe that the true bluesmen (all black) could be counted on two hands; blues democrats argue that Moses, Beethoven, Gandhi, and all disappointed lovers know the blues.

The evidence is on the side of the democrats. As musical form, the blues emerged less than a hundred years ago out of the peculiar institution of slavery of Africans in America; they are now a metaphor for emotions felt by people all over the globe. Blues are at the essence of a wide range of American musics, and have influenced all modern composers. Whatever the bastardized or attenuated idiom or style they get shoved into, they always maintain their integrity against depredation.

The blues are first the music of black Americans. Their technical basics evolved in the meeting of black slave and white master cultures; in time they accumulated a vast range of meanings, subjects, and styles. The blues have become the aggregate expression of black Americans, detailing every facet of their lives, reflecting every change in their fortunes, and speaking, often obliquely, their self-assertion in a world that tries to trap them in invisibility. The fundamental requirement of the blues is absolute honesty, and they are accurate to the last nuance of black life in America. Aesthetically, they *are* black America, and to love them, to find expression of oneself in them, is to identify with the black American experience.

That experience is as diverse as the blues, but its unifying fact is displacement—simply not being at home. The blues are the music of a people profoundly alienated, a people making their way in a foreign land—Babylon, Eldridge Cleaver calls it—to which they were brought as captives. On one hand attempting to deal with the cruel or absurd reality facing them as best they can, they are also searching for a surer, more essential reality—their past, their historical, racial, and primal selves, and the web from which they were ripped. One feels the earnestness of that search, its yearning and frustration, in every blues chorus with its Sisyphus-like climb away from the tonic chord, the brief reaching of an unstable peak, and the inevitable fall back to the tonic.

But so powerful is the world black Americans live in that the search must be carried on within its terms. Though the blues are always played on Western instruments, the "blues scale" is not Western. The notes that give blues their emotional tonality are not the "do re mi" that white Americans call "the scale." Guitars are not fretted to include them; "blue notes" are between the keys, as pianists say. A blues musician can only reach them by distorting the sound their instruments were built for—bending a guitar string, fading open trumpet valves, "overblowing" a harmonica, or grace-noting across several piano keys. He must twist and restructure the reality he is given to find his way through to those tones that soothe and inspire him. Using the tools of the West, he over and over again recreates those haunting notes that seem to be an elusive key to a past and self remembered only well enough to make its disappearance agonizing. The tragedy of the blues is that you can't go home again; their hope is that through them, maybe someday, somehow, you can. And right now, you can make where you are a lot more homey.

The dialectic of displacement and the yearning for home is universal, a theme as old as man's expulsion from Eden and as new as our own births, yet the popularity of the blues indicates that it has particular relevance today. Did we know it no other way, the worldwide acceptance of the blues would prove that millions of men now feel robbed of their homes, cheated of their birthrights, lost and oppressed. A lot of people in this world of all colors and cultures are niggers, and they have the blues.

In a century the blues may be a form like the sonata form, something to be learned from a book. Today they are living truth. And an American one; while the world is being Americanized (i.e., accepting the technology of the white master culture), it is also (maybe therefore?) learning the other side of American life, the loneliness of displacement. Blues truth runs counter to hysterical confidence in progress, machines, and human power. It is a darker, more fateful, though ultimately more relaxed and humorous truth that has its own sober and sensual comfort. "When it all comes down," say the blues (here in the words of Memphis Slim), "you gotta go back to Mother Earth." The blues tell that truth with the ease and grace of folk tales, as well as with raunchiness, anger, and despair.

This simple music bears that truth's burden easily, because it is not quite an "art," but the vital creation of men of very human genius.

King is one of those men. He had been on the road for almost twenty years, but the day when he was a James Brown, a sex symbol with top-10 songs, has been over for a decade. Soul music, with a heavy beat, strong gospel influences, and glamorous stars, is the staple of the best-selling charts, not the blues as played by older men who won't change the rhythm to suit the latest dance steps. Blues are "roots": recognized as the basic source but ignored because they merge into the cultural background. It is the Otis Reddings, Bob Dylans, Rolling Stones, and Janis Joplins who, working changes on the blues, get the hits. Even when folk enthusiasts in the late fifties and early sixties were "discovering" blues singers like Son House and Mississippi John Hurt, B.B. was passed over as too urban and sophisticated. His blues are all music created by city artists in the past twenty years; few date directly from the oral tradition of the country blues singer. But B.B., long caught in the middle, is now getting full attention.

On one hand, educated blacks who had scorned the blues as dirty music, as an opiate of the people, and a result of an oppressed past, are turning to them to express their blackness; B.B. is both funky enough and modern enough for them to dig. For a Negro to say, "B.B. is my main man," Charles Keil wrote in *Urban Blues,* "is to say, 'I take pride in who I am.'" On the other, the millions of white kids going deeply into rock 'n' roll, led by young white guitarists like Michael Bloomfield, Eric Clapton, and Elvin Bishop, began to discover the blues in the mid-sixties. The touted "New Rock" is as much a blues revival as it is electronic psychedelia. What the Beatles are to the latter, B.B. is to the former. For blues fans, black and white, not only is King a beautiful musician, he is the essence of the lead guitarist, the soul man alone with his guitar, a breed that for cultists has all the misterioso allure of the cowboy, racing driver, or bullfighter. Both audiences recognize him as a proud and intelligent man, an artist who presents himself with no apologies and no put-ons.

"I'm different from the old blues people," he says. "I don't smoke or drink on stage. And unlike the new ones, I don't dance. I'm just not electrifying. I figure that it's the singing and the playing the people come for and that's what I give 'em.

"My only ambition is to be one of the great blues singers and be recognized. If Frank Sinatra can be tops in his field, Nat Cole in his, Bach and Beethoven and those guys in theirs, why can't I be great and known for it in blues? It's been a long time, and the fellas that made it before me with the twist and rock, I'm not saying they don't deserve it, but, I think I do too."

In Port Allen recognition seemed a long way away. The group had just started forty-five straight one-nighters in clubs on the "chitlin' circuit" that would have them crisscrossing the Deep South. They would get good crowds because it's blues country, but they knew they'd been doing it for years and that you don't make money from people who don't have it themselves. And that night, right after the Club Streamline promoter said he didn't have the $650 promised and B.B. wearily took four hundred dollars, there was trouble.

They left the club at 3:00 A.M.—B.B., his road manager Frank Brown, and Wilson in the green Cadillac Fleetwood Brougham, the band in a Ford Econovan (a disparity exactly expressive of their business relationship to B.B.; despite it they are all friends). They planned to drive the two hundred miles to the motel in Mobile by morning, sleep until early afternoon, then drive to Montgomery for the date that night. While they gassed up in Baton Rouge, Wilson and two guys in the band walked over to a café for sandwiches. No eating at the counter, said the door attendant as a dozen white toughs watched over their beers; no takeouts either. "We're Wallaces," shouted a tough. "Great, man," sneered Wilson from the door. "Whah, you nigger," said a tough, coming out after him and punching him to the gravel. "Git 'em!" cried another, and suddenly the whites were outside, one swinging a heavy chain.

The three fought back, and when Frank, a giant, came running and grabbed away the chain, the whites scattered. But tenor sax man Lee Gatling had been stabbed in the arm and trumpeter Pat Williams was bleeding from a chain wound on the forehead. The police who gathered asked a few questions, said they couldn't find any suspects, and stood under the blue-white gas station lights eyeing the band suspiciously.

King, who had missed the action because he was in the men's room, quickly took charge, ordering the ambulance, calming his men, and talking to the police, but his mind was somewhere else. "Wanted something to eat, just something to eat and a man'll hate you so bad he'd kill you. You think things are getting better," he said to no one in particular, staring at the "I Have a Dream" stickers on his bumper. "Thought you knew how to get along, never anything like this happen before. Oh, man, this hurts so bad. And they tease me when I sing the blues. Hah! What else can I sing?"

They all waited at the hospital until six before a doctor appeared and said Williams was all right. As the sun rose they started for Mobile, getting there, sleepless, in the glare of early afternoon.

B.B. got a few hours' sleep in before they started out for Montgomery. The anger of the night before was beginning to recede, and as the Cadillac swept north, he talked about his life. He had told his story before to other interviewers, often in the same words, as if he had saved it all up, knowing it would one day be worth telling. His mother had left his father when he was four, taking him to the Mississippi hills and her churchgoing family. She died a few years later, and he spent his boyhood as a fifteen-dollar-a-month hired hand for a white tenant farmer until his father found him and took him back to the Delta, where he chopped cotton and drove a tractor on a plantation.

He had sung in church since he was tiny and learned guitar from a minister uncle, first sneaking the guitar off the bed where the uncle put it while he ate dinner. In the Delta he started singing and playing regularly in a gospel quartet.

At eighteen he was drafted and then deferred—the plantation owners wanted good workers on the homefront—something B.B., who misses having no formal musical education, is still bitter about: "If I had been let stay in, I could have gone to music school on the G.I. Bill." But then it meant getting Army equivalent pay instead of fieldhand wages and having money in his pocket. "I'd take the extra and buy a bus ticket for as far as it would take me—Jackson, Oxford, even Hattiesburg—and play the blues on street corners, making more on a weekend than I could all week. 'Course, I was sneaking away; playing blues if you were in a sanctified singing group was evil, consorting with the devil. But I didn't mind 'cause of the money, and all those cheering me as I played, that made it worth it."

After the war he moved to Memphis, determined to make it. He lived with his cousin, the great bluesman Bukka White, and landed a ten-minute spot on WDIA, one of the first radio stations anywhere with Negro per-

sonnel, advertising Pepticon Tonic and playing his blues. He was immediately popular; by 1949 he had the best-known blues trio in Memphis, his
own show as a disk jockey, and his first big record, "Three O'Clock
Blues," which stayed at the No. 1 spot in the rhythm and blues charts for
eighteen weeks.

"I was a star from then on, getting good guarantees, making every
record—'Sweet Sixteen,' 'Rock Me, Baby,' 'You Know I Love You'—a hit.
Always traveling, too. One year we did 342 one-nighters, me and Lucille,"
patting the guitar case behind his head. The present Lucille, a red Gibson
with gold frets and mother-of-pearl inlay, is Lucille No. 7; a label on the
case says, "My name is Lucille, I am a guitar. My boss is B.B. King. Please
Handle Me With Care."

"Lucille got her name in a nothing town by the name of Twist,
Arkansas. We were playing some club, and some guys were fightin' and
they knocked over a kerosene barrel and burned the place down. I was
almost killed going back in to save my guitar, and when I found out the
fight was over a gal named Lucille, I named my guitar that to tell me to
keep her close and treat her right."

The car slipped through miles of forest. Frank had the radio on jazz
softly. . . . Harder times came in the late fifties and early sixties. When
Top-40 programming swept radio everywhere, replacing specialty shows
like blues hours with solid pop, B.B. didn't get much air play. Most bluesmen either moved to rock or went off the road; blues became the music of
country people, the old and the poor. He always had work, but the clubs
and money weren't good, especially compared to the standards set by
black stars making it in white markets. He still recorded, but the albums
sold for $1.99 on drugstore racks. One car crash wiped out his savings;
another almost took off his right arm.

"Then my second wife left me and it like to killed me. I really loved
that gal, but she wanted me off the road. I wanted to, too, but I was
behind to the Government so I couldn't, but she didn't understand. Just
being a blues singer was hard. People thought they were all illiterate,
drinking and beating their women every Saturday night. I'd fight for the
blues, but they wouldn't listen, and since I didn't have school past ninth
grade I didn't feel too confident of myself. I'm still a country boy, a little
scared of people who can make you feel bad. It's like since I was a boy
going to bed with no lights 'cause there was no electricity, I've been afraid
of the dark."

That night B.B. was magnificent. The Montgomery Elks Club,
Southern Pride Lodge No. 431, was packed to the walls with a good-time

crowd, and he worked for them. His face beaded with sweat, Lucille brought up under his chin, his eyebrows going up and down, B.B. pulled out the notes, starting solos with just the rhythm of organ and drums, and building slowly to the full power of the band behind him, Lucille always showing the way. When you thought Lucille had said it all, King sang, his voice both tough and vulnerable. Young white audiences marvel at his guitar playing, but for the blacks he is a blues singer, first and last. "I've been down-hearted, baby, every since the day we met," he began one song softly, ending in full-blown shouting. . . . Before cheering had died down he was into a slow and very funky "Don't Answer the Door," that ended in more screaming. . . . And then the next song and the next, fast ones, slow ones, setting up moods and dissolving them for new ones; everything was real and true. "There's no signifyin' jive with B.," shouted one delirious listener, his glass held up in salute, as King went off.

"I wish they had something could measure the pressure inside a person," King said in the cramped dressing room. He spoke softly but intensely. "Like at times when you're in a strong mood, if you've been hurt bad by a gal or your best friend. It's like that when I'm playing and I know exactly what I want to play, and it's a goal I'm trying to reach, and the pressure is like a spell—oh man, I don't have the words.

"But I know this, I've never made it. I've never played what I hear inside. I get close but not there. If I did, I'd play the melody so you'd know what it was saying even if you didn't know the words. You wouldn't know when Lucille stopped and my voice began."

A beautiful woman with a wig of rust-colored curls came in. "Hello, B., how are you?" she said.

"Happy to see you, beautiful," he said with a big smile, and kissed her.

"Haven't seen you for a year, B. Are you staying over?" she said, rearranging her curls.

"No, baby, we're going to Atlanta soon as we're ready." She looked crestfallen. They chatted a few minutes and she left. "Man," said B.B., wiping his brow. "Gonna have to do something about those pills!"

By the car the guys in the band were talking about the fight; they hadn't stopped talking about it. They couldn't figure out the why of it. Nothing like it had ever happened to any of them; its ferocity had astonished them. B.B. joined them.

"You never saw anything like it before, B.?" asked one.

Never, and he couldn't explain it for them, he said, but things are better now. You didn't stay at Holiday Inns when he started, but in black fleabags; you kept food in the car and relieved yourself beside the road.

"If you had that fight a while back, you'd be in jail now. Only one thing I regret about that fight: you fellas didn't put one of them in the hospital."

"Next time, B.," said Lee.

It was a long drive to Atlanta and B.B. felt like talking. T-Bone Walker's clean sound and Elmore James's swing were his big guitar influences; church preaching for his singing. But he always loved jazz, especially Count Basie. "I just *love* to swing, man," he said, "and nobody swings like the Count." Charley Christian's guitar was an inspiration, but "the man who won my heart" was Django Reinhardt. "He had a singing guitar, gypsy Spanish, soulful. It really filled my soul."

Classical works are too long for him, but there's no music, he said, that if he listens to it, he can't see what it's getting at, even Japanese Koto music. When he retires he'd like to have a disc-jockey show again and play whatever he liked. "All music is beautiful. Man, I got twenty thousand records and I never buy ones I don't like. I even have a record of Gene Autry singing 'T. B. Blues.' He's a rich man now but there was a time when he was saying something.

"Old bluesmen, they didn't listen to anything but blues; I do and I'm more polished than them. But blues can't be too polished; they have to be raw and soulful. They started with a fella singing to you like he was telling you a story; if he kept up the tempo, he could make a chorus fifteen, even twenty bars long if he wanted to say his piece. I was like that, but when I got a band I had to stay within twelve bars to keep with the other fellas. And man, those bars went flyin' by! But blues can't be perfect. A lotta white people can't sing the blues because their English is too good. Blues and correct English don't sound right. You gotta break the verbs for it to be blues.

"Some say the blues are backward, but I think they can he'p black people now. If something is bothering you and you got a friend, it he'ps if you can talk about it. It may not solve it, but it he'ps. You can talk about your problems in the blues and you find people have the same problems, and then you can do something. Blues' words are usually about men and women, because that's where it all starts—men do most things on account of women—but if you hear the blues, you *know* it's about a lot more."

B.B. doesn't have a home; Memphis is home base, and he has a farm there that his father lives on, but in Memphis, as elsewhere, home is the motel room he's in. The one in Atlanta looked it. Spilled over the bed, tables, floor, and sink were briefcases full of contracts, letters, unfinished songs, notes for a book to be called "How I Play the Blues," by B.B. King; an electric pan in which he makes oatmeal for his ailing stomach; a tape recorder, a tape-cassette-radio, a dozen changes of street clothes and another dozen stage outfits, books about flying (B.B. is almost qualified as a pilot), two big red volumes of *Joseph Schillinger's System of Musical Composition* from which he is learning to write his own arrangements, copies of *Billboard* and soul-music magazines, and empty packs of Kools. "I've been doing this a while," he said, padding around the piles in his black silk underwear. "I own an apartment building in Memphis, wouldn't mind moving in, but whites live there, and if I moved in, they'd move out and my property wouldn't be worth a thing. That's the truth."

He found what he was looking for, a sheaf of unfinished songs. "This one I've been working on. It says what I think about myself. *'I ain't no preacher/Not trying to be no saint/Because I don't get high every day/Don't mean I don't take a drink.'* That's all now, but it's gonna be a song saying, I'm just B.B., take me as I am."

"Maybe soon I'll just work weekends, maybe even have a club of my own. I got four kids by various women; they're all grown and have children. Maybe I'll enjoy my grandchildren like I never had a chance to with my own. But I'll never stop playing. As long as people'll hear me, I'll keep playing."

The next date was at the Lithonia Country Club, a place at the end of a dirt-road maze twenty miles from Atlanta. "This is a real funk," said Sonny Freeman, unbelievingly. The club, a shack, was half empty, the decor made the Club Streamline look like the Stork Club: bare wooden chairs and tables, a cracked cement floor, and a stage, incongruously lined with ripped tin foil, lit by one fixed spotlight. It was a tough night; the audience seemed to like the blues but just wouldn't clap. "You know we're working hard for you," B.B. pleaded several times. "Whyncha' beat your hands together for us," but all he got was desultory applause.

"Man, you see what it's been like for us all these years," he said at the break. "It's so hard when people ain't with you. But if they can't be satisfied, man, I play for my own satisfaction."

He did. Coming back on at midnight, the club even emptier than when he had begun, he played roughly, slashing his pick across the strings in harshly vibrant chords, even breaking two strings. But as he was bringing the show to a close, he changed moods. Singing in a pure falsetto, leaving the roughness behind, he made his voice all sweet pleading. . . .

The riffing of the band built through the second chorus and exploded as he started the third. "Someday, baby," he sang, his voice almost squeaking, "someday, baby, someday, baby." He stood there, a big, powerful man on a sagging stage lost in the scrub woods of Georgia, singing to thirty people, all black, poor, middle-aged or old, a little drunk, and only a few hours away from work the next day, singing "Someday, baby," as high as he could over and over again. One knew that for every "Someday, baby" he sang, there were many somedays on his mind. . . .

He said his thank-you's, left the stage, changed, thanked the band for playing well (as he does every night), and got into the Cadillac, turning on the portable television he keeps plugged into the cigarette lighter.

"What's happening?" he asked Frank, who has been driving for him for ten years, as they pulled out.

"Another day done passed by," said Frank.

It was a fine social night backstage at the Fillmore West after a year of days passed by.

B.B.'s stomach troubles were long gone. Two lovely young women had dropped by especially to see him; a huge black man named Ernie who he had once played with in Memphis was there and had brought a fifth of scotch. B.B. sent out for some beer. Someone else was passing around a goatskin flask of red wine.

When everyone was pretty high three young blacks came to the door and shyly asked if they could enter. B.B. waved them in and offered one his seat. No, they said, they didn't want to take up his time, but they were representatives of the San Francisco State Black Students Union, and wanted to tell B.B. that they thought he was the greatest, a real soul brother who told it without any jive. He thanked them, but their manner somehow implied a "but," and he waited for them to go on.

"I hope this isn't rude," said one, "but I wanted to ask you, if it's not too personal, why you now wear your hair natural."

"I'll tell you," said B.B. "Because I'm beginning to get a feeling for who I am. I had a process for years, partly because it was the fashion and 'cause I thought it looked good, but I always knew it wasn't quite right; it was a mask I wore to hide something. Now I don't feel I need it anymore."

Another one said it was still pretty short, but B.B. said he had it the way he wanted it. The tall thin BSU-er, whose name was Tony and who seemed to be the leader, asked if B.B. would play for the BSU. Not this trip, he said, and they'd have to wait until he was in California again, but he'd be glad to do it free. Tony didn't quite seem to trust him; B.B. said he was a man of his word; Tony looked doubtful, and then the conversation started to get a little ugly.

It was hard to tell what the students wanted. They kept needling him with questions, often all three speaking at the same time, bursting out with an impatience both nervous and angry. What was success, why did he play for whites, did he think whites understood the blues, what was the blues, did everyone have them or only black people, did he think black people had suffered more than any other race, did he believe in violence? They were at once apologetically self-abasing, acting as if their questions were unloaded, and openly antagonistic. B.B. was remarkably polite.

He knew a lot of white people who were worse off than blacks, he said, and what the students knew from books about plantation life he knew from his own life. He had walked, he reckoned, about sixty thousand miles behind a mule plowing cotton. But they cut him off before he could finish, and he pleaded in vain to speak his mind.

"You say you lived on a plantation," screamed one student, "but was your mother and wife raped before your eyes?"

"You know they weren't because I'm still alive," said B.B., "and that would only happen over my dead body."

"But *that's* the blues," shouted another student, "and that never happened to no white man."

"You come here to ask me about the blues, and then you tell me what they are?" B.B. asked in disbelief.

"But how can you really have 'em if you say anybody can have 'em?" said Tony.

"I didn't say anybody, I just said no race got a monopoly on suffering," said B.B.

They continued at an impasse for twenty minutes, a strange spectacle: young men whose own sense of pride and dignity as humans and blacks had in large measure been awakened by B.B.'s artistry having to reinforce that still shaky confidence by attacking him. Finally they were almost calling him an Uncle Tom. For the first time, he showed anger.

"Listen," he said, "I've got only one more thing to say. You're upset now, but it don't bother me. You know a lot more about who you are than I did at your age, and I'm proud of you. You are going to be leaders and we need leaders. But there's one word I don't want you to forget, and that's justice. Be just. *Please* be just. That's the lesson of suffering and it's the lesson of the blues. I try to be just when I play my song, and if you can't be just, *that's* when you don't really know the blues."

"But, but," Tony started to stammer.

"No buts," said B.B. "Now let's shake hands and don't bother me no more."

This article documents the meeting of two blues legends in a double interview full of playful interactions.

John Lee Hooker and B.B. King, the world's preeminent bluesmen, met at Fantasy Studios in Berkeley, California, during March 1993 to record together for the first time. The session was for B.B.'s *Blues Summit* album, a star-studded affair featuring duets with Ruth Brown, Robert Cray, Albert Collins, Lowell Fulson, Buddy Guy, Etta James, and Koko Taylor. No track comes closer to celebrating B.B.'s Mississippi roots, though, than his mesmerizing "You Shook Me" with the Hook.

While B.B. and John Lee have similar backgrounds—both were raised in the Delta, idolized the same musicians, migrated north, and began recording in the late '40s—their styles are remarkably dissimilar. A master of single-note solos punctuated with his signature hummingbird vibrato, B.B. has typically worked with a jumping, well-rehearsed big band. Much more of a lone wolf, John Lee tends to perform solo or with a small, hand-picked band, matching his deep, deep voice with propulsive, trance-inducing rhythms or raucous boogies. Performing together, though, the bluesmen easily found common ground during the "You Shook Me" session.

A few weeks later, on April 4th, the B.B. King Band played the Circle Star Theater in San Carlos, California, just a few miles downhill from Mr. Hooker's Redwood City home. We had just 35 minutes between sets to score the interview and photo shoot. After a thrilling performance before a packed house, B.B. cooled down for a few minutes and then settled into an easy chair alongside the couch where John Lee Hooker was holding court. Their exchange began with a hearty handshake.

B.B.: John, you did me a great favor. I owe you one.

John Lee: Look, B.B., there ain't nothin' in the world . . . I could never give enough to do what I did with you.

B.B.: Same here.

John Lee: All my life, I wanted to sit down with one of the great masters.

B.B.: Oh, listen to that! [Hitches up pants legs and pretends he's wading.] *Now go ahead, John.* [Both laugh uproariously.]

John Lee: He's a genius. I been on the stage with him a lot, but this is the first time I recorded with him. That was a pleasure too. I never will forget it as long as I live. We did "She Shook Me, Like The Hurricane Shook The Trees." We played the hell out of that tune.

Was B.B. hard to work with?

John Lee: Just like takin' candy from a baby. I been talkin' about wantin' to do that for years and years. We come up together—I don't want to say how far back—but we were youngsters. We would party, go out together. But something I dreamed of was wantin' to sit down with this man, side to side, face to face, and just play. It was such a tribute, to me, and I just felt it will be with me until the day that I go, tryin' to be with one of the greatest musicians alive, one of the most famous persons alive, and one of the nicest persons. He just like a lamb, he's so easy for people to talk to. He's such a nice gentleman. He'll talk to anybody, anywhere. He's not the kind of person that run, duck, and hide from his fans. That's what I like about him. I said, "Well, here's two mah-sters." You know what a mah-ster is? Like two great men.

The two of you have probably made more blues recordings than any other pair of artists in history.

B.B.: I would think so. I think John has made many more than I.

John Lee: Oh, yeah, I have. I did a lot before he did.

B.B.: See, John was playin' when I was plowin'. I was still on . . .

John Lee: What is a plow? [Both laugh uproariously.] *You down there in Indianola.*

B.B.: *I was still in Indianola. Just come to Memphis, and John was makin' records then.*

John Lee: *You know who I met you through? [Promoter] B.B. Beaman.*

B.B.: *B.B. Beaman, Atlanta, Georgia.*

John Lee: *He was* thin *[points to B.B.]—weighed about 125, 130 pounds.*

B.B.: *Yeah.*

Is that before you had a hit with "Three O'Clock Blues"?

B.B.: *Yeah. That was about the time of [1952's] "Three O'Clock Blues." I'd made about six or seven records before "Three O'Clock Blues." The first four sides I made was for Bullet Record Company out of Nashville. It's funny—when I made those four sides, they went out of business. So I was that bad!*

John Lee: *You know the first thing I heard from you? "C'mon, Baby, Take A Swing With Me."*

B.B.: *That was one of the first four sides.*

John Lee: *[Sings "C'mon, baby, take a swing with me."]*

B.B.: *Yeah! Then after that I recorded several other tunes. I'd been listening to Lowell Fulson. I got his "Three O'Clock Blues," and when I did that, that was the one that did it.*

John Lee: *Yeah, I love that Lowell Fulson. Still do. "Everyday I Have the Blues"—he really did a good job on that.*

B.B.: *Yeah. You know, a lot of people don't know it, but after Memphis Slim wrote it and recorded it, Lowell Fulson was the first one that ever* *made a hit on it. 'Cause I don't think Memphis Slim called it "Everyday I Have The Blues." He called it something else, but it was the same lyrics.*

John Lee: It was the same, same thing.

Do you hear traces of the Delta in John Lee Hooker's music?

B.B.: I don't think of John as a lot of people do. I think of John Lee Hooker as John Lee Hooker. And he play the blues like I heard 'em when I first started to play. And he still plays 'em. He plays the blues like John Lee Hooker does. It was two or three people that I knew before—in other words, that was older than John—and that was Lonnie Johnson, Robert Johnson, and Blind Lemon. I didn't know them all personally, but I did get a chance to meet Lonnie before he died. But these people, the way they played, they were so themselves. Well, in the modern times—and what I call modern times is the time I started to play—John Lee Hooker was one like that. Lightnin' Hopkins was like that.

John Lee: Oh, yeah.

B.B.: You know who they were the minute you hear 'em play. When John Lee Hooker plays, it's like writin' his name: "I'm John Lee Hooker." So I don't necessarily think of it as Delta or city or any other type . . .

John Lee: No, me neither. It's just blues.

B.B.: I just think of him as John Lee Hooker playin' the blues. It takes me home, of course. Yes!

John Lee: You know people ask me about Mississippi blues, jump blues, big city blues, Mississippi boogie—it's all the blues to me. The blues is all over the world now. People that don't speak English love the blues. I'm so happy for myself and other blues singers out there that the blues is beginning to get so popular.

Is it better now than during the 1950s and '60s?

John Lee: Oh, yeah! Are you kidding?

B.B.: Yeah, because nowadays people don't class you so much. It's not always thumbs-down, as it used to be. It used to be back in that time, in some places, the minute you say you a blues singer, it would be thumbs-down.

John Lee: Yep.

B.B.: It was just like, "Oh, he's a nice guy, but he's a black."

John Lee: Yeah, yeah.

B.B.: "He's a nice guy, but he's white." Nowadays there's not so much of that. You do find it, but . . .

John Lee: It's very rare.

B.B.: The only thing I kind of take issue with a little bit is when people say, "Oh, that's city blues, that's Delta blues, that's Mississippi, that's Chicago," and so on. Muddy Waters, for example, is to me the first of the so-called Chicago blues.

John Lee: That's right.

B.B.: Muddy left Mississippi, went to Chicago. John left and went to Detroit. I left and went to Memphis. We was still migrating, and wherever we went, our identity was pretty strong, like Muddy's was and the people surroundin' him. So you had a lot of the new guys to be born and started to play later. But to add to that, to me, blues is that label again. For instance, when John Lee made "Boogie Chillun," that wasn't blues. That was get up and get it!

John Lee: Get up and go! That was the first rock!

B.B.: *That's right!*

John Lee: *You get rock and roll from that.*

B.B.: *So when people say blues and you say "Boogie Chillun," how in the heck could he be blue? He's havin' a ball! He's havin' a good time.*

John Lee: *That's right.*

B.B.: *If I sing "I got a sweet little angel," I'm not blue at all.*

But when you were growing up, wasn't blues used as party music in the Delta?

B.B.: *It still is. You didn't only just hear it in the roadhouses. You could hear it on the streets of Indianola, Sunflower. You could hear it in most of the places around. Even in Memphis, you could find it on Beale Street then. When I first went to Beale Street, there was . . .*

John Lee: *Look, B., okay, I want to say something now. The blues was here when the world was born and man and woman got together. That's called the blues. Rock and roll sayin' the same thing that me and this man are saying: "My woman gone, she left me." See, rock and roll, you have the same thing, you just cut 'em in a different form. Cut 'em hopped up and shined and polished up. You sayin' the same thing. You talkin' about a woman that left him. You could make it a ballad. [Croons "My woman have left me, she gone away."] You wouldn't call that blues, but we all sayin' the same thing. But I'm gonna tell it in a different way. You understand that, B.?*

B.B.: *Yeah. Another thing, see, like they use words today that if I'd have used them around home comin' up, I'd get smacked in the mouth.*

John Lee: *Oh, you get you teeth knocked out!*

B.B.: *Like, for instance, if a guy say, "Man, make it funky!" If I said "funky" around home, my mother would knock the hell out of me!* [Both laugh.]

John Lee: [Like he's talking to his mom] *"I wasn't makin' funky!"*

B.B.: *Now you hear guys quite often, and nobody pay any attention: "Here, make it a funky beat, man. Put a funky beat." Well, now we accept it. But during the times I was growin' up, man, that was a bad word. That was like a kid swearin' in the house.*

John Lee: *It sho was. You say "funk" around my mother* [Laughs] . . .

B.B.: *Smack you! "Boy, what are you saying?" Bam!*

What can someone gain by listening to B.B. King play guitar?

John Lee: *Well, I'll tell you what he just told you about me. There only one B.B. There's a lot of imitations, lot of people pick up the guitar and follow this man—many, many of 'em. Used to be everybody that pick up a guitar try to sound like B.B. King. But you can tell when the main person, the main man, hit it. You know it's B.B. There was a boy in Chicago called Little B.B.*

Andrew Odom?

John Lee: *I think so. Tried to sound just like B.B., but I know it wasn't B.B. He be playin' with my cousin a lot, Earl Hooker.*

B.B.: *Yeah! That's a bad man. Ain't been but one other person play slide like Earl Hooker. You know who that is, for me?*

John Lee: *What, Bonnie Raitt?*

B.B.: *Bonnie Raitt. She is the best that is today, in my opinion.*

John Lee: *Yeah. So let me finish. So you can tell in a minute if you hear B.B. from an imitation—I can. What they don't know, maybe—and I think you know this, B.B., you know it* [points to Jas], *and I know it— anybody can sound like John Lee Hooker, but it ain't the real John Lee Hooker. He make it real good, but I can come along and just hit it, and they gone. They'd rather see me. Like B.B.: Lot of B.B.s out, but it ain't* like the real one. You can tell it's B.B. King. He had one song I never will forget, but everything he do, I love it. Come to my house, I got stacks of B.B. I've got his six-pack. What they call it?

B.B.: The box set.

John Lee: I got that. And he got one in there: "You breakin' my heart, and there ain't anything I can do."

B.B.: "There ain't nothin' I can do," yeah.

John Lee: Boy, people used to play that thing!

It's interesting that both of you play Gibson's B.B. King guitar.

John Lee: Yeah, I went and bought one.

B.B.: John has played so many different guitars through the years, though. So many different ones, and they all sound like John.

John Lee: I got my identity. I got my style. I got nothin' to regret. I got nothin' to try to gain. I got nothin' to try to change. I wouldn't change for all the tea in China and all the money in the world. Who else you gonna sound like?

B.B.: It's just like one piano that sits over in the corner. If John go and play it, he gonna sound like himself, 'cause that's the way he play. If I go play it, I'm gonna sound like myself, 'cause that's the way I play. Now, if you don't believe it, you can hear Ray Charles play it or Pinetop [Perkins] or Elton John—they gonna sound like themselves. That's just one of the things that we're lucky we were blessed to be able to do—to be ourselves and do our own style. Like, when I heard John, I know it was John. If I hear Jimmy Reed, I know it's Jimmy Reed. My cousin Booker White—know it's him. Even in jazz and rock and roll, certain guys—not all—have that identity.

It's just like you as a journalist—certains styles people have of writing, singing, whatever they do. Like an architect or some of the Old Masters *painters, da Vinci and all these guys that was doin' whatever they did. You* knew *the way that they did it. Same with the classical musicians— some of 'em you knew. Well, that's what I think of John. John couldn't change if he wanted to.*

John Lee: No.

B.B.: I couldn't change if I wanted to.

John Lee: I'm like in the old way. I couldn't change if I wanted to. But if, like B.B. said, if I did it, it wouldn't be me.

B.B.: It's just like a way of talkin'.

Is it a waste of time for someone to try to play like you?

John Lee: I would think so.

B.B.: Well, not really, John. Think about it. 'Cause when we first started—I know I did—when you first started, you heard somebody you liked.

John Lee: Oh, all the time. I did, I did.

B.B.: So I liked somebody when I first started. We had our idols then, just like kids do today. So there's nothing wrong, I don't think, with lis- tening to or trying to play like someone—in the beginning. But then as you learn, you start to think that there's already one of those. So you try to play as you play.

John Lee: Don't play like Jimi Hendrix or B.B. King or somebody else. Play . . .

B.B.: As you feel yourself. Put you in it. We all like somebody. Everybody did. John, who was your idol? Who did you like when you first started to play?

John Lee: Well, when I first started to playin', T-Bone Walker was my idol.

B.B.: Me too. [Both laugh.]

John Lee: Boy, I used to follow him like a little puppy followin' his mama.

B.B.: Yeah, me too. I tell ya somebody else I liked—I was crazy about Lowell Fulson.

John Lee: Whooo weee! "Everyday I Have The Blues," and then "Blue Shadows Fallin'."

B.B.: Even before that, Lonnie Johnson.

John Lee: Oh, man!

B.B.: I was crazy 'bout him. Lonnie Johnson and Blind Lemon. Those were my people, along with T-Bone Walker.

John Lee: Lonnie Johnson, he sing, but it didn't sound like deep blues. What would you call that?

B.B.: I don't know. He was so versatile, he did some of all of it. Lonnie Johnson. Now, most of the kids today are crazy about Robert Johnson. Now, I think Robert was great. I think he was really great, but he wasn't my idol.

John Lee: No, he wasn't mine, either.

Why did Robert Johnson have a gold record in 1990?

B.B.: Well, that's from the same thing I just got through sayin'. Johnny Winter swears on him. [Laughs.] He says he's the greatest thing ever happened—that's what he told me. And a lot of the kids are crazy about it because they say it's authentic.

John Lee: It's authentic. Let's put it like this: The man has been out of existence so long that they really built him up a lot just talkin' and writin' about it. Then when they did put it out, everybody went for it. He get so much publicity.

B.B.: There you go. You just hit it.

Publicity?

B.B.: Of course!

John Lee: So much publicity!

Do you like Robert Johnson's music?

John Lee: Some of it, yeah. I'm like B.B. I'm not a fan of his, though. But I listen to it.

B.B.: And I like some of the things he did. I just didn't idolize him like I did Lonnie Johnson.

John Lee: Lonnie Johnson and T-Bone Walker. I would have dust his feet if he'd have said so.

B.B.: Here's what happens in a lot of cases. We'll take John as an example. John has been great since I first heard him. He was doin' great things all the time, but he couldn't get the publicity . . .

John Lee: That's right.

B.B.: Until he got this manager he have today and Bonnie Raitt.

John Lee: This man right there [points outside of the room to Mike Kappus of San Francisco's Rosebud Agency].

B.B.: So that was the same thing with me. My manager's name is Sid Seidenberg. So when Sid and I got together, that's when things started to change. Gosh, as great as Bonnie Raitt is—I've known her all her career—and as great as Robert Cray and Roy Rogers and a lot of the people we hear today are, John has been like that since before they were born.

John Lee: *It's true.*

B.B.: *You understand? But, thanks to John's manager and other people that know how to package it, the people that knew Robert, that knew Roy, that knew Bonnie—many of the people—now can hear John. Like a guy told me not long ago: He said his son came home and says, "Daddy, you got to hear this guy I just heard!" And his father say, "Who is it, son?" He said, "Oh, you wouldn't know him. You wouldn't know anything about him." Said, "Well, who is it, son?" He says, "You got to hear B.B. King! You just got to hear it!" [Laughs.] So his father said, "Son, long before you was thought of, I was listening to him." He said, "Yeah, but dad, you don't know about things like that! This is new!" So it's the same thing. John and myself and a lot of us that's been playing for a long time just never got the break.*

John Lee: *Never got the breaks, and then they just didn't push the blues like they should. They still don't, like they really should right now. But they pushin' more than they used to. They used to just push it under the cover.*

Does recording with rock stars make that big a difference?

B.B.: *Oh, yeah. Of course, of course! That's why I mentioned Bonnie Raitt. It's like U2 and myself. Had it not been for U2, a lot of people wouldn't know. But thanks to Sid, we were able to have this happen.*

John Lee: *The same thing I say about my manager. Thanks to Mike. You know, I had give up recordin'. I said, "I'm not gonna record no more." The record companies, they rob you blind. Like Modern Records and Vee Jay and them—they just robbed you. You know they was takin' everything you had. Well, I think you know that too. [B.B. nods and laughs.] They were! I said, "I'm gonna get out of the business." And I had been out for about eight years. I was still with Mike. Mike says, "Let's get you a record deal." He worked hard, got me a* record deal. Got me pulled together. And that's how I come to be . . . I never was forgotten, but I got disgusted. I said I wasn't gonna record anymore.

B.B.: See, Mike's a very good man, as Sid is to me. They always lookin' out for things that'll help us, that will get the publicity that we . . .

John Lee: Never was able to get.

B.B.: Now, don't misunderstand me. Nobody gave Bonnie nothin'. Nobody gave Robert [Cray] anything. They earned it. But today they are superstars. What I'm trying to say is that had people known John in the beginning as they have known him now, he would have been a superstar years ago.

John Lee: Right. Just wasn't gettin' that push.

Like Muddy Waters, you're both making very good records during the second halves of your careers.

John Lee: Well, Muddy gone now, but he . . .

B.B.: But he was makin' them then, man!

John Lee: Yeah, he was makin' them, but they wasn't bein' pushed.

B.B.: Even today—take it from me—if I wasn't on the record with U2, nobody would have played B.B. King.

I don't know about that.

B.B.: Can you take my word for it?

Yes, but I'd listen to your record even if it were just you and an acoustic guitar.

John Lee: You know he's a monster. You know how good he is. But you're just one.

B.B.: Look, I'm not trying to be false modesty or anything of that sort. But today listen to the radio. Watch the T.V. And every time that you hear a new B.B. King record play . . . Of course, I don't think it will be like that with this album John and I just got through doin'. I think this is gonna be played.

John Lee: I think so too. I'm prayin'.

B.B.: But prior to that and prior to John and Bonnie Raitt—understand? —I bet you wouldn't hear a John Lee Hooker record played.

John Lee: I don't think so either, B.

B.B.: I have to eat my words. I said that if I ever had a record played on MTV, I would eat the cover. [Both laugh.] So I had to eat my words because they did play me with U2. We did "When Love Comes To Town," and they played it. I said, "Well, I'll be darned. I might as well go start eatin' covers." [Laughs.]

John Lee: Gettin' back to Bonnie Raitt. She was on about 20 years that nobody ever knowed her. Remember that?

B.B.: Yeah. Used to be an opening act for me.

John Lee: Me and her used to party together. She used to drink liquor like water.

B.B.: One of the nicest people I ever met, though. One of the nicest.

John Lee: Oh, she's nice. Whoooo wee.

B.B.: She's a great person. Nobody gave her anything. She earned it. I was so happy to see it.

John Lee: Nobody give her nothin'. She earned it. Like this man here, nobody give him nothin'. He earned it. Nobody give me nothin'. I *earned it. But they just beginnin' to play us now, but not like they should.*

B.B.: *I think what we're talkin' about now is, today the blues is known better. One of the things I take issue with quite a bit, you hear people say, "Oh, the resurging of the blues."*

John Lee: *Resurgin'! It ain't never went nowhere!*

B.B.: *It never left, as far as I can tell. I've worked on an average of 300 days a year since '56, many concerts every year. What they fail to realize, though, is that when you have superstars like Eric Clapton or Robert Cray or Jeff Healey or Stevie Ray Vaughan, when they came on the scene, they had their new thing goin' and they played the blues, so that made a difference. But they hadn't left nowhere. It's just each time we got a new disciple.*

Does it seem like there's something fundamentally wrong with this?

John Lee: *No, it don't bother me. Not at all. I don't know about B.*

B.B.: *No, the only thing that bothered me is that we didn't have nobody like that at first.*

John Lee: *That's right.*

B.B.: *That was the thing that bothered me. We wasn't recognized. So today, to find that we have some people that's playin' the blues and not ashamed to say it . . .*

John Lee: *Right. Then they had the right people to push it.*

B.B.: *That today makes me happy. Very happy.*

John Lee: *Me too.*

B.B.: *So today we got superstars. John's a superstar today.*

John Lee: I know I could have been . . . That older stuff we did? It should have been . . .

B.B.: There was a lot of good stuff done. When you did "Boogie Chillun," man, everybody should have known about it.

John Lee: Yeah. And "Boom, Boom," "Dimples," and stuff like that.

Do you remember creating "Boogie Chillun"?

John Lee: Yeah, I do. I used to hear my stepfather, when I was a kid. My style—I got it from him. He'd do stuff like that [sings "boom-da-boom, boom-da-boom, boom-da-boom" while snapping fingers], "Boogie Chillun," different things. I do remember that. I got people to do something like what rested in him. Everything I do is direct from Will Moore, my stepfather. He play just like I'm playin' today. I learnt from him. He played that kind of stuff—foot stompin'.

Open G?

John Lee: Yeah. "Mama don't allow me to . . ."

B.B.: "Stay out all night long."

John Lee: "Boogie Chillun" and all that kind of stuff. It used to be "Boogie Woogie," and I changed it to "Boogie Chillun." I didn't know it was gonna . . . You know, it was just a old funky lick I found.

B.B.: But it was a monster hit.

Were you writing about your mom?

John Lee: Nah, it's just a song. There's so many kids, their mama don't allow them to stay out all night long, you know. I couldn't just be talkin' about my mama. Lot of people have kids don't stay out all night long, but they gonna stay out anyway. [Sings "Mama didn't allow me to stay out all night long."] I didn't care what she didn't allow, they would stay out anyways! They knew they would get a beatin' when they get home, but they still stay out.

Does playing guitar bring you as much joy and satisfaction as it did when you were younger?

B.B.: Yes. I think it brings even more today . . .

John Lee: It do.

B.B.: Because I'm more concerned about what I'm trying to do. Then, I was just havin' fun.

John Lee: Havin' fun, drinkin', stayin' out.

B.B.: [Laughs.] As you said, stayin' out all night long. But now today I'm concerned about it, because if I get out there now and I hit something that don't sound right, I know that there are a lot of people that are listening to me.

John Lee: Critics.

B.B.: Well, not only that, but a lot of the kids that are listening to me. Reminds me of a story I heard once. There was a trumpet teacher teachin' trumpet to his class. And one little boy, the teacher was tryin' to teach him to play non-pressure, where his jaws wouldn't balloon out. So the teacher was talkin'. So there's one little smart egg in the class [laughs], and the teacher say, "Why are you playin' like that? I keep tryin' to tell you that when your jaws pop out like that, that's not good." So the little smart egg, he said, "Well, Dizzy Gillespie plays like that!" So the teacher thought about it for a moment, and he says, "Yeah, but there's only one Dizzy Gillespie." So I think about it a lot of times now when I'm playin', that the kids out there idolize me, like me. And not just kids, but people that are starting to play or the people that's already playin' and maybe came out to admire what I do or be critical of what I do. And if I make them wrong notes or put them in the wrong way or hit something I don't intend to hit . . .

John Lee: I have never heard anybody as true as you, man. Nobody.

B.B.: Well, thank you. But I make mistakes, though. So when I make 'em now . . .

John Lee: Everybody do.

B.B.: Yeah. To answer your question, when I make a mistake now, it hurts [thumps chest]. Oh, yes. It hurts.

John Lee: You're right.

B.B.: Because, see, I'm supposed to be professional—that's what I think to myself. I'm supposed to entertain. I'm supposed to rehearse, practice enough to not do that.

John Lee: But some people, when you look out into the audience, they don't even notice what you did, they so excited about lookin' at him. But he know it [points to B.B.].

B.B.: Yeah, and that hurts, don't it?

John Lee: Yeah, that's right. They may not know, but you know you made that mistake. And you lookin' back at the fellows, and some of them look like they kind of smile, you know, because they know I did.

B.B.: But when you're able to run it into something else . . .

John Lee: To cover up.

B.B.: Yeah, like you and I, say we talkin', and we got a male conversation goin' on and all of a sudden a lady walked in, you gotta change to something else! [Laughs.] That's the way it is with playin'. Here's another thing: When guys start to gettin' to be our age, John, they're not quite as fast as they used to be.

John Lee: I know.

B.B.: And as you get a little older, you think more about it. Remember when you was young and somebody said, "Come here," you get up and start running? Now you think about it—do I really want to run, or will I just walk on over there?

John Lee: Yeah, walk to the car!

B.B.: And a lot of the youngsters that come around can play rings around me—this is not false modesty!—but what they do, they think of what I did that gave them a chance to think beyond that. You think Graham Bell thought of what his work would be doin' today? There was that first foundation. I was able to go and see one of my idols, Lonnie Johnson, and I was able to shake his hand and thank him. Because he was one of the people that made me want to play. I don't know. Here I am, still doin' somethin' with it.

John Lee: Well, B., time for me to go.

Is this the first interview you've done together?

B.B.: Yes. The very first.

John Lee: I've did it with a lot of people, but this is the first I ever did with B.B. And I couldn't wait for tonight to come!

B.B.: It's an honor to me. What you are doing for us will even help it to go further. We appreciate it. Thank you. And thanks to a couple of other guys named Mike and Sid.

THE INFLUENCE OF B.B. KING (1968)
BARRET HANSEN

Better known nowadays as "Dr. Demento," Barrett Hansen is the host of a nationally syndicated radio program of "mad music and crazy comedy." He has also produced several compilations of novelty records, most typically emblazoned with his own name. Published in 1968, this was one of the first articles to adapt the model of comprehensive literary criticism—writing about the total work of someone whom the writer has never met—to a blues performer. Nonetheless, Hansen asks readers, especially those familiar with his recent work, to consider that "this piece was written early in his career, when blues scholarship (not to mention its author) was in its infancy."

Hiya, blues fans and all you other people! Last month we went to Chicago in spirit to tell the story of Muddy Waters, Little Walter and the original electric blues band style. This blues scene was closely restricted to Chicago, as far as the live action was concerned. And the people who bought the records were mainly natives, transplanted and otherwise, of the lower Mississippi Valley, from whence came the singers and musicians. This month's brand of blues also springs ultimately from that musically fertile place, where the Blues Boy, Riley B. King, was born a few years after Muddy's entrance.

You could make a case for B.B. King's style having been born in Memphis, where he got his start. But we soon find that we can't really talk about B.B.'s blues, and the other great music that it has inspired, as a Memphis scene. This is the whole nation's blues we're talking about now. Muddy's music remember, grew out of a strongly-localized blues tradition, and inherited its limitations as well as its strengths. Mississippi people loved it to death, but millions of blacks around the country never could quite get into it. B.B. King never really had any of these limitations, because the blues style he developed was really a brand new bag. And it's about 101% authentic.

Rather than relying on any preestablished blues style, B.B. created a whole new style which drew on the totality of all blues that had gone before, plus elements of many other kinds of music, from gospel to jazz. Others had tried the same thing, and are still trying it now. But it was the unique genius of this man B.B. that made him emerge, after a scant three years on records, as the living symbol of the blues for practically anyone who ever cared about blues.

B.B. King is really the first and greatest blues man of the modern age of communications. Though his music is soul music in the best sense, it was influenced in many subtle ways by records that he heard. Not just blues records, but records of every conceivable kind of guitar playing. He was considerably influenced, for example, by records made in France by the legendary gypsy jazz guitarist, Django Reinhardt. Then again, it is modern communications that have made B.B. a byword in every ghetto in the country. The incredible rapport he has with live audiences is based to a great extent on those people's familiarity with his records. It was the records that made him a bigger star than any previous blues singer had ever been, and did it faster than had ever been known in this traditional kind of music.

Records were B.B.'s profession even before singing was; he earned his first fame and his nickname "Blues Boy" as a disc jockey in Memphis. He was still spinning other people's records when he made his own disc debut.

This was on the Bullet label, which has the distinction of being the first record company ever to headquarter in Nashville. (It was known mainly for country music, of course). This company was nearing the end of the line, and B.B.'s sales didn't exactly help the situation. But when Modern Records, a big West Coast R&B label at the time, set up the subsidiary RPM label, they went straight to Memphis. Howlin' Wolf was among the local talent they captured there, and so was B.B. King. The Blues Boy's sales, unspectacular at first, gained slowly. Then, in 1952, they got their gold mine. RPM #339, "3 O'Clock Blues," was ordinary stuff on the surface, a slow blues about a guy who can't sleep for worryin' about where his baby is. But it was on this record that all the elements of B.B.'s style really came together. People couldn't get enough of this new sound to suit them; the record was on *Billboard's* R&B charts for five months. But what is even more amazing is that the people have stuck right with that sound ever since, and never tired of it. "3 O'Clock Blues" is going on seventeen years old now, and still sounds fresh as ever today. (The original disc has been reissued many times, most recently on a Kent LP.) Moreover, B.B.'s new records continue to put out the very same kind of blues. Today the backup bands are sharper, the recordings are better, and (on his live albums anyway) B.B. stretches out a bit more, but like the Volkswagen company he has refused to tamper too much with success. Now and then he has tried other things (like pop ballads with choruses and orchestras) but he never strays from that old "3 O'Clock" sound for very long.

So it's about time we went into a little more detail about what that sound is, and where its various elements seem to have come from.

On "3 O'Clock Blues" you hear B.B. singing with his guitar, and a backup band consisting of two saxes, piano and drums. The backup band is the most conventional part of the sound (this remains true today). The horns-piano-drums combination had been used in blues since Big Bill (Broonzy) and the Memphis Five ruled in the 1930's. Some of the Harlem blues singers of the 1940's had regular big bands behind them, but in the South a simpler instrumentation had always prevailed. B.B.'s band on "3 O'Clock" is in every way a typical band of the period. The horns stick to close harmony parts, droning away through the record in what seems to us today a rather listless fashion. The drums just keep time. The piano seems to be divided between the old style in which the left hand carries the rhythm and the bass line, and the newer band piano style in which the right hand predominates, playing fill-ins and such ornaments.

But the crucial thing here is that all this happens off in the background, and what is up front is B.B.'s guitar. And this guitar is in every sense a lead guitar. Just as happened with Muddy Waters, the presence of a band relieved B.B. of the necessity to play both bass and melody parts at the same time, a necessity that had shaped the whole world of country blues guitar.

B.B. wasn't the first to play blues lead guitar. In the late 1920's Scrapper Blackwell, accompanying the blues pianist-singer Leroy Carr, helped create a sound that was as revolutionary, and almost as successful, in its day as B.B.'s was in the 1950's. Many other artists tried the same guitar-piano combination. But the acoustic guitar was hard pressed to be heard above the heavy piano styles of that era. Only when the guitarists played the simplest possible lines were they able to make any real contribution to the sound. Saxophones were much better equipped to make lead lines heard.

But the coming of the electric guitar changed all that. Not as fast as one might think, because a whole generation had grown up with the saxophone for a lead instrument. Memphis Minnie, and later Lightnin' Hopkins, John Lee Hooker and of course Muddy Waters, adapted traditional country acoustic guitar styles to the electric box with success. But for the antecedents of B.B.'s sound we look to the urban blues, and especially to T-Bone Walker, a very popular performer in the 1940's. Walker came out of the big-band scene, like Jimmy Rushing, but he made his electric guitar a prominent part of his recorded sound. And on this guitar he played not country blues, but lines strongly influenced by jazz guitarists like Charlie Christian.

Walker gets off some excellent solos on those records from the 1940's (there's an LP of them on Capitol) and does some fine singing; his "Stormy Monday" is an alltimer. But to modern ears that big-band accompaniment seems much too busy; horns keep popping in and distracting us from what's really going on. With B.B., the band parts are much, much simpler, and they are kept way off in the background. Whether this is due to design, or whether it is just because B.B. had no big band available, we can't quite be sure. But what we are sure of is that it concentrates all our attention on the central instrumental sound of the guitar.

B.B.'s guitar style itself is a big step beyond T-Bone Walker's or any other blues guitar that was around in 1952. Jazz, of course, influenced B.B. enormously. His technique is just like that of a jazz guitarist, built on fast single-note runs, which move melodically like a horn does. Moreover, it is very free rhythmically. Except in fast shuffle numbers, B.B. almost never plays in any kind of even rhythmic pattern. This distinguishes him from all country blues guitarists, and all the white guitar-boogie men whose style formed the basis of early rock guitar.

Yet, with all this, B.B.'s guitar doesn't come out jazz at all. It comes out blues. The main reason for this is in the notes that he chooses, which always stick close to the blues scale with its flatted thirds and sevenths. Essentially they're the same notes that he sings, though in different patterns. And the free rhythms, unconventional as they may be for blues guitar, fit in perfectly. Bernard Pearl, a Los Angeles guitar teacher who has studied B.B.'s style intensively, points out that his guitar rhythms are very close to the rhythms of speech. B.B. once made an instrumental called "Talkin' the Blues," and his "talkin'" could hardly be more profound if he had used his voice.

His voice. In many ways that's the greatest thing of all about B.B.'s music. His first few records (before "3 O'Clock") didn't have any guitar at all, and he still frequently makes them that way. Coming into an era when blues voices were either rough and primitive or soft and genteel, with very little middle ground, B.B.'s singing style was at least as revolutionary as his guitar. Though very strong and powerful, his voice has none of the rough-hewn attack of such traditional blues singers as Howlin' Wolf and Elmore James, his contemporaries on the Memphis scene. B.B.'s tone and phrasing are actually much closer to gospel music than to any other blues that was around in 1952. This means an open-throated technique, rather than the "gravel voice" favored by the older bluesmen. Thus the higher notes ring out as loud and clear as an opera singer's. Gospel style also involved considerable use of *melisma,* which means singing quite a few notes, without a break, to one syllable. At slow tempos, B.B. does this quite a bit.

But it would be a grave mistake to say that his whole style in gospel music was a much softer, swingier kind of sound. It's quite possible that B.B., along with such great gospel singers as Sam Cooke and Archie Brownlee, helped make gospel what it is today.

So that's as close as my mere words can come to describe this man's music. You can probably hear it best, if not in person, on "Live At The Regal" (ABC-Paramount). If you explore some of his innumerable other LP's, you will find much music that lives up to what we have been saying, and some that maybe doesn't. Some of his early recordings appear to have been hurriedly done for the 88¢ lines maintained by his former record label, RPM (later Kent); and he has made a number of ballads in the vein of recent Ray Charles. But he always comes back to the blues.

And as far as the 1968 style of blues is concerned, a lot of it goes back to B.B. Bobby "Blue" Bland and "Little" Junior Parker, to use their earlier stage names, were two of the first singers to move into the area B.B.

had pioneered. Though neither is as much into instrumental music as B.B. is with his guitar, both sing in the same sort of gospel-blues blend. More recently, several fine younger bluesmen followed his footsteps both vocally and instrumentally; outstanding here are Buddy Guy, Otis Rush and Freddy King. It is interesting that all these musicians have kept their sound rougher and louder than much of B.B.'s work; there are no sentimental ballads, and less prettiness in general. You could simply say that they are more traditional than B.B., which is undoubtedly the case. But it's also noteworthy that in passing up the more refined, eclectic aspects of B.B.'s style, they are making the same choices that B.B. himself did in 1952, when he chose not to emulate the big-band aspects of T-Bone Walker's bag.

Bland and Parker, as well as B.B., are righteously celebrated in Charles Keil's *Urban Blues,* a work which chooses only a small slice of the blues world to work with, but covers it so objectively and straightforwardly that it emerges as the best book on blues, period. But the most celebrated black urban bluesman of today doesn't figure much in that book. Three years ago, Albert King was strictly minor league, working most obscurely in St. Louis. Now that Stax-Volt has made him famous, he emerges as the archetype of modern B.B. followers. His whole vocal-guitar bag is full of what are probably inevitable borrowings from B.B.; these borrowings are as natural as modern rock's reuse of Beatle ideas, or Bluegrass' reuse of Bill Monroe's. But he has taken the idiom in a certain direction, with the result that he has reached thousands of young white blues fans much more powerfully than B.B. ever did. These are young people who tend to grow impatient with B.B.'s forays into non-blues, and subconsciously or otherwise reject the survivals of their parents' music that crop up now and then in his backup bands. B.B., with a huge bag of tricks, will conserve his best blues licks, separating them with music of lower intensity. Albert, much more limited, is *on* all the time, packing heavy, heavy stuff into each tune. Though less subtle than B.B., he gives young audiences quite a bit more of what they really want to hear. And on recordings he has the peerless support of the Stax-Volt house band, a far heavier sound than anything B.B. has ever used.

Our final point of history also concerns young whites, the musicians this time. The white blues band movement, in the U.S.A. and in England as well, started out with the Muddy Waters sound as a model. This was the case even though black musicians, and the black public, had already swung solidly over to the B.B. sound. The reasons for this are interesting. The outstanding white musicians were linked with the folk revival and/or the rock music of 1964, both of which were much closer in instrumentation and to Muddy's music than to B.B.'s. Muddy's vocal style proved easier for whites to imitate. And of course the old-time Mississippi roots of Muddy's style were attractive. The original Butterfield band was itself a part of the latterday Chicago scene; Canned Heat and the English groups learned from records but achieved hardly less satisfying results. But more recently the B.B. sound has made converts out of nearly all of them. Horn sections have been added, harmonicas and bottleneck guitars have been deemphasized, and vocals emphasized. Notice that when Mike Bloomfield left Butterfield to form his own band, *both* men moved in these directions. Canned Heat has stuck closer to the Chicago-Delta bag, but frequently gets into the streamlined straight-time formula Albert King favors. And with Albert as the magnet, great hordes of young white kids are learning the licks he plays on his lovable Lucy, licks which are often intensified, concentrated remakes of the licks B.B. created long ago on his original Lucille.

With a little help from his friends, that man B.B. has done more than any other man to keep the blues alive and healthy today. Aside from his influence, direct and indirect, on the white audience that suddenly is the music's main financial support, B.B. has proven to be the one charismatic figure, the living legend that was needed to keep the black blues audience hangin' on. May he go on forever.

REMEMBERING MY 1980 BIOGRAPHY (1995)
CHARLES SAWYER

Charles Sawyer wrote King's first full-length biography, *The Arrival of B.B. King*. In an addendum prepared for a 1996 German reprint, Sawyer remembered the difficulties he had in getting his manuscript (and, by extension, King's importance) accepted by a major publisher.

Since its first publication in 1980, my book *The Arrival of B.B. King* has enjoyed a life far beyond any reasonable expectation. The English language edition has been in print for all but a brief time during these fifteen years and I still get letters and postcards from new readers who find that the book has touched them in some personal way. This success is in stark contrast with the pre-publication story of the book. The difficulties it encountered finding its way into print reflect the special obstacles faced by blues music and its most famous practitioner in particular. Between 1970 when I began circulating a proposal and sample chapters for a book on B.B. King among publishers, and 1980 when Doubleday announced the publication of the hardback edition of this book, fifty-three publishers passed judgment on the prospects for this book and fifty-two declined the chance to publish it.

The reasons given for rejecting the book were the usual smoke screen of ambiguities intended to blunt the author's disappointment, but the sub-text of the rejection letters and the editors' comments by telephone revealed the deep skepticism verging on cynicism with which the conventional wisdom looked upon race, music, and the connection between intellectual values and popular culture. What was missing from their calculations was the willingness to believe that B.B. King had become a true hero of the American public. To book publishers B.B. was merely the best artist from a musical genre they had relegated to the margins of pop music culture. Like the pundits and public moralists of the mid-1950's who considered Elvis Presley and Rock N' Roll to be only passing fancies, they considered the rise of blues and B.B.'s emergence as mere trends, just secondary side-effects, "epiphenomena" philosophers would call them, in the flux of the entertainment industry. A few publishers declared firmly that they understood the paramount importance of blues to our musical heritage and B.B.'s place in that context, but did not believe that these facts translated into ringing bookstore cash registers. These few who grasped B.B.'s historic importance rated the market for a book on Eric Clapton to be worth hundreds of thousands of sales, but believed that a book on B.B. King would sell too few copies to pay for its printing costs. The life story of the white superstar was a guaranteed success but the life of the black master from whom he had learned a substantial part of his craft was only grist for the ghostwriter's mill which would be ground down to a page or two in the bestseller about his white disciple.

Matters stand differently now. Today, because of the great stature B.B. has attained in the meantime, publishers would vie for the right to offer the book, if it were unpublished. Except for the brief few years during the mid 1970's when he experimented with self-management, his popularity has risen steadily from the time of his arrival in 1968 through today, and continues to rise. This feat should not be taken for granted, for 1980 might as easily have been the zenith of B.B.'s rise. Instead of continuing toward the stratosphere of superstars he might have slid into obscurity and become the marginal figure that publishers in the 1970's were so sure would be his fate. The history of popular culture is littered with stories of brilliant artists like Little Willie John, the inspiration of James Brown, who burned brilliantly and then burned out, or curiosities like Tiny Tim, who held the American public in rapt fascination for one television season with his strange persona, quavering soprano voice, and furtive ukulele strumming, only to slip into an oblivion so complete that today, walking through an airport terminal, he can't even draw a second look.

In September, 1980, backstage at the Beacon Theater in New York City a small party was held to celebrate the publication date of the first hardback edition of this book. B.B. King said the greatest pleasure in seeing the book published was knowing that when he is long gone there will be something left of him, something people can read to learn how he lived and how he made his music.

PART THREE

Lucille
Talks Back

CONVERSATION WITH B.B. KING (1986)

JERRY RICHARDSON and ROB BOWMAN

King has been especially generous in his interviews in guitar magazines and with fellow guitarists, exploring not only his own techniques but contrasting them with what others do. Both a musician and a musicologist, Richardson has the understanding to write in detail about B.B.'s guitar techniques and to elicit from him unique information.

Riley "B.B." King has made his mark in the blues world as a great innovator and unique blues-guitar stylist. His strong determination to continuously improve his technique and enlarge his repertory has assumed him success and earned him the well-deserved sobriquet King of the Blues.

Paradoxically, King was given this long-overdue recognition only after several of his early recordings had animated a group of blues-rock guitarists in the late 1960s—Mike Bloomfield, Elvin Bishop, and Eric Clapton, among others—who proclaimed publicly that he was the their mentor and inspiration, that he was the greatest living blues-guitarist. King also had had moderate influence in the 1950s on the style development of several black blues guitarists, including "Magic" Sam Maghett, "Buddy" Guy, and Albert King.

The casual listener may gain only a glimpse of the talented B.B. King. The student who takes the time, however, to carefully scrutinize and analyze King's style will find it to be of great complexity, and will realize that his technique serves to enhance and verify his uniqueness and his stature as a blues performer.

Like most of the bluesmen of the Mississippi Delta, King was raised in impoverished circumstances. Born Riley B. King, 16 September 1925, on a plantation near Indianola in northwest Mississippi, he was the eldest of three sisters and a brother. His mother died when he was only nine years old, and he subsequently bounced around from one family to another, although he resided most of the time with his maternal grandmother, a sharecropper. After completing the ninth grade, he left home and settled in Indianola, where he worked as a tractor driver by day and sang and played guitar on street corners on weekends.

In 1944 King lived for a short time in Memphis, Tennessee, with his cousin "Bukka" White, a noted, Delta bottle-neck guitarist. In 1948 King found employment with a blues group in West Memphis, Arkansas, which played on radio station KWEM. Soon thereafter he became a disc jockey and had his own show on the newly formed radio station WDIA in Memphis. It was during this time that he acquired the title Beale Street Blues Boy (later contracted to "B.B.").

King began recording in 1949 and produced his first hit, "Three O'Clock Blues," in 1951. Over his long career of almost forty years, he has produced more than thirty albums and over 130 singles; he has appeared on numerous talk shows, television specials, and radio programs; has done many television commercials; and has made several global concert tours. He is the recipient of two honorary doctorates and a plethora of national music awards. He is indeed King of the Blues. Despite his performing demands, however, King has found time to actively engage in civil-rights and humanitarian work, such as prison reform.

In the following interview B.B. King offers insight into his evolution as a performer/musician and the development of his guitar technique. We also learn of the myriad sources and influences that have contributed to his diversified style and how he perceives himself as a blues performer, guitar stylist, and songwriter.

This interview took place on 7 June 1986 at Natchez, Mississippi.

* * *

Richardson and Bowman: We should like to cover several areas in our questioning. One question has to do with influences: we want to get very specific in terms of what you picked up from individual people. We want to talk about your guitar playing as it has changed over the years. You've mentioned your aunt and her records many times in various interviews; we want to know more about her influence on you during your formative years. At what age did you first begin to visit her?

B.B. King: *About five or six. I was around her until [I was] about twelve or thirteen, maybe.*

Had anything else captured your musical interest, or was she really the first one that got you interested in music?

I think that [my interest in music] came almost like an inheritance, because when I learned to talk and learned to know anybody other than my mother, people were singing and playing guitars around me. I think I was interested in [music] long before I ever thought I would try to become professional at it myself. So I would think that mostly it was just something I grew into—in other words, just like here I am, and the music is here already. If that makes sense.

Certainly. The sounds you said surrounded you, [were they] both blues and gospel music?

Blues and gospel, some country, and a little jazz—it was mostly gospel. In the area in the Mississippi Delta where I was born, there was a lot of white people around that sang country music, so the blacks would sing gospel and blues. Not all of them sang blues, but I mean the majority would sing gospel. Some sang blues, and a few would sing country, and jazz was just starting to kind of come in a little bit. Well, all of the whites sang gospel, some would sing country, and a few would sing blues. So it was kind of like a balanced type of thing. But everybody sang gospel, because down there there were a lot of religious people—at least, you thought they were. I learned some of it and liked all of it.

But growing up, my aunt (not the aunt that used to buy the records, but her sister) was the one that I lived with a lot of times, and was around and influenced by quite a bit, along with my mother until she passed. They were very religious; no blues was sang around them. You would get smacked in the mouth if you did so. You had to sing gospel, so you got a lot of training, a lot of rehearsals.

Whether you preferred it or not, that's the way it went?

It had to be gospel.

What about the aunt with the record collection?

She collected records, yes. I think she did it just for her own amuse-ment.

Just like anybody buying records?

Right. Like I do today.

Sure. When people have asked you about her [records]—you often men-tion Jam Gates, Lonnie Johnson, and Blind Lemon Jefferson.

Those were the ones that I liked.

O.K. What I am trying to get at is how extensive was her collection, how many records were you getting to hear? Did she have fifty records, 200 records?

She wasn't wealthy, so she wouldn't have a whole lot of records. I imag-ine she probably would have had seventy-five or eighty, maybe even a hundred. But not any more.

That is clearly a large collection of 78s for the time.

Yes, because like kids are today, she would buy records for her own amusement. And she couldn't know about the new hits—the new release that one might know about today—because there was no radio playing. There was no Billboard showing the next release of blues tunes. So when she would go to the little town, she would have had to inquire— you know, what's new, or whom. And so I would think maybe she would buy a new record maybe each time she went to town on the weekends, if she could afford it.

Considering the fact there was no blues on the radio back then, was radio important at all to your development as a musician?

The time we are talking about now, the time when I was five or six years old, I [had] never heard a radio. I heard about them, but never heard one.

When would you say you first heard radio, about what age?

About ten or eleven. My boss had one, but all I ever heard most times then was [when] my boss lady used to listen to Stella Dallas while I was working around the house.

I am curious as to exactly which country influences were absorbed into your playing?

I listened to Gene Autry, and I listened to Jimmie Rodgers and Roy Acuff. Most of the country stars I was around then, I was able to hear them on the radio later. My boss had [recordings of] country players like Hank Snow, and I could go on and name quite a few that was popular at that time.

Were there specific things or songs of theirs that you would later incorporate into your playing?

I didn't do it intentionally. My first books that I used—I used to order them from Sears Roebuck—when I was trying to learn to play guitar—. I would get these country tunes in these guitar books [and] I was learning country even when I didn't intend to. Those books had mostly country songs, like "My Darlin' Clementine," "You're My Sunshine," "Walking the Floor Over You."

So you learned a number of songs in the country repertoire?

Yes, that is the way I learned to read music in the beginning, because most of the songs—. I think they had "Green Eyes" and a few other popular songs like that. [They] were country songs. So I learned to read them before I could play "Three O'Clock Blues."

When you were singing on the street corners in Indianola and people would request songs, were they just requesting blues, or did they request pop songs and country?

Anything that might be popular at that time was being requested, but mostly it would be gospel songs because, as I said to you earlier, most of the people in the little towns and suburban areas usually were very church-going people. A guy that was known to be as I was—a gospel singer quite active in the church—if I was caught by my church members [singing the blues], I would have been scolded about it. Maybe even almost like in the Army—"written up." But, usually the ones that I would come in contact with would be people that thought or lived similar to my own way of life—which means, you won't tell on me and I won't tell on you.

When you did get pop or country requests, could you virtually play most of the hits of the day in all styles?

That is the one disadvantage I've always had—I have never been able to play anybody's tune as it was supposed to be played, [not] even my own. I've always been, if there is any such thing as being, an original. The way I hear a song usually is a little bit different from [the way it was] written, unless it is on paper. If it is on paper and I am trying to play it, I would naturally read it as it is. I have never yet been able to sing a song as the author wished it to be sung, because that is where the originality comes in.

It is not because I am trying to be—. This is the way I hear something, the way only B.B. King hears it. Like, if I do a commercial—I've done several commercials, one for Coca Cola, one for Anheuser Busch Beer Company, one for Frito Lay. Where I am supposed to follow the script or the melodic line as laid out, [I don't]; but they always wind up saying that it's B.B. King, so go ahead (laughs). I guess maybe they kind of pet me a little bit in some ways, but they seem to get the best work out of me when they allow me to be myself.

What was the role of your guitar when you were playing on the street corners? Were you accompanying your singing with chords?

Even then I would [first] sing and then play; play and then sing. I've never been able to actually accompany myself with chords like a guitarist would do. We use the words "to frail along the guitar," which means just strum it. I can do that, but to properly play the chords—. No, it just never happened. In fact, it don't happen today.

That makes sense. One is an extension of the other.

That is the way I hear it.

When you were playing on street corners and frailing or strumming, so to speak, you would literally sing a cappella, and then play a guitar response?

No, I strum it. But I may not play the proper chords is what I'm saying. But after the melodic line leaves the lips, the serious part starts on the guitar. And then the facial expression takes over as if it is the guitar being strummed. In other words, it leaves from here and goes here [gesturing towards his face]. When I am serious singing the melody, then I am strumming the guitar, which is not very serious. After I stop singing, I am singing through the guitar.

That's interesting. And it actually makes sense, based on the way I've seen you play.

It's not something I am trying to do; it's almost like the exorcist.

You say that whenever you learn songs, you have always done it in the B.B. King way, you haven't been able to reproduce exactly what was on a record. Did you ever try to learn specifically from records, especially your guitar playing? Did you ever try to learn recordings note-for-note, like a lot of young people learn?

Yes, I did. That is what turned me out to be the B.B. King that I am now, because I could never play like anybody else. I guess I just can't hear, and [I] have stupid fingers that just don't work.

For somebody who can't hear and has stupid fingers, it works incredibly well.

Well, what I am saying is, I would listen to T-Bone Walker, I listened to Blind Lemon, I listened to Lonnie Johnson, I listened to all of these people that I loved. And if I could have played identically like [any] one [of them], I would have, but it just never came out. I have never been able to do it. I guess that is one of the reasons why I have kept a group with me all the time, because I have never, even from the beginning, even now—unless I've got an arrangement on it musically where I could study it—I've never been able to do it. Somehow it just doesn't come out.

But I see young kids today and, Man, they are playing note-for-note what George Benson would play or what Chet Atkins would play. But I personally have never been able to do it. Now, maybe a lot of that is laziness on my own part. Maybe. I never put enough initiative into it to try. A lot of times, I have heard people say, "I sure would like to play guitar," and I say to myself, "If you would really try, you could." Maybe I have gone about it in the wrong way or [have] not put enough effort [in it]—could have been either—I am not sure, but I know that I tried.

Maybe B.B. wouldn't have evolved the way he did if you had done that.

That is possible, too.

T-Bone Walker is great, but instead of having a second T-Bone Walker in the world, the world did better by getting a B.B. King.

Well, thank you. But, if I could have played like him note-for-note, I would have.

About the age of eighteen, when you were playing street corners, were you playing single-string lead responses at that point?

Not as I do now. I was just starting to, because at that time I wasn't into T-Bone Walker as I later learned to try to be. It was then more a Lonnie Johnson or Blind Lemon effort, or Lowell Fulson even. He was one of the guys I idolized as well. It was a lot of the guitar players—my cousin, Bukka White. But I never could play with a slide—I still can't— so I didn't go too much in that direction.

Lonnie Johnson was my number-one person—he and Blind Lemon, because of something they had. Now I could also extract from many other people a bit of what I was feeling from Blind Lemon or what I felt from Lonnie Johnson. So that is how I could easily incorporate Charlie Christian and Django Reinhardt [in my playing]—even though they were far-advanced jazz musicians. It was that certain little something, that cer- tain little sound, that certain little feeling that seemed to be kind of like a sword that went straight through me right through here.

You mean the magic hit?

Yes, that is the way [it hit me].

There really is that magic in some of their music. You must have really had a high when you first listened to Django and Charlie Christian?

Oh, God, yes! But I started to feel then something that they were doing quite often, because I am jazz-oriented, I guess. I don't try to play it publicly, because I don't think I play it that well, but I enjoy getting in a jam session. Like, last night we had a kind of jam session, and I really enjoyed it because I was able to improvise—just got turned loose.

But in most cases, [when] I [go] on stage, usually with a group, there is an audience there, everybody is going to say, "Oh, Man, play 'The Thrill Is Gone,' play so-and-so"; and so I am never allowed to actually be myself. And when I say be myself, don't get me wrong. Sure, there is nothing I enjoy playing better than a good slow-down and dirty one [i.e, blues]. I like that because it is kind of like talking— I am not very good at talking, my diction and everything else is terrible. To try and say, "I am B.B. King," it takes a whole lot, really. But I can do that through the guitar, playing slow things. A long time ago I learned that my speed was not good, so I decided to play economy for speed.

To opt for slower blues?

Yes. One picture is worth a thousand words. So, [for] me, one good note [put] where it should be put, will say what it will take some people many notes to say. I hope I'm making sense.

You do. And that is reflected in your guitar sounds. It is all so ironic when you think of the trend within rock circles, which is to play a million notes a minute. It was "the fastest guitars in the West"—especially in the late sixties and early seventies. And many of those people who were heavily blues-influenced would say that you were one of their prime influences. Yet you were never that sort of guitarist. I heard the women mention Son Seals to you earlier. He is much more a player who plays in that style. I believe a younger generation of Chicago players do that because of the influence of rock, but it has always been different with your playing.

You mentioned tunes like "Stormy Monday" by T-Bone Walker. Is there any specific thing you learned from that tune?

Yes, that nobody else can play it like him [laughs]. He starts off—I have a copy of the original—and he plays twelve bars first, which sets it up, kind of like a pitcher on a great ball team that sets up the batter. Well, T-Bone Walker did that to me with the first twelve bars of "Stormy Monday." He set me up—I let the melody do it. I am here on the edge of my seat, [and] he kept me like this the whole three minutes or so of what he's [playing].

Anytime a person gets my attention like that, I couldn't sit here and be writing a letter, or sit here and talk to you and continue listening to that. I got to listen to it. You know, as we are talking now, the conversation can just flow. It is kind of like a rhythm section—a good rhythm section is playing good, and it continues like this. Quite often I tell my group, if you are playing and you have a rhythmic pattern going, if you keep doing that, nobody can beat you. They just have to join you, they can't beat you.

This is what you try to do in your tunes, too. Do you start them with a guitar prelude?

Well, I learned a long time ago to do something jazz musicians usually do now, and that is just play what you feel like playing. Now, don't worry whether this is properly played or whether the progressions are intentional, but just play what you feel. There's another thing I'll tell my group: if we screw up, and all screw up together, it's right [laughing]. Somebody may criticize you, but if you do it together, it is still right because that is what you are doing. Well, that is the way I like to play.

A lot of times people expect me to end a song properly. I may not want to end it like that; I may [want to] hit a few more licks on it and then end it. Of course, my group works with me. They know what I intended to do, and we have worked together long enough that I can signal them and say, "Hey, I got a couple of more things." And people in the audience, especially musicians, may think, "What the heck is he doing?" But I am doing what I feel; I don't feel like it should be chopped off right then, so that is the way I play.

And if it works, it is proper—nobody can say it isn't.

Well, sometimes [laughing] it may not be. I tell my group I have never made a perfect record yet, and I have never made a perfect beginning or ending. So, it just stops whenever I tell it to.

I'll give you another thing that I rarely talk about, but I will have to tell you this and be honest. The musician that starts off playing alone—especially if he is a folk, country, or blues player—usually doesn't depend on bars to keep a rhythmic pattern going. You hear it in most all players. I had some friends of mine to tell me from time to time—Robert Junior Lockwood, for instance, who was a good friend of mine. When I first met him I was playing over in a little place called Hughes, Arkansas, not too far from West Memphis. So I had been hearing Robert Junior and admiring him all the time. He used to be with a guy called "Sonny Boy" Williamson [= Willie "Rice" Miller], and they used to be on radio station KFFA in Helena, Arkansas—the King Biscuit Time Show. So this particular night, the three of us were playing—myself on guitar, a drummer, and a piano player. We were having a ball, and the people were dancing; we had a little place the size of this room almost, and Man, the people were rocking.

So, I would sing the song for ten bars before I decided to make the change. I may stay on the "I chord" for ten bars the first time, because I have to get that feeling going good. So, getting started off is like [having a] heavy load, Man. So you grab that first thing you are saying, like "Mama, the baby's leaving," you know. And you stay on that until it is moving good, and then finally you change to second gear [the IV chord]. You getting ready to come back later to the V chord, but you've got to get it moving first. But if you've got a good beat going, the people that are not trained to music aren't thinking nothing about the bar [i.e., the harmonic rhythm]. You got the beat going where they can dance, [and] the melodic line is going good. That is great; that's all they want.

So, when Robert Junior came in that particular night, he listened to me and tried to play with me. [But he] couldn't follow; he just sit there. So when the tune was over, I said, "Man, come on." And he says, "Man, I can't play with you." So I said to him, "Why?" So he told me there is order to playing—you got to have some order to what you are doing. And he went on to tell me about the bars, which I had read about in my guitar books. But I had found that, to me, the important thing wasn't to play the songs out of the books as they were [written], but to try to keep those people happy. I am not a fast sight-reader, but I do read. Most of my guys are, but I'm not; I'm the worst thing out here. Once I've learned a tune, I will then have to play it as I feel it.

One of the things we wanted to ask you about was what were the specific influences of T-Bone Walker, or Bill Jennings with the Louis Jordan Band. Would you talk about those people, specifically about their guitar playing, and how it affected your guitar playing—harmonically, rhythmically, technically. What sort of things did you learn? Let's start with T-Bone.

T-Bone was very technical to me in his way of playing soulfully. He seemed to measure each pick precisely to get exactly what he wanted. In other words, [his tone] was not blurred, it was a good clean tone. To me [it seemed that each of] T-Bone Walker's tones was carefully placed—each finger placed properly behind the fret to get the exact tone that he was looking for. And it just seemed to me, Man, his transmitting seemed to hit me each time where I lived.

Now, there were others. Take, for instance, Bill Jennings: he was very technical in some ways but then swinging in another. In other words, he seemed to be daring—both rhythmically and technically— more so rhythmically, because he would start a groove to going, and then whatever it takes to keep that groove going, he would do it. Not only was that exciting to me, but he was also a left-handed guitarist. And, the way he played—. I only saw him a couple of times with Louis Jordan; he seemed to get his kicks playing, and I am getting mine along with him. So actually he would go ahead and improvise where T-Bone Walker wouldn't.

T-Bone really mapped things out for himself before he would play?

T-Bone, I like to think, played what he knew and didn't experiment. In other words, what he played had been played in his room or was already in his head.

Bill Jennings would take more chances like jazz guitarists do today.

Oh, yes. They play it even if it ain't right—because it is right to them. [Jennings] seemed to be one of those people like Oscar Peterson and a lot of other people that play what they think. Anything they think, they play it.

Now, a lot of us can't do that, and I am one. If you give me three or four bars to think about, maybe I can get it under my fingers, but I don't play everything I think. I wish I could. But, I will hear something that leads to something, that leads to something [else], and I can follow that. So it is almost like mapping out a road as I go. Now, if I can do that, fine. If I've got a good rhythm section, and I'm able to just float along with it—in other words, not try to keep the rhythm the way I want it myself but try to pull them, [then] I can just play my ideas, lay out what I want as I go.

That's what happened in "The Thrill Is Gone." The rhythm section seemed to just float, and they were just there. Those four guys were like a water bed. But I have had to play a lot [of times while] trying to pull the rhythm section. I hate to do it, but in a lot of cases, I think it has helped to give me a sense of rhythmic timing, or stops, or syncopation, that have helped me even when I didn't want it to. A lot of the time I would be angry.

I have seen you at times on stage. Where it appears you want to say, "Come on, band."

Right, that kind of thing! I tell my nephew, who's my conductor, when he is writing, "You don't write things simply because you can play it, because everybody may not be up on the instrument as well as you are. Someone else may have a problem with it."

Simplicity, to me, rules. Now, you can get a guy started, and then you bring him up to what you want. So, when I am playing even now with my own group, and some of the guys have been with me eight years, we still have some tunes some nights where I feel the need to kind of bring them together. I like to think that I'm the kind [of musician] that brings everybody together. Sometime I will go to the horn section, go to the rhythm section, and then I will look at them all, and this is my way—like a mother hen getting everybody to come on, not to play any harder, but [to play] together. And that is usually the way I wind up a lot of nights. The group is great group—the best band I have had. They want to play and love to play, but I can see why you have a conductor standing in front of an orchestra.

Maybe this would be a good time to talk about your conception of solos. We were talking about T-Bone having everything mapped out before he hit a stage. What about you? When you are up on stage, when you record, how much is worked out and how much are you improvising?

When I record, everything is improvised. I never play anything that I planned to play.

So if you are doing a seventh take on—. Whether it's "Back To The Night" or "The Thrill Is Gone"?

I play exactly what I feel then. I am not going to go too far out on the limb to record. I am not going to go too far out on the limb to play tonight. I will try to play from feeling. So, tonight when I play from feeling, I will never hardly screw up because I am only playing what I feel. Now, I don't feel the same way every night, and I don't feel the same way every day, so that in itself kind of polices me. It keeps me from playing the same thing all the time.

A lot of times people will say, and I've heard some of the critics say, "I know what B.B. is going to do, I just don't know what order he is going to play it in." But if they are real critical and check out what I have done, they will find it was different, because I never feel the same way. Nobody does. You may feel good, but if you define good, what is good today, and what is good tomorrow? How do you feel then? Was it just good or extra good? So, what I have to do, other than being a musician trying to satisfy my audiences, is be pretty good at being a programmer, to be able to keep the people happy today compared with the people yesterday. So if you will listen tonight, you will find that I will do a fast tune, a slow tune or in-between tune, and another. And you will find that if you really dissect that, you will find a new tune, an old one, and one in-between. And that is how I manage to make it.

Now I think when someone asked me earlier about my success, this is one thing I forgot to mention. I try to play songs according to the situation. Certain tunes I wouldn't play to this audience, I would play to that audience. I am not talking about black or white, I am talking about the audience itself, or the place where I am playing. I wouldn't go to Carnegie Hall now and try to play "Misty" or "Stardust" without playing "Three O'Clock Blues." But the point is, I would be careful about where I put "Three O'Clock Blues," and I would be careful about how I tried to play "Stardust," because I don't play it all the time.

I feel that the people that come to hear me at Carnegie Hall would be some of the same people that would come to hear me in Fayette [Mississippi]. But there are some that are not familiar with me, so I would try to not bore the people that have been with me all the time by playing something that they haven't heard me play. And then, of course, I would try to introduce myself to the people that are not familiar with me at all.

I noticed a tremendous difference in your playing when I first moved to Memphis. I saw you at Club Paradise, at Sunbeam's Fiftieth

Anniversary, and I have seen you many times in Toronto at Massey Hall, and there is a tremendous difference.

But, if you had went down to the theater there in Memphis, you would have caught me playing different. I remember a critic came to the Apollo Theater and said that I didn't play blues at the Apollo Theater, that I had them watered down. Well, naturally, this person being a journalist, I couldn't rebuttal, but I am saying to you that—no, I wouldn't play even to the same audience the same way twice.

But, if you have gone on stage—both of you being musicians—and played everything you knew to play, the best you could play it at first, what the hell are you going to do when you come back the second time? So, what you have to do then is think in terms of trying to make them happy a second time. So, what I've found is that is the time you try to be a musician/entertainer, if you will.

I think this is what hurt some of my colleagues, some of the best blues players we've ever had, because they would do the same thing, and it don't work. [If] you are going to have an audience—like last night down stairs—sure, you can play one or two slow, real bluezy things, but I could very easily see as I was playing that the people were in the mood to "boogie." They wanted to get out and do something. So if you keep playing all of your best blues, the good ones, you are going to lose them. I would rather somebody would criticize me to the point of saying, "Well, he didn't play here like he did there," and they would be right. But I still kept my audience.

To me that is not a criticism, that is a compliment. You can see a performer five times, and if it is the same show five times, why go the sixth time, no matter how good he is. Whereas, I have seen you twenty or thirty times in my life, and I am still not bored.

Well, I would be bored myself if I had to do the same thing—that is one of the things about doing a Broadway show or something like that. But I have learned from some of the actors and musicians that even though they have the same road map as we do—. Like I play through dawn every night, more than anything else, and if it was going to be any tune I hate to play, if I had to play it the same way that I played it the first time I recorded it, I'd probably jump out the window [laughing]. But don't get me wrong, I still have the same road map. But I sing it with the energy, play it with the energy and the feeling that I feel now, not like I did last night, or not like I recorded it. I think that is the one thing that keeps me from being bored; anytime I can keep myself from being bored, I can probably make somebody else feel good.

Would you consider some of these "licks" you play to be road maps? Is there a framework to some of your "licks?"

No, when I am playing, that is the one thing I have never limited myself to, trying to play the same thing each time I play. No. Now, one of the things that helped me to learn more about music, it seems to me, is believing in my mind. In other words, if I can graph it out and see it—I learned through the Schillinger system that when I can graph out what I want to say, then it makes more sense to me. Basically, I can take four notes and permute them twenty-four different ways. So, even if some of them don't sound good, they are still there to be used. I would pick the ones out of those twenty-four tones that sound best to me and play them, not just play them simply because they are there. But I would pick the notes that sound good to me. That I do nightly.

I'm sure you are familiar with Charles Sawyer's book, *The Arrival of B.B. King*, regarding the use of "riffs" in various ways, or licks, or whatever word one wants to use. Charles Sawyer tries to make a point that there are a couple of "riffs" that you use more often than others.

Tom [Charles] is a friend of mine. I will finish reading the book eventually, but one of these things is that we have been friends for quite some time, and when he started to write the book he told me he was going to write about B.B. King the man, not the musician. One of the things we dealt with was as long as he tells the truth in it, I wouldn't be worried about it.

But, what makes identity? What makes persons be themselves is being what they are continually, as far as I am concerned. In other words, that is who you are. Now, if I listen to the Beatles, I know it is the Beatles because I know what they sound like. Nobody else to me sounds like the Beatles, even the new people that are trying. Nobody to me sounds like Elvis but Elvis. Same thing with Blind Lemon, same thing with Memphis Lemon.

So, I would say, yes. Of course there are certain licks that I am going to hit, because that is me—I have to do that. It's kind of like trying to talk to you; I say the clichés or something to try to get my point over. I think the same way when I am on the stage. I am carrying on a rapport with my audience. I am trying to say something to identify me. On stage, I try my very best, and I sometimes try to describe it this way: I feel like I am on stage with long rubber arms around a dancing partner, which is the audience, and I like to be able to lead the audience.

When we ask you about using certain licks or riffs over again in different ways, that is in no way a criticism. Any good musician is—. I guess part of what we want to know is where some of them came from?

If we were going to go back to the same people I mentioned were my idols, I am sure that some parts of that have been there all the time. But it has grown to be such an intertwining with my own personal feelings. When I do it I might touch upon Blind Lemon or Louis Jordan or any of the people, not knowing it. That is B.B. King.

That is no different than the "terms" we all use in speaking. We all use things that our friends use, and that our parents use, that are now part of us. Part of what we want to do in this interview is to establish what is B.B. King's guitar style, and where various elements of B.B. King's guitar style came from.

The very beginning of B.B. King was "Three O'Clock Blues." I was starting to learn a little bit, I was starting to walk—crawling in the beginning—if you were able to put it together, you would say, "Oh yea, I know what he will sound like in '86."

I started teaching guitar to little kids in 1966, and these kids would come in with a B.B. King recording, saying that is the lick they wanted to learn. That, in many ways for many years, was sort of a signature lick or identity or part of what you were. Do you remember how that came about?

When I first got my electric guitar—it was a little black Gibson with the "F" holes in it, acoustic—I got a DeArmond pick-up for it, and the first amplifier was a little Gibson amplifier, just about the size of that tape recorder. I don't remember now what it was called, but it had this ten-inch speaker in it. I couldn't hear low bass sounds, like most people do. Today, my bass player can fool me very easy; I can hear treble sounds better. So, in order for me to play and make sense to myself, I played with a lot of treble on that first little electric guitar.

Finally, I bought the first Fender that they made, and that really gave me treble. So that was the beginning of this treble sound that you hear today. With the stereo guitar I am able to mix the sounds somewhat as I go along, so one of my little secrets has been, from the beginning, to open up the amp and set it from the guitar as I play.

Usually when I record they give me some leeway: I never like straight in, I like to have the amp where I can hear it myself. I am able to mix the sound, not to look down and see what I got it on, but the way it sounds good to me. And that little stereo flipping switch from one speaker to the other, I never move. It stays in the middle; rare thing for me to move it. The other little thing, the control knob, which seems to change the sound from bass to complete treble, I never use, because to me it takes away the energy that I need.

Another thing I like about the Gibson Guitar (ES-135) is, I can ease my big old hands under there, touch the one that I want, and get it just like I want very easily without making a noise. And most times people don't even know I've done it—they just hear a difference in sound.

So, that is the sound that started B.B. King to become the B.B. King, along with a lick or two. All came from this treble sound and certain things, [such as] not knowing one bar from the other. So, when I start with an intro, and the rhythm section starts playing from feeling, I might let the rhythm section get to the fifth bar before I realize it, so I have to make a quick move to the IV chord. I think that was the beginning of it. Usually now I am aware in most cases, but I still get out in space sometimes and caught out there. Even now I am terrible if I try to play or sing a cappella or sing along, so I always need a guide, I always need somebody out there—that rhythm section.

In a "Gambler's Blues" (1966) recording I have, you did a jazz type of pull-off.

We recorded that at the Burning Spear in Chicago.

I'm curious: how often do you play that lick where you touch the strings and lift your fingers off? Is that a pull-off? To me that is more a jazz approach to guitar playing. I listen to both Howard Roberts and Barney Kessel. They do it all the time. I wonder where you may have picked up that way of playing?

I don't know, but I guess I am somewhat like Barney Kessel quite often. He stated that he thought that Charlie Christian was the father of the electric guitar. Barney listened to him, so did I. I don't know—I'm just being honest with you—I really don't know.

You have talked a lot in various interviews, and even earlier today, about Django, Charlie Christian, and the other people you've listened to quite a bit. If you will remember when we talked to you about Bill Jennings and T-Bone Walker, we were asking about specific things you got from those players. Can you talk in the same sort of specifics about the elements of their guitar playing you tried to incorporate into yours?

During the time of Charlie Christian, most people weren't aware of chords like ninths and thirteenths. So, what Charlie Christian was really known for was using those progressions. He used what we call diminished chords, and, Man, he could break them up so pretty. He just lay 'em out—breaking up those diminished chords—and still had a good rhythmic pattern going along with it. Well, that to me started the improvising. That was one way even horn players could improvise something. So the guitar doing those diminished chords made it stand out just a little bit different from what some horn players had been doing.

When you're talking about his breaking down into diminished chords, are you talking about simply running a diminished chord as a single-note solo?

Yes. You can do that even today, and it sounds pretty. And if you keep within the diminished structure, you're never going to screw up really, because if you know your instrument you can go all over the neck and just keep going. Well, Django seemed to have had a different conception of progressions, and his single string was superb—it still is today.

I think one of the things that made him [different] was because he started off studying to be a violinist, and due to an accident in his trailer he got his hand burned, [and] started playing the guitar. So now, when he started to play guitar, to me Django had a trill that he would get on his guitar. Each time he would hit a note, it was just like there was not going to be another one—so I'll take care of this here, and milk this one as long as I can. So each time he touched that [note] it was like touching a lady, you know; this is it! And I would feel that certain little something [when I listened to him], and I still do.

It is a little bit of something extra: like the note is B-flat, sure it's B-flat—bang, it's B-flat. But it's B-flat with just a little bit of a grace note with it. That is the way I feel. So, that is the part that Charlie Christian had, the certain little touch that Django had. I can't describe it any further than what I have told you. There is a certain little something [put] on each note, and to me each one of them is important. Each note! You don't just play it because it is a note to be played.

You have spoken about non-guitarists being influential on you. I believe you mentioned Louis Jordan's alto-sax playing, and you talked about Lester Young a few times. Would you talk specifically about their saxophone-playing and the sort of things you've tried to incorporate in your guitar-playing?

Louis Jordan had a way of hitting a note that he really stayed with; for instance, if the note is in the key of C, he would stretch the note to D-flat or C-sharp, [then] down to the C—slur it down. O.K., let's assume that we were starting on the 5th, [then move from] the G to the A, to the C, then push the D out back to the C—that is Louis Jordan. He would do that same sort of thing. So that is the part I would have borrowed from him. It is B.B. King. But what I am trying to say is that is what I would hear Louis Jordan doing, even if I don't hear him.

What about "Prez" [Lester Young]?

The same way I described Django Reinhardt—only ["Prez" was] just slower getting there, but very dominating in doing it, mellower with it, in other words. Again, like [there] is not going to be another note and I may be a little late getting there. But I'm coming, and the waves are like Jaws [the whale] moving in the water.

Guitarists, like other instrumentalists, prefer to play in certain keys. Are there certain keys you like to play in?

No. I like to think about my playing, the little bit that I can play, all keys is good. I won't tell anybody, because I don't want my band to know it, and they will—the only key that I might would be a little short on would be E. They are going to kill me, 'cause anytime a guy gets in my group, I find the weak key that he plays in and I'll keep him in it.

When he leaves me, he will be able to play whatever he knows in all the keys. So my shortest-coming would be in the key of E, but I do things quite often in E.

With regards to tuning, you use standard tuning all the time now. Have you always done that?

All the time.

One last question: can you break down into any time-frames the evolution or development of your guitar style? Are there times you've made quantum leaps that you can sort of mark off?

Well, it's kind of like every record I've made: I always thought there was something special on it. I've never made a perfect record, but each time that I played a record, I always felt that I played something that I never played before—even if I didn't like it afterwards. I think I am quite critical of most things I do. In fact, the guys that work with me—. [No one] has ever heard me playing my own records in my room unless it was something that I was working on. I play them, but nobody else is going to hear me do it.

I have never practiced like musicians usually do. I practice different in that I don't pick up the guitar a lot of times. But since I've been sitting talking to you, I looked at the neck of it quite a few times and saw things that I would like to do that I haven't done, that I wanted to do and haven't been able to do. That is my way of practicing in a lot of cases—seeing a picture of a guitar in my hand. Good thing God put our brains where nobody sees what we are thinking [laughing].

I did that quite a few times when I was trying to describe to you a few minutes ago about the notes—like starting, for instance, the B-string, starting with G to go to C, and all that. I'm visualizing the neck of the guitar. In fact, if I hear you play or hear a record, that's the way I get it into my head what is going on—I start looking at the neck of my guitar and associate what I hear with it. That is the only way I can get it straight. But anyway, I hope I was able to say something that makes some sense to you.

Thank you for sharing with us your candid perception of B.B. King the artist.

Steinblatt, an editor of *Guitar World*, asks other relevant questions about King's relation to his instrument, lovingly known as Lucille.

It's been over forty years since he first arrived in Memphis to play the blues, but B.B. King still has the fire.

B.B. King sits munching on a chicken leg in his plush suite at the New York Hilton. He is a long way from Beale Street, the one-time blues mecca of Memphis, where, in the late 1940's, he developed the golden tone and unearthly vibrato for which he is envied by blues and rock guitarists the world over. He is even further removed from Indianola, Mississippi, the small Delta town where he sharecropped cotton as a youth. Anyone unfamiliar with the details of King's incredible career need only conjure an image of the young B.B. working the fields of Indianola and then see him couched in five-star splendor to appreciate the great distance he and his beloved Gibson ES-355—universally known as Lucille—have travelled.

More than any other bluesman, B.B. King has enjoyed mainstream success and recognition. Adults whose eyes glaze with pure mystification at the names Buddy Guy, Albert King and Otis Rush will instantly identify B.B. as the "King Of The Blues." Few of his peers are ever booked at the kind of large venues B.B. regularly plays. No other bluesmen are television regulars—besides his frequent spots on Johnny Carson's "Tonight Show," King has guested on such sitcoms as "Sanford and Son," "The Cosby Show" and "Married . . . With Children." And he is the only bluesman to have an honorary doctorate conferred upon him by Yale University.

Perhaps most significantly, however, B.B.'s international reputation, brilliant musicianship and unparalleled guitar artistry have caused him, more than any other bluesman, to suffer the singular anguish engendered by young journalists asking old, old questions:

GUITAR WORLD: I imagine you've been asked this a thousand times before, but how is it that your guitar came to be called "Lucille"?

B.B. KING: You're wrong; I've been asked that question ten thousand times before. [Laughs.] But here it is: I used to play a place called Twist, Arkansas, on weekends, mostly at the beginning of my career. It got quite cold in Twist, so they would take a big garbage can, half-fill it with kerosene, and light that fuel for heat. One night in 1949 two guys got to fighting, and one of them knocked the other over on that container and it spilled on the floor. It looked like a river of fire. Everybody started running for the front door, including B.B. King. But when I got outside, I realized that I left my guitar, a Gibson acoustic, and I went back for it. When I did, the building started to collapse around me. I almost lost my life trying to save my guitar. The next morning we found out that the two guys had been fighting about a lady. I never did meet her, but I learned her name was Lucille. So I named my guitar—and every guitar I had since then—Lucille, to remind me never to do a thing like that again.

It's a wonderful tale; every element—women, jealousy, guitars, fire—screams the blues. Of course, B.B. recreates that rural Southern blaze every time he bends a note or plays one of his patented vocal-like phrases. I was about to ask the guitarist to recall some other outstanding anecdotes of his early touring days, when a loud, repeated alarm interrupted me.

"What the hell is that?" asked King. I ran to the door, opened it and smelled smoke. Apparently, the walls of the New York Hilton have ears; so impressed was the luxurious hotel with King's tale of Lucille and Twist, it decided to catch fire. We were on the forty-second floor.

"We'll take the steps, the elevators aren't safe," said B.B. I followed; you don't question the King Of The Blues, certainly not in an emergency. My thoughts, as the King and I descended through an acrid haze of smoke and semi-panicking guests, were understandably disjointed. On the one hand, I was fleeing a fire with a man I'd only come to talk vibrato with. It hadn't occurred to me, while preparing for the interview, to write my will.

On the other hand, I was secretly thrilled. There was a fire, yes, but my comrade through all this was *B.B. King.* I knew that years thence, whenever some odious acquaintance would namedrop to sickening excess, I would in an appropriately bored voice say, "Yes, that is interesting. It reminds me of the time B.B. King and I fled a fire together in the New York Hilton."

Truthfully, the greatest dramas of our escape more involved my companion than myself. We were joined on every landing by other guests running from the fire. On almost every floor someone, eyes widening, would exclaim, "You're B.B. King!" And the legendary bluesman would respond graciously—even as he continued running down the stairs.

By the time we reached the twentieth floor, the fire department had arrived and quickly isolated and extinguished the blaze. No one was injured, but I was exhausted by my brush with immolation—an unpleasant way to go, albeit in the company of a great bluesman. B.B. King, however, appeared unscathed by the adventure. "So when can we finish our conversation?" he asked cheerfully. I didn't have the nerve to voice my great hope. After that fire in Twist, King named his guitar "Lucille." Now, after the Hilton . . . isn't it perhaps time for a new name?

GUITAR WORLD: Give me your reaction to this statement: The blues is doing great.

B.B. KING: *I have to agree; it was never accepted in the past like it is today—not in my lifetime. I don't know why. It seems to me that there were many people playing the blues in the Sixties that left to do other things. Only a few remain—I think Eric Clapton still plays blues. But now you got new kids on the block like Robert Cray, Stevie Ray Vaughan, God rest his soul, Jeff Healey, Joe Louis Walker and quite a few other people who are playing.*

GW: Apart from the blues phenomenon, there's very much a B.B. King phenomenon that stands apart from any other blues artists. You still play almost 300 gigs a year. Your energy is hard to believe.

KING: *Nothing has driven me so much as my trying to bring respectability to the blues. In the early years, it was put down so much. When I was growing up there were a couple of types of music that were put down by the educated "majority"—country music as well as blues—but blues seemed to be at the bottom of the totem pole.*

GW: Maybe that's a reflection of its being black music.

KING: *That was it. I like to say, "If you're white and you play the blues, you're black once. If you're black and you play the blues, you're black twice." [Laughs.]*
Some people have pronounced ideas about blues players as a whole. Blues musicians should be a guy my size, sitting in a chair, a broken chair, looking north, with a jug of liquor on his west side, a cap turned

south and a cigarette pointing east, hanging from his lip. The rear end of his pants are worn out—not for style like the kids today. He has a guitar that has four good strings. Two of them are tied by wire so he has to have a pencil or something to keep the other strings from rattling, so he can use the good part—from the pencil to the bridge. The smoke is so thick, you can cut it with a knife. And he should be half-drunk at the same time . . .

GW: You perform so often. How do you prevent your material from becoming stale—if not to the audience, then to you?

KING: Because I play it each night like I'm playing it for the first time. Meaning, I know the chords, but I never go note-for-note on the melody—ever. You play it some nights a little faster, some nights slower, but generally you play it with a feeling that you haven't played it with before.

GW: Do you ever change keys? Do you take risks?

KING: I improvise, yes—I love to improvise. I couldn't do it like Charlie Parker, no way. But in my own way, I improvise. I play what I'm feeling now, not what I played yesterday and felt then.

GW: How often do you practice?

KING: I don't practice for half a day like some people, but maybe that's why I'm not the musician that some people are. It's a sure thing that practice makes perfect. If you practice anything enough, you can play it. I do practice quite a bit, but nothing like I should. If I'm able to be with my guitar each day, I'll practice—maybe half an hour.

GW: What do you practice?

KING: Scales. Chords. I'm never good with chords so now I've been concentrating quite a bit on them. but I'm a single-string player, mostly, and most of my practicing or rehearsing or whatever has generally been running the scales.

GW: When most people pick up the guitar, they start with chords. Did you concentrate on your soloing?

KING: *Always on my soloing, very little chords. I didn't ever practice playing chords as an accompaniment. I've never been very good, and I'm still not.*

GW: Is it something you consider a liability?

KING: *I always depended on playing with someone, and that's why I always kept a band and had the rhythm section play the rhythm while I played the lead. So that kind of made me the featured person all the time. I got used to doing that, and I guess I got lazy about being an accompanist to myself.*

GW: Who would you say is good with chords?

KING: *There's a guy called Robert Jr. Lockwood—I think he's a master with them.*

GW: His blues playing is very jazz-influenced.

KING: *Why not? I've always liked that. I love jazz. I like country. I like rock and roll. I like to think that you should be able to incorporate anything you want to in what you do. Play your feelings. Like, I don't feel that I am a country blues singer or a blues musician or an urban blues musician or city blues . . . I don't think anything like that. I think one thing: I'm B.B. King and I play what I feel—or at least I try.*

GW: You're well known for your ability to say worlds with just one note.

KING: *When you're a soloist, you don't just play a note simply because you can find one. You do it because it makes sense. To me every note is important. Some people are very fast, they have speed, they play many, many notes. And I have to listen carefully to understand them. You ever hear of a trumpet player called Bobby Hackett, or an alto saxophonist called Johnny Hodges? Those people, when they played just one note, they seemed to live it. That's the way I like to play. I can hear those guys play and it seems like their one note is like a sword—it just goes through me.*

GW: I think you've managed to become a pretty good swordsman your-self. You have, in the past, cited Django Reinhardt, Lonnie Johnson, T-Bone Walker and Blind Lemon Jefferson as important influences on your style. Is it possible to break down their respective contributions to your playing?

KING: *If you dissect everything that I've done, you would probably find bits and pieces of each one of the people that I idolize. T-Bone Walker—man, that was the prettiest sound I ever heard in my life, hearing electric guitar playing single-string blues. It seemed to me that every time I got a guitar, the notes that T-Bone and all my other idols played, they weren't on my guitar.* [Laughs.] *Just my luck.*

GW: What do you think of players nowadays?

KING: *To me, it seems that the young kids who are around today are playing more, sooner, and better than we ever did. There are reasons for that. Today there are many things you can get that we didn't have—for instance, the tape recorder you're using right now. And synthesizers. Now, all you do is go down and get a small synthesizer keyboard, program your own rhythmic pattern, sit down with your guitar and play. At home I have a computer that I can compose with, and the computer will play everything back for me—the many different voices. I can hear what my band will sound like long before I tell them, "This is what I want."*

With us, back then, we would pick up a guitar where we could find one. There were no other instruments in my neighborhood. The only time I saw a keyboard was in church. There were no music stores anywhere nearby. There were no bands.

GW: How long have you been playing the Gibson ES-355?

KING: *The 355? About, oh, 20 years. Prior to that I used the 335. The difference between the two is that the '55 is a solidbody. I like to think of it as the big brother to the Les Paul.*

GW: Have you ever played a Les Paul?

KING: *I've played practically every guitar that was available to me over the years. Some years I couldn't afford anything else, so any guitar I could get, I played.*

GW: Do you remember the first guitar you played?

KING: *Yes, the first guitar I had was called a Stella.*

GW: That was an acoustic?

KING: *Yes.*

GW: What did you use when you recorded your earliest sides?

KING: *In those days, it was hard to keep a good guitar, so I played anything I could get . . . I had a Fender, a Gretsch, a Silvertone and a Gibson.*

GW: How do you keep the action on your guitar?

KING: *Low. Very low. I don't like my fingers to hurt. They used to bleed sometimes, so I keep the fingering very close to the fret. I use pretty heavy strings, I guess, for a blues player. That's an outgrowth of my Stella days—the days I played acoustic guitar. At that time I knew nothing but Black Diamond strings, and they were very big. Now I use a .010 on the E string, an .013 on the B string, .017 on the G, .032 or .034 on D, the 5th string I use an .046 and a .054 for the E.*

GW: The technique for which you are particularly renowned for is your vibrato. How did it evolve?

KING: *In the early years I used to hear a lot of slide guitar players. I've never been able to use the slide myself. So, I found that when I trill my hand, my ears tend to be fooled somewhat by that sound—as if it's a person using a slide or steel guitar. I can sustain the tones, get overtones and do quite a few of the things you couldn't do otherwise. And I've been doing that to this day. Though I'd have to say that I still haven't perfected it.*

Wheeler and Obrecht are two noted journalists who write on guitar history and technique; not surprisingly, this article focuses primarily on that aspect of King's career, and how he learns new
material and adapts it to his style.

Riley B. King is the world's preeminent blues guitarist. There is hardly a
rock, pop, or blues player anywhere who doesn't owe him something,
although because much of his influence has been indirectly transmitted
through rock stars, more than a few may be unaware of that debt. His
dedication is as inspiring as his talent, and it's hard to imagine someone
working harder at music, or anything else. For decades Riley, better
known as B.B., has worked a staggering 300 nights a year or more, in part
because he feels that he must live up to a long-held title. They call him
King of the Blues.

"There are days when I don't feel like going onstage," he admits, "but
whether I want to go on or not, I *must* go on. Usually when I'm up there,
I try and do like an electric eel and throw my little shock through the
whole audience, and usually the reaction comes back double-force and
pulls me out of it, because the people can *help* you entertain; they become
a part of it. It's something like radar: You send out a beam, and it hits and
comes back with even more energy."

Sweating in the spotlight, working on the freeboard, B.B. seems like a
string-bending surgeon with his deft and confident left-hand technique.
Unlike many self-taught guitarists, he plays very efficiently, without the
wasted effort that comes from using the wrong fingers. He takes a breath.
From his expression you know that in a split second Riley B. King will lay
himself bare. He extends an irresistible invitation to share in the simple
transfer of joy and pain which he has perfected: He stings Lucille; Lucille
stings you. David Bromberg recently put it this way: "Usually in a good
concert you'll hear people say 'ooh' or 'ahh' at various times, but when
B.B. plays they all go 'ooh' at the same time and 'aah' at the same time.
He doesn't just play his guitar; he plays his audience."

Many of the post-Beatles guitars stars were of course technically
accomplished and innovative, but in most cases, beneath the arrangements
and the special effects were guitar licks unmistakably attributable to B.B.
King and other American bluesmen who, in the U.S. at least, were then

known only to limited numbers of blues buffs. Aside from phrases and blues scales, the dynamics of rock guitar as a communicative vehicle also owe much to the originality of B.B. King. He can make Lucille talk in an almost literal sense, with screams, sassy put-downs, cute little tickles, or an unabashed plea for love. He can articulate the hopelessness of poverty or a love gone wrong with a poetic subtlety rarely matched by mere words.

When he was developing what has become one of the world's most readily identifiable guitar styles, B.B. borrowed from Lonnie Johnson, T-Bone Walker, and others, integrating his precise, vocal-like string bends and his patented left-hand vibrato, both of which have become indispensable components of rock guitar's vocabulary. His economy, his every-note-counts phrasing, has been a model of taste and style for thousands of players. Mike Bloomfield was awestruck upon hearing Eric Clapton in the mid '60s. Later describing his impression, he groped for superlatives: "He was as good as . . . *B.B. King.*" For Bloomfield, an ardent musicologist, it was the ultimate tribute.

According to one prevalent view, there is some quantum of suffering that must be endured before an entertainer "qualifies" as a blues artist. Under anybody's standard, B.B. King has qualified many times over. He was born on a Mississippi plantation and earned 35¢ for each 100 pounds of cotton he picked; he once calculated that he had walked thousands of miles behind a plow during his years as a farmhand. It was only during the rainy season that he was allowed to leave the farm to attend school, and he walked ten miles to join his 85 classmates in their one-room schoolhouse. For two decades he took his music to scores of obscure and often sleazy bars throughout the South, where isolation crushed the dreams of many a performer.

At age 24 King was performing in a bar in Twist, Arkansas, when two men started a fight, kicking over a barrel-sized kerosene lamp. The building erupted in flames, and the panic-stricken crowd scrambled into the street. Not having enough money to replace his $30 guitar, B.B. raced back in to save it. The man who was later to acquaint much of the world with the blues was almost burned to death, and just after his escape the building collapsed, killing two other men. When he learned that the fight had been over a woman named Lucille, he gave that name to his beloved instrument and its many successors "to remind me never to do a fool thing like that again." The story is the stuff of legends, but legends sometimes spawn stereotypes, and B.B. King is a complex man, one who in the interview that follows disavows several popular images of blues entertainers.

The young B.B. King spent countless hours in the small recording facilities used by Kent (later Kent/Modern), Crown, and Blue Horizon, turning out regional hits in the early '50s. He estimates that he's recorded over 300 sides in all, although because of poor distribution and low retail prices he never reaped much profit on many of them.

He cut more LPs after signing with ABC-Paramount in 1961, one of the best of which is *Live At The Regal*. He was transferred to ABC's now defunct Bluesway label in 1967, and he made the R&B charts a year later with "Paying The Cost To Be The Boss." Producer Bill Szymczyk contributed much energy to *Live And Well* in 1969, and it was hailed in *Down Beat* as "the most important blues recording in many years."

Finally in 1970, over 20 years after cutting his first records, B.B. scored a nationwide hit with "The Thrill Is Gone." Though it employed a string section and thoroughly modern production, he is suspicious of the emphasis so often placed on elaborate recording techniques, noting that many early blues classics were cut in garages or mobile facilities. In fact, his first major R&B hit, RPM's "Three O'Clock Blues," was recorded in 1950 in the Memphis YMCA. It stayed on top of the regional charts for four months, and as he discusses below, it changed his life.

B.B. has been acclaimed in virtually every music poll, and his affection for music of almost all types continues off-stage. In his hotel room, a bed or table is usually covered with mounds of cassette tapes, perhaps 50 of them, "just for my own listening enjoyment." He often practices long into the morning hours, even during periods of grueling roadwork, and spends much of his free time listening to the records in his mammoth collection at home.

B.B.'s approach to his art is not only the cornerstone of a distinguished career but also a metaphor for a remarkable philosophy of self-improvement and universal brotherhood. In 1973 he and Fayette, Mississippi, mayor Charles Evers co-sponsored a memorial festival commemorating slain civil rights leader Medgar Evers. B.B. was a founding member of the JFK Performing Arts Center and has received public service awards from B'nai B'rith and many other organizations. He co-founded the Foundation for the Advancement of Inmate Rehabilitation and Recreation. He has played many prison benefits and been cited for his service by the Federal Bureau of Prisons. He is a licensed pilot and an accomplished player of several instruments other than guitar. He received an honorary doctorate from Mississippi's Tougaloo College, and his hometown renamed a park after him and painted a guitar on the street near the corner where the King of the Blues used to play for dimes.

The town turned out to see him put his large hands in the wet cement, and the tribute was a highlight of B.B. King's life.

In the following interview B.B. reflects upon his professional standards, his guitar techniques, and his more than 30 years as a bluesman. He rejects certain public perceptions of blues performers and explains the evolution of his relationship to his art. B.B. King is witty, gracious, independent, and significantly more eclectic than his contemporaries. At the core of his career is a dedication to his ideals, to his fans, and to his belief that music is a social tool, a vehicle for bringing people together.

When were you born, and where did you grow up?

I was born in 1925 in the country outside of Itta Bena, Mississippi, which is not too awful far from Indianola. My parents separated when I was around four, and I spent some time in the hills of Mississippi, up around Kilmichael. That's where I lost my mother, when I was nine. I was a farmhand all of my life, until I was inducted into the Army and sent to Camp Shelby near Hattiesburg, Mississippi, in 1943. I was plowing, driving tractors and trucks, chopping cotton—everything that one does on a farm, I did some of it.

When did you first encounter music?

The first music was in church. From that time until now, that . . . certain something was instilled into me. I had been baptized as a Baptist, then I was in the Holiness—the Church Of God In Christ—and the singing and the music in the churches was something that a small boy, even in his fifties today, will never forget.

What did your family think of you playing the blues when you started?

I couldn't play them at home. I was formerly a spiritual singer, and they wouldn't go for the blues, not around the house [laughs, shakes his head], not then. That's one thing about the early days of the blues. A few of the spiritual people liked blues, but they would play their blues after 12:00, when they were in their room and nobody could hear them. But you always had a few devils like myself and a few others that would listen to anything. You played it and it sounded good, we would listen to it. I was singing spirituals in my first group, the Elkhorn Singers, but I'd love to go to juke joints at that time.

What made you choose the guitar?

I think that a lot of that has to do with the Sanctified Church, because this preacher played guitar in the church, and that was one thing. But also, guitars were kind of available. The average home had a guitar and a harmonica, usually; you could always find them around. But saxophones, trumpets, pianos, and thing like that were rare. Only the middle class families would have a piano. Sometimes a lot of us would like to sneak in the church to play with the piano, and many of us got jobs as janitors, because this enabled us to be near it. We'd be cleaning up the church or something like that, and get a chance to fool with a piano a little bit.

Do you remember your first guitar?

My first one was a Stella, about two-and-a-half feet long, with the big round hole in it, and it was red, one of their little red guitars. I was making $15 a month, so I paid seven-and-a-half the first month and seven-and-a-half the next one. I kept it for a long, long time. It was stolen, but I don't remember when. The next one was a Gibson I bought in Memphis with the help of my cousin, Bukka White. It was an acoustic, but we had just learned about DeArmond pickups. I didn't have enough money to buy the regular electric, so we bought that and put a pickup on it that cost $27. The very first Fenders—I had one. I used it when I first went out on the road, '49 or early '50. I also had a little Gibson amplifier that was about a foot wide, and about half a foot thick [chuckles at the recollection], *with a speaker in it of about eight inches, I suppose, and that was my amplifier, and I kept it for a long time.*

When did you begin playing professionally?

In the middle 1940s, in Indianola, on the corner of Church and Second Street. Second Street is like the main part of town, and Church Street crossed it and went into the black area, what we called "across the tracks." I never passed the hat, but the people knew that I'd appreciate a dime if I played a tune they'd requested.

Why had you picked that particular corner?

I was afraid to sit in the square near city hall, because I probably would have been run out of there. I forget the name of the sheriff that we had then [laughs], *and on my corner both the blacks and the whites would see me. It wasn't something I planned; it was just like a good fishing place—it seemed like a nice spot to be. You'd find me on that corner on Saturdays, and sometimes after I got off work I'd take my bath, get my guitar, and hitchhike to other little towns like Itta Bena or Moorhead or Greenville. Most times I was lucky. I'd make more money that evening than I'd make all week driving tractors. I'd probably have enough money for a movie. Next day, go to church, then back to work. At the time I was making $22.50 a week with the tractors.*

Do you remember your first paying job as a musician?

I don't remember my first paid gig, but I remember the first gig where I started working for like a week at a time—1949 that was, in West Memphis, at a place called the 16th Street Grill. That lady was paying me $12 a night, room and board. I was 24 years old, and that was more money—I didn't know there was that much money in the world. So that's how that started. That was me alone up there—sing, and then play, as I normally do. Sing and play. Working there made me think about going on the radio as a disc jockey, because the lady at the grill told me that if I could get my own show like Sonny Boy Williamson and Bobby Nighthawk and quite a few of the guys, she would give me a steady weekly job, and I loved that idea.

How did you acquire the name "B.B."?

The idea came from the local radio station where I was working, WDIA. I was singing some advertisements for Pepticon, one of these cure-all patent medicines. Later, when I became a disc jockey with my own one-hour show, they would call me "the blues boy," or "the boy from Beale Street." A lot of times they'd shorten it to B.B., and I liked that, and it stuck with me all this time.

Before you were nationally recognized, was there much contact between you and your contemporaries such as Muddy Waters? Were you aware of each other; did you have each other's records and so forth?

No. I had their records, but see, Muddy Waters and John Lee Hooker and all of those guys were playing before me, and they didn't know me from Adam. I was plowin' when they was playin' [laughs]! I liked them, and I imagine that they were aware of each other. But they didn't know anything about me, no. Like Ike Turner was about 14 years old when I first met him, in Clarksdale, Mississippi. I had this great big band at that time, which consisted of my guitar, a set of drums, and a saxophone. That was a big band, wasn't it? When Ike saw me [laughs], he said, "Oh, man, you need help!"

What was it like gigging for years in small, segregated clubs all over the South?

Well, you hear this term "chitlin circuit." That's not one of my terms, but they're talking about the joints where we used to play before we started to play the white establishment. These clubs were small, most of them, and always across the tracks, in the black area. A lot of the promoters couldn't afford to pay you very much money, and if they didn't have a pretty good crowd, sometimes you didn't get paid at all. I only have about $180,000 owed up to me from my playing during my career. I'd say 90% of the promoters were for real, just like they are today. But then you had the other 10%—the young promoter, probably his first time to give a dance or concert. If he didn't make it, that was it, because he had thrown in everything he had to do this one concert, which he felt would be a gold mine. He'd say to himself, "Well, if I can get B.B. King or Junior Parker or whoever, this night they're going to pull me through," and a lot of times that didn't happen, and when it didn't happen for that promoter, you didn't find him. He wasn't around afterwards.

When you started entertaining, did you think of yourself mainly as a singer, as opposed to a guitar player?

When I first started, couldn't nobody tell me I couldn't sing. See, if you told me I couldn't sing then, I would have an argument with you. Later on, I found out how little I really knew, how bad it really sounded. I then found out that my guitar playing wasn't any good either [laughs]. It's funny how this happens, because at first, you believe that you really have it, like you're God's great gift. I mean I felt like that, I really did, and had someone told me I wasn't, well, I would just ignore them because I figured they didn't know what they were talking about. My singing was more popular in the early years than my guitar playing. I was crazy about Lonnie Johnson, Blind Lemon Jefferson, Charlie Christian, Django

Reinhardt, T-Bone Walker, Elmore James, and many, many others, and if I could have played like them, I would have, but I've got a thick head that just don't make it, and my fingers—they don't work either. Therefore, I think my playing was very, very, very limited, more so than my singing, because I did have a kind of style of singing at that time.

Compared to many electric guitarists, you play few notes.

I was at the Apollo Theater one time, and there was a critic there, and to me what he said was one of the great compliments that people have given me. The critic wrote: "B.B. King sings, and then Lucille sings." That made me feel very good, because I do feel that I'm still singing when I play. That's why I don't play a lot of notes maybe like some people. Maybe that's the reason why most of my music is very simple—that's the way I sing. When I'm playing a solo, I hear me singing through the guitar.

How did people like Django Reinhardt and T-Bone Walker influence you?

In the way they phrase. They still do it today. Even though they may be in different categories, even though some are jazz and some are blues, when I hear them phrase, each note to me seems to say something. And it doesn't have to be 64 notes to a bar. Just one note sometimes seems to tell me a whole lot. So that's one of the reasons why I like them. Same thing with Louis Jordan; even though he plays saxophone, the way he phrases seems to tell me something, and that can just stop me cold when I listen.

Did you play rhythm guitar first?

No, I never accompanied myself, still can't. I cannot play and sing at the same time; I just can't do it. I've always been featured from the very beginning. I still can't play rhythm worth anything, because I never had the chance to really play in a rhythm section. But I know a few chords.

Did you invent the fingerstyle, perpendicular-to-the-neck vibrato?

Let's put it this way: I won't say I invented it, but they weren't doing it before I started [laughs]. I will say that I'm still trying. Bukka White *and quite a few other people used bottlenecks. As I said, I got stupid fingers. They won't work. If I get something like that in my hand and try to use it, it just won't work. So my ears told me that when I trilled my hand, I'd get a sound similar to the sound they were getting with a bottleneck. And so for about 32 or 33 years I've been trying to do it, and now they tell me that I'm doing a little better.*

What about the idea of hitting the fret a step lower than the intended note and bending it up—were people doing that before you?

Yes, but I'd never heard anybody do it the way I do it. My reason was that my ears don't always hear like they should. I'm always afraid that I might miss a note if I try to hit it right on the head, so if I hit down and slide up to it, my ears tell me when I get there. But also it's more like a violin or a voice; you just gliss up to it.

Were there any milestones in the evolution of your technique, specific experiences or events that made you alter your approach?

I don't think so. It was like this cancer that got hold of me and started to eat on me. Like when I heard T-Bone Walker play the electric guitar, I just had to have one. I had to play, but it's been a gradual thing, and it still goes on. In fact, if you went to my room right now you'd find a Blind Lemon tape that I've been listening to whenever I'm lying around.

Do you take many cassettes on the road?

I take quite a few in order to hear the old things. I listen to the radio to hear the modern music, but I like to go back to some of the old things so that I can keep the same feeling. I like contemporary things with slick changes, but even if I play them I like to put in the feeling of yesterday. You're lost with either extreme, so I try to make a happy medium and do them together.

Your record collection is something of a legend.

Well, I've got over 30,000 records now. You won't believe this, but even though they're not alphabetized I can always tell if one's missing. One day I plan to get me one of these home computers and enter them all into that. Every time I go home I just tape, tape, tape. [B.B. has since donated his record collection to the Blues Archive at the University of Mississippi.]

Do you play visualized patterns on the fingerboard, or do you hear a note or phrase in your head before you hit it on the guitar?

I hear it first, sure do. It's like some guys use an electronic tuner and just look at the needle on the meter, but I can't buy that; I have to hear it, and it's the same with a phrase. No one else can set your hat on your head in a way that suits you. I don't think I've ever seen anybody that when you put their hat on their head they didn't take their hand and move it, even if it's just a bit. Well, I'm like that with the guitar. Do it your own way. When I play it's like trying to describe something to someone; it's a conversation where you say something in a certain way. A lot of times I play with my eyes closed, but in my mind I can still see the people paying attention to what I'm doing. I can see them as if they're saying, "Yeah, okay, I get it." Playing the guitar is like telling the truth—you never have to worry about repeating the same thing if you told the truth. You don't have to pretend or cover up. If someone asks you again, you don't have to think about it or worry about it. To me, playing is the same way. If you put yourself into it, instead of something else, then when you get out there on the stage the next time, you don't have to worry, because there it is. It's you.

Today you're doing things on guitar that sound different from what you were doing only six months ago. Your style seems to continue to grow.

Well, I hope so, because I do study. People hold it against me sometimes. They say, "You're not playing the same thing that you played the last time." But I don't want to play the same thing I played last time. That would get boring. I always try to add something, or maybe take something away, to give it a little twist.

Do you play instruments other than guitar?

I try. I was doing pretty good on clarinet before I got ripped off for one. I got to where I could read faster on clarinet than I could on guitar. I know a few scales on the violin, and I fool with that a bit. I'm a little better with piano, and better than that with bass. Drums—I did some time with them too. Also harmonica.

Does working with other instruments alter your approach to guitar?

Yes, it affects my phrasing, and it makes me a little more fluent. It's something for me to do when I'm not practicing like I should. I usually practice mentally, but when it comes to physical practice, I'm a little lazy. I don't know how it is with other musicians, but with me sometimes I don't play like I want to, and then I get a little bit disgusted and lay off for a while. Then one day, something happens, and I can't wait to get back to it.

You mentioned mental practice.

Sometimes I hear something—someone will walk by and whistle, or I'll hear it on the music in a restaurant—and I'll start to look at the fingerboard in my mind to see how I'd do it. I visualize the different ways to do it. That's a good thing to do; it helps you learn the guitar. Just don't do it too much when you're driving, or you'll forget where you're going [laughs].

Do you ever stick your neck out onstage, or do you usually reassemble a series of notes, a scale perhaps, the structure of which is already known to you?

In my room, you'd be surprised at all the things I try, but I never go out on a limb, not onstage, no, no, no. I make enough mistakes without it. The guys in the band always tease me. But if you're in the key of C and really don't want a Cmaj7—that B note—if you should hit it, you can flatten it and get the dominant 7th, which sounds all right, and if you make a mistake and hit the A, it's the 6th, so it's still relative. I learned through these many years of being out there and hoping to get everybody working with me that if you make a mistake, please work something into it, so that it's not a mistake.

There's a very unusual melody line near the end of "Chains And Things" on *Indianola Mississippi Seeds,* where . . .

I made a mistake. Now you're getting all the secrets. My bandleader and I have laughed about it many times, but I made a mistake and hit the wrong note and worked my way out of it. We liked the way it sounded, so we got the arranger to have the strings follow it. They repeat the phrase the way I played it. If you've got a good take going and then hit one wrong note, you don't want to stop, so I was in the key of Ab, and when I hit [hums E, Db, Eb, Eb], which is #5, 4, 5, 5, we just got the rest of the band to follow right along.

Do you read music?

Reading music is what I call spellin'. I spell; I read slowly. If the metronome is not goin' too fast, I can do it pretty good.

"Three O'Clock Blues" was your first major R&B hit. How did it change your life?

I could go into the important theaters. As far as the black people were concerned, when you were getting into show business there were three places you had to go through to be acclaimed: the Howard Theater in Washington, D.C., the Royal Theater in Baltimore, and the Apollo Theater in New York. "Three O'Clock Blues" enabled me to go into these places, and it opened other areas, like one-nighters. I had been making about $85 a week with my playing and being on the radio and everything else could do—$85 total—and when I recorded that first big hit, I started making $2,500 a week. I didn't get to keep all of it, but that was the guarantee.

In the early years, how widespread was racial prejudice in show business?

In the early years—you mean right now?

Well, I was talking about . . .

Well, I do. It still happens. A lot of things are not happening for us as blacks as they do for the whites. It's a fact. It's a natural fact. I've been one of the lucky few. A lot of things have happened for me, yes; a lot of things have happened for a lot of blacks. But when you compare it to what's happening for the whites, it's a big difference, a great big difference. Fortunately, though, it has gotten much better over the past few years. Blacks get better breaks. We're getting there.

Does racism exist predominantly in one field—radio, recording, club work?

You find it in all of them. I can't say which is more, one or the other. But the problem is never with the musicians themselves; it doesn't matter to them. Even when it was very segregated down south, the players always got together and had a good time. Still do. The trouble's been more with the companies, the establishment. Being a blues singer is like being black two times—twice. First you've got to try to get the people to dig the blues, and then to dig you. As a blues singer today, yes, I'm very popular. The FM radio is usually very fair with us, but you won't hear B.B. King or blues very often on AM radio. And I'm not only talking about the white stations. I'm talking about the black ones, too.

Your music is kept off of some white stations because you're black, and off of some black stations because it's blues?

Yeah, of course! I remember once I went to a black dude, a disc jockey that had a program in the South, and he said, "You know, every day we have an hour of blues." I said, "Really? Who do you play?" He said, "Well, I play you, Bobby Bland, Junior Parker, Albert King," and so on. I said, "What about Jimmy Reed, or John Lee Hooker?" "No," he said, "they don't fit my program." And that really got me uptight, you know. This guy is lord and master. He knows what everybody wants. I guess by being a Virgo, I'm a little sarcastic sometimes, so I said, "Well, how long is your station on the air?" He said 12 hours. And I said, "And you play a whole hour of blues?" He says, "Yeah." I said, "Well look [laughs], why be so nice to us blues singers and give us a whole hour? Why not play a record or two during them other 11 hours?" He didn't like what I said, but I didn't really care, because that's the way I felt and that's the way I feel today.

Have the attitudes of black people toward the blues changed over the years?

They're changing. Today they're not ashamed of it. We've always had black people who like blues, but if I had to try and put it into categories, we had the people that were down here with me, that did the work, you know. Then you had the middle and upper classes, as we called them in Mississippi. The people that worked on the plantations, the regular working class people—they understood. They were never ashamed. About 90% of them were a part of it in the beginning; they knew what I was doing. A lot of them could do it even better than I do. But then you had that middle class. A few of them would be down with us, and then the others would play our records, but like I said before, they'd only play them after 12:00, you dig? They felt that blues was kind of degrading a bit. They were made to be ashamed of it. They liked blues, but they weren't particular about everybody knowing about it. It's just like me. I like to eat sloppy, and I'd rather eat it in my room rather than let people catch me. Among the upper class, the college graduates and the ones who had money, only a precious few would acknowledge my kind of music in the early days. That is changing today, and they're listening.

Early on, were you more popular among younger listeners?

Some of the people have stood up and been counted all along, of course. This is a funny thing to say, but it's the truth: When I was young, young people as a mass didn't dig me. When I was, say, like 20 years old, it was always people my age and older. But today, we are gaining ground because black kids will come up to me and say, "Hey, I don't dig the blues, but I dig you." So I think we're making progress. At some concerts we'll have all ages and colors. That I like. Lately we're starting to have not just blacks and young whites, but older whites too. I'm surprised, but we have them.

You once complained about the notion that in order to be a blues singer you have to be in torn clothes, you can't be successful, and you've got to be high on something. Do you still encounter that attitude?

I think that that's the one thing that has been the big mistake about people in the blues. They seem to think that you have to be high or just completely smashed or stoned out of your head to be able to play blues, and that's wrong. And then I don't think that a guy has to be in patched trousers. That image that people seem to put on us is wrong. Blues music is like any other kind of music. Some of us excel, and some of us don't. Some of us are really able to please people, and some of us are not. But we all have the blues. Red, white, black, brown, yellow—rich, poor—we all have these blues. You can be successful and still have the blues. I have been fortunate, and yet now I have more to sing about than I ever did before.

You're referring to the world situation?

Yes. I look around me and I read the papers, and I see what's happening in this country and all over the world. Here, there are money troubles. Food's running low in other places. There's been price fixing, and oil problems. I go to the prisons, and I see what's happening there. Look at what's happening with the people that we pay our taxes to. Look at Asia, at Cambodia. There was bombing going on for years after the Vietnam War was supposedly over. They weren't bombing trees. They weren't bombing ditches. I think of my people, the ones I left behind in Mississippi, and all the people in all the Mississippis. We are a part of each other, you know. Those problems used to affect me individually, directly, and now they affect me indirectly. When one person is hurt, it hurts me too. When I see their condition, I know what they feel, and I feel it, and it hurts.

Comparing the earlier years when you were playing to limited blues audiences in the South and in the black theaters in the North to your present success when you are known all over the world, have the blues taken on any new meaning for you? Do you feel the same when singing and playing as you did then?

My blues mean more to me now than it did then, because in the early years, sure, I wanted other people to like what I was doing. But at times, I was singing for my own personal amusement. A lot of times I'd get it in my mind that nobody understood me, to be honest with you. A lot of times, the people were there, but they really weren't there. The bodies were there, but I didn't think they were with me. And whenever I felt like that, I would go ahead and sing to amuse myself. I'd close my eyes and visualize all of those beautiful people out there enjoying themselves. But as I kept playing and years started to pass, I started thinking a little different from that. I started to feel that it was my job to make people interested in what I was doing, to make them be able to understand what I was doing, to make them see that I wasn't just teasing, that I was really for real, you know. And this took a while to do, and it takes time today too.

In purely artistic terms, do you relate to your music any differently?

Yes, it's more of a creative art form now. Before, when I made a record I really didn't think that that's exactly what it is—a record of what you're doing and who you are on that day. And once it's out, it stays. I'm much more conscious of that.

What do you do differently?

It's not just music. It's kind of like a selling job, public relations. Sometimes audiences don't pay attention unless you present it a certain way. No matter how good it is, you seem to need to put a catchy title on it. A lot of people, especially blacks, won't like it if you call it blues, but if you go ahead and play it and call it a different name, they'll like it. That's the truth. So the blues are more important artistically, and also because I feel that I've got a message that should be heard.

What's your message?

Well, here I am. I'm trying to work. I'm trying to bring people together. I'm trying to get people to see that we are our brother's keeper. So there are many, many things that go along with it. I still work at it.

You once deliberately chose a spot to perform that was located between black and white neighborhoods of a small Mississippi town so as to draw a racially mixed audience.

Yeah, I got 'em all. We never would have had any segregation if people would've had enough music around. If musicians from all around the world could get together, country to country, that would be a good thing. Like when I toured the Soviet Union in March of '79, the other people who got together thought about politics, but the American and Russian musicians didn't think about anything but music. It was a tremendous experience.

Do you find that your goal of using music in order to bring people together is a common attitude in the entertainment business?

Yeah, I think most of us are doing it. As musicians we feel that if we can get people together just on a social level, having fun, then they can go ahead and get to know each other in other ways too. They can discuss their differences. We get them together and then something good can come from it, because that's when people start communicating.

What brought about your recognition on an international scale?

That has to do with many things, like the changing of times, like the marching, and like the people getting together and trying to stamp out prejudice and all of the many, many things. It seemed to bring people together. It started out to make people think, to see that everybody had something to offer, and that if you listen carefully you could learn something from others. People started searching for the truth . . . while I've been diggin' all this time. Black awareness—there was a time if you called me black, it was insulting [nods], oh yeah, insulting. In Mississippi we always did call white people white people but we, as a whole, really didn't want to be called black. We felt that at the time it was degrading, because it seemed that the person calling you black was really saying more than what they said. But later on we started to think about it. If the Indian is a red man, and the Chinese is a yellow man, and you're a white man, then why not be a black man? Everybody got aware and became proud of the fact that we are what we are. We began to feel that we did have something to be proud of. Like when James Brown made "I'm Black And I'm Proud," this really hit a lot of us, and I think all of this has to do with the blues. There was a time when we felt that nobody else had dirty clothes in the closet, you know—the troubles of life. We were sort of made to feel like we were the only ones that had dirty clothes in the closet, and anytime somebody said something to us or about us, we always felt that we should close the door and not let 'em know what we had in the closet.

And that finally began to change?

Yes. After the early '60s and all that, it's a funny thing, we come to find out that everybody has dirty clothes in the closet, and if the people in Nashville and Kentucky can be proud of bluegrass music—which is real music about the way they live, and about their problems, and their happiness and all—why not be proud of the blues? This kind of transition caused people to recognize the blues singers. Even the people who don't dig blues come up to me and say that they respect what I'm doing.

Many guitar players discovered you by reading comments by Eric Clapton, Mike Bloomfield, and your other musical descendants.

I talked in terms of black people. Now, as far as the white part of it is concerned, when the Beatles came out, they started people to listening again. See, when Elvis came out in '54, they'd scream—yaahhh, you know. They never did hear half of the lyrics. If you could move or shake a bit, if you could twist a bit, rock and roll, that was it. Even though the Beatles' fans used to yell their heads off, their songs said something. People listened again for lyrics. All of this seemed to come back, to be re-imported, in a manner of speaking, because I heard many Beatles tunes that had been recorded by some of the blacks over here. They were re-imported with a different sound. Then Michael Bloomfield, Elvin Bishop, Eric Clapton, and quite a few of the other guys had been listening to myself, Muddy Waters, and many others. Their followers started getting inquisitive about their playing, and they said that they had listened to me. That's when the white youth started listening to us. And then another thing: The white youth never did have to feel, say, inferior when they were listening to blues, because they never did have to go through the thing that a lot of the young blacks did—things that made them feel that blues was really degrading to them.

Do you ever get a chance to jam with some of the younger musicians whose careers you've influenced so greatly?

Jamming is something that I rarely do, but we have done it, yes. I have jammed with some of the guys that say they idolize me, but most times I'm rarely around them, or if I am it's just for a short time, like playing the same job. But who knows about the future?

Did you ever jam with Jimi Hendrix?

Yes, we all jammed together at a place called the New Generation in New York City. Any guitar player in town would usually get off work long before us, so they'd come by to see if I was really like someone had told them I was. Everybody would have their guitar out, ready to cut me, you know [laughs]. Jimi was one of the front-runners.

Do you ever listen to any of the guitarists who have become famous by playing a style that was originally derived from you? Do you ever find that you are influenced by their playing?

Actually, I'm influenced by anybody that I hear. I don't think that I've ever heard anybody play something that didn't intrigue me at one time or another. If they have been influenced by me, I still find that they have put their *feelings* into what they did, and my things which have influenced them sound different when they come out again. There's only been a few guys that if I could play just like them I would. T-Bone Walker was one, Lonnie Johnson was another. Blind Lemon, Charlie Christian, and Django Reinhardt: Those were the only guys I ever heard—well, there's Barney Kessel, and Kenny Burrell [laughs]. If I could have played just like them—not today, but when I first heard them—I would have. And there are also things that they do today that if I could do, I probably would, but not the way that they did it. Instead of playing it A, B, C, D, I'd probably play it A, C, D, B—not the exact same thing, because I think that there are very few people that play the same ideas identically as you would feel it yourself.

How long have you been using semi-solid, thin-body guitars?

Since the first one I saw, about '58. I have been using Gibson ES-355s for a long time because they're stereo and I like the highs. I can't hear lows too well—my ears don't tell me much—but highs I can hear very well. My new guitar, which Gibson is planning to release as the Lucille model, is sort of like a 355 but with a few changes.

How has it been modified?

It has a closed body with no f-holes, so you don't get the feedback. I used to have to put towels in my 355 to cut down the resonance, but with the new Lucille I can crank right up. Also, I can tune the tailpiece [a Gibson TP-6] at the back. I usually wear sleeves most of the time, and on the other tailpiece, because of where the strings were wound, I always snagged my sleeves, or I'd wind up hurting my hand a little. With this one, my sleeve doesn't get caught, and when I cup right on the bridge, it doesn't hit the end of the windings, so I don't hang up my sleeve and I don't hurt my hand. Also, the neck is a little bit thinner.

What kind of circuit does it have?

There's a Y cord that lets me bypass the stereo.

Which pickup do you use?

I usually go through the stereo circuitry, with both pickups working against each other. With just a quick shift of the hand I can set the volume or change the tone. To tell you the truth, I'm not even sure which pickup does what. I just put them both on and use my ear.

Did you ever use the vibrato tailpiece on the 355?

No. I think the reason people came out with vibrato tailpieces was because they were trying to duplicate the sound that I was getting with my left hand, and they forgot that I don't need it [laughs]. I always took the handle off. The new guitar is really something. I can't put it down, and it has really got me wanting to play again, just like when I started.

Have you had many guitars over the years?

Yes. I was in an accident once, and the insurance company gave me a Gretsch, and then I was in another accident and that one got busted up, and they gave me an Epiphone. Somebody stole that. Then I got some Gibsons, and about four of them got busted up. I've been in about 16 accidents. On the thirteenth or fourteenth one, an accident right outside of Shreveport, Louisiana, I remember seeing the bone in my right arm. They took me to the hospital and sewed it up, and the doctor told me that I nearly lost the use of the arm because of some nerve in there. But we drove to Dallas, and I played that night with my left hand. I still made the job.

Weren't you also injured in Israel?

Yes, I fell about nine feet and messed up the side of my face and shoulder, and busted a blood vessel in my left hand. My teeth went right through my lip—seven more stitches. But I went swimming that evening in the Dead Sea. I couldn't miss it, man, because we were sold out in Jerusalem. The Holy City—I had to make that!

What kind of strings and picks do you use?

I use Gibson's 740XL set, with the .009 for the first string. I use a fairly stiff pick. Sometimes it's hard to get good amplifiers, and since I almost always play only with downstrokes, I find that I don't have to hit the strings quite as hard with a stiff pick to get the volume I want.

What kind of amplifiers do you prefer?

Whatever the promoters set up for us ahead of time on the road. I used to request Gibson SG amps, and the second choice was a Fender. Lately I've been trying the Gibson Lab Series amps, and I think we'll be using them from now on.

Of your own records, which ones do you think are the best? Any favorite solos?

I've never made a perfect record, never. Although I'm not ashamed of any of them, there's always something that I could have done better. I know the critics always mention Live And Well *or* Live At The Regal, *but I think that* Indianola Mississippi Seeds *was the best album I've done artistically.*

How seriously were you criticized for using strings and pop songs and more sophisticated chord progressions on some of the recent albums?

I have had some people that weren't thinking. They'd come up and say something about it, but they didn't realize that I was using strings in the early '50s, with things like "My Heart Belongs To Only You," "How Do I Love You," "The Keys To My Kingdom," and quite a few things like that. We were using strings long before "The Thrill Is Gone," many years before. But those critics didn't say much about that. They thought that you were being Mr. Big or you were being jazzy. My answer is this: If the song needs just a guitar and me singing, we use that, and if you need something else to make it, then you should use that. Whether it be a full orchestra or just a harmonica and guitar—whatever's needed, that's what you should use, though I don't think that one should put a lot of stuff in there just to put it in there.

Were you criticized when you decided to have a large stage band with nine or ten pieces?

I have been criticized, yes, but again, a lot of the people who are criticizing didn't know that I had a big band back in the early '50s. It's a great thing to have a big sound from time to time. Years ago, Blood, Sweat & Tears and Chicago showed that if you've got a good band, a band that shouts and plays well, you can get a great thing going. Count

Basie and them—that's all they did. They'd swing you to death, man, they'd swing you crazy, and I've always liked that.

What do you look for in a musician who comes to work for you?

A man. I look for a man first, and a musician second. I must respect what he has to offer. I wouldn't say that a guy that can really blow the roof off a building is necessarily the best musician. He may be firey; he's the type of guy that can really move an audience in a hurry. But an audience don't like to stand on its nose all the time. They want to get down and be something else from time to time. Then you've got another guy that has a touch when he's playing that can really move people, like in a slow groove. Well, you don't want that all night. Each guy is good for his one particular thing. Everybody in my group is behind me to push me. I need their cooperation. But I look for someone who's 100% man. If he's only 50% musician, that's okay; we'll turn him into 75% musician after a while. But if he is not 100% man, there's nothing I can do.

Do you have much of a problem with discipline, members not showing up on time and so forth?

I've had guys in the band that screwed up from time to time, but I feel kind of like their father or uncle, and unless they do it very bad I won't do anything to them. I may fine them today and give it back tomorrow. They can tell you such fantastic lies: "Man, the train, like, came by, and one of the cars ran off the track, and they wouldn't allow nobody to come across." So I laugh, and if he doesn't screw up tomorrow I don't say anything about it. All of the guys are very good musicians and very dependable. I've been fortunate to have dependable men. But I got a thing: Three days of screwing up in a week's time, and you're out. No more fines. So these guys are cool. I tell them that if I can make it, so can they.

You've toured the world and worked 300 nights a year for over three decades. What is the source of your strength and energy?

You've asked me a hard question. I guess one thing is that when I first became popular and started going to many, many places, I always felt kind of bad about stopping school in the tenth grade. I always felt that I wanted to be able to talk to people everywhere I went, to really partic-

ipate in whatever was around. As I moved about, I found then that my education was really far off. I started learning how much I didn't know. That was one of the reasons why I really started to push myself, and I've done it through the years. Sometimes a lot of people wouldn't expect a blues singer to know certain things, and I do know them. I won't mention them, being a Virgo, but it just knocks me out for people to cut me short, thinking that I may not know. I work a lot of times just to have that little bit of pleasure. That might not sound like very much, but to me it kind of knocks me out for people to think, okay, the B. didn't go to college or he didn't do this or he didn't do that, and certain things they don't expect me to know—I know about. I pay attention, and if I hear something played or hear somebody say something, I'll put it on the tape recorder and listen to it and work with it. I wouldn't say it as he did, but I liked what he was doing and I would do it this way, my way.

How do you maintain your health and keep up the pace?

It's part of my job. It's like this story about the snake who's lying by the road all cold and muddy. This guys sees him, picks him up, and takes care of him. He gets home, around the fire, and the snake warms up and pokes his head up and says, "You know what? I ought to bite you." The guy says, "You wouldn't do that. I took care of you." And the snake says, "Yeah, but I'm a snake, and that's my job—I'm supposed to bite you!" [Laughs.] It's the same with being on the road and keeping up with the schedule. Sometimes it's a part of your job to eat, and sometimes it's a part of your job to get some sleep.

Many people call you the King of the Blues. Does that change your outlook on your work or make you feel obligated in some way?

Well, I guess I look at it both ways. First, I never think of myself as King of the Blues; I happen to be a guy named B.B. King, and he plays the blues. Of course, I think I know my job pretty well. What keeps my feet on the ground is that there are people who haven't had the popularity that I've had who are just as talented, or even more so, some of them. But I have so many young fans now, white and black, that come up to me. They trust me; they have faith. You know how it is when you do something and it's appreciated by your girlfriend or your father or mother or whoever it may be. You can see it in their eyes. I can't explain it; it's a feeling that I can't tell you about. You have to see for yourself to know. Maybe like your little brother or your daughter or your son, maybe even like your pet, your little puppy or something. When you look at them, there's something that tells you—I know it seems a little deep, and it's hard to explain—but you know that this pet or this person or whoever is really serious about what you've done.

I wish I knew the words—now I'm really at a loss. You're hurting when you can't say what you really want, but there are times when no one else can tell you that they dig you like this special person can. This feeling has happened to me as a musician through the years. It's made me think a lot of times when I go out on the stage and guys come up and want to play guitar with me. You can look in their eyes, the young musicians, and know that you have been something that's going to help them go much further than probably what they would have without you. It's like seeing your own children or your neighbor's children. You don't want to mess up, and this makes you really buckle down and try to do it a little better. I look at my own kids sometimes, and my nephews and nieces. They won't say it around me, but I can tell that they've been whispering, "That's my daddy! That's my daddy!" That within itself is enough to make me really go out and try to do better. I try and live and be a certain way so that each day I meet a person, they can't help but say, well, he's just B.B. King. And that's all.

July 1991

A decade after Tom Wheeler's B.B. cover story, Billy Gibbons flew up from a break in his ZZ Top tour schedule to join Jas Obrecht and Mr. King for *Guitar Player*'s July '91 cover story interview. The meeting ground was the Embassy Suites in Indianapolis, Indiana. On hand was a cassette of early B.B. King guitar highlights from Ace Records' *The Memphis Masters* and a copy of Stefan Grossman's *Bottleneck Blues Guitar* instructional video, cued to a scene of Bukka White playing a lap-style "Poor Boy" with a metal rod slide. Bedecked in a splendid silk three-piece, B.B. shook our hands warmly and settled into a chair.

Billy: Word's out that you're opening a nightclub on Beale Street.

B.B.: Yes, it's called B.B. King's Blues Club. I'll be playing at the opening soon.

What led you to choose that location?

B.B.: *I started from Memphis. Beale Street was very good to me in the beginning. When I came to Memphis from Mississippi, the first place I thought of, because of hearing so much about it, was Beale Street. I come to find out that Beale Street was like a college of learning. You had everything goin' on [laughs]. Beale Street was like a little town all of its own. Good musicians in the park playing various styles of music. In fact, the first time I ever heard a black guy play a Hawaiian steel guitar was there in Beale Street Park. He was playing the steel like lots of the country people. It drove me crazy!*

Billy: Let's show that little piece of film we peeked at, which shows someone you know playing lap-style slide. [*Starts video.*]

B.B.: *Bukka White! That's my cousin. [Laughs heartily.] Thank you! Old traditional blues song. I sure appreciate this. You don't know what you're doin' to me.*

Billy: He's got some real power in his forearm; the way he's shaking that thing takes some strength.

B.B.: *He was a big guy. Not just fat like I am, but big.*

Had you seen people in the Delta playing that style?

B.B.: *Yeah, that's what I grew up with. That's why I feel that I've got stupid fingers, because I could never do it. I could never do it. It's sort of like trying to play the piano—my right hand, pretty good. The left hand, it just seems like the only reason I've got it is to help the other one out.*

When you first moved to Memphis, you reportedly lived with Bukka for ten months.

B.B.: *Yeah, I suppose so. He was working over at Lauderdale and Vance at a place called Newberry Equipment Company. He got me a job working with him. We used to make tanks that they used in service stations, what they put the fuel in down underneath the pumps. Yeah,* *that's what we were doin'. These big transfer trucks that carry fuel from place to place—we made those too.*

Billy: You were playing on the evenings or weekends?

B.B.: Mostly weekends. I would go out with him sometime [nods to Bukka]. When I first came to Memphis, I kind of left in a hurry because [laughs] . . . This is a funny story. I was a tractor driver in Mississippi, and there was nine of us that drove the tractors on the whole big plantation. I was considered pretty good. See, if you were a slow learner, you was choppin' cotton—you'd pick cotton by hand. But if you a pretty fast learner or you want to advance, first you plow the mules and then you learn to drive the tractor. Once you drive the tractors, man, you in; that's doin' it. You're kind of pampered a little bit when you're a tractor driver. You big stuff. Well, I wanted to be a tractor driver, so when I was about 14, man, I was a regular hand at it.

At the beginning in that part of the Delta, the old houses was way up off the ground because the Mississippi River would flood around there. So the boss' house was way up, and when he moved to town, that left this building to be something like a tractor barn, and we'd put the noses of all nine tractors underneath it. The tractor has a big muffler, and exhaust comes up through the top of about the center of the engine.

Billy: The pipe's sticking out.

B.B.: Right. When a tractor has been running a long time, usually it's hot. So you use magnetos on it for your fire. You have a battery to start it, but the magneto runs it. Well, when you cut it off after it's been running a long time, a lot of times it will backfire. It'll do two or three times back or forward. If it's in gear . . .

Billy: Oh, no. I know what's coming.

B.B.: [Laughs.] I thought you'd get it. This particular evening, boy, I'd been flyin' all day, man, and everything was cool. I'm thinking about a lady I'm going to go see that night, ran the tractor up like we usually do, cut it off, get off there, and that sucker turned over a few times more. And when it did, under the house it went! That broke off the exhaust. Scared me so bad—I knew my boss was going to have a fit! His name was Johnson Barrett, I love him, but I knew he was going to have a fit. I didn't go to see the girl. I got me a bus, and I left and went to where Bukka was that night. Now, that was the first time I went to Memphis. I stayed away for about ten months, you're right. But then I started to thinking about it, because I missed my family and I missed everything. So I went back down there and told him what happened. He laughed then. I told him, "I'm sorry, and I came back to pay for it," which I did. I stayed there a year. I left legitimately the next year, which was the last of '47. I went back to Memphis, and that's when I started living on my own.

I'd been listening to Sonny Boy Williamson, the harmonica player on the radio. He used to be on a station in Helena, but at this time he'd moved to West Memphis, Arkansas. He had his little program on KWEM, I believe. I felt like I knew him. You know how we are with entertainers—you meet a person that you heard so much about . . .

Billy: You know him.

B.B.: *Yeah. So I went over that day, and I begged him to let me go on the radio with him. He made me audition, so I sing one of Ivory Joe Turner's tunes called "Blues At Sunrise," and he liked it. I didn't know anything about chords—still don't. But I had a good loud voice, strong, and I could keep a good beat. But if you thinking in terms of the changes and everything, I was terrible. Still is. [Laughs.] But he liked it. And that day, as fate would have it, he had two jobs. One what was payin' him a couple of hundred dollars, maybe, where he was making $15 or $20 down at the 16th Street Grill. The lady's name was Miss Annie. He had 15 minutes, and when he was off the air, he called Miss Annie and asked her did she hear me. She said yes, and he said, "Well, I'm gonna send this boy down in my place tonight, and I'll be back tomorrow." He hadn't asked me anything! She said fine, and when I went there to play for Miss Annie that night, I found that West Memphis was then like a mini Las Vegas. Wide open.*

In front of her place they sold sandwiches, burgers, and stuff like that, but in the back of it they gambled, shoot dice. My job was to try to entertain the people that was up front. Me being young, slim and crazy about the girls. And I could holler real loud then, man. So she said, "You know, the people seem to like you. If you can get on the radio like Sonny Boy is, I'll give you this job. You play six nights a week, you have a day off. $12 a day, room and board." Well, man, I didn't know there was that much money in the world! Drivin' a tractor, *when I thought I was big stuff, you made $22.50 a week. But she was gonna pay me $12 a night? And them girls?*

Billy: That's why we got into this business!

What were you playing?

B.B.: I was playing anything you mention, but nothin' right. During that time Louis Jordan was very popular, Dinah Washington, Roy Brown. I could mention a lot of people that was popular in the vein of stuff that I could do. I never did any of it right, but my way of doin' it was me, and it came off pretty good.

Were you performing by yourself?

B.B.: Yeah, I had a guitar with a DeArmond pickup.

Billy: Just the add-on kind, wasn't it?

B.B.: Yeah, you just put it on. I had me a Gibson amplifier and an old black Gibson guitar, the first one I ever had with the f-holes in it. And, man, that was the thing at that time.

Not long after that, you started to record.

B.B.: Yeah. After Miss Annie telling me that if I could get on the radio like Sonny Boy was that she would give me the job, that's when I first heard about WDIA in Memphis. That was the first all-black-operated station. So I went over there a couple of days after I had talked with her, and I saw Nat Williams on the air. I actually had started off singing as a gospel singer, so I was pretty up on radio stuff. So I asked for Nat Williams, this black disk jockey in the picture window. His question was, "What can I do for you, young fella?" I said, "Well, I'd like to record, and I'd like to go on the radio." So he said, "Maybe we can help you with one; I don't know about the other." So he called Mr. Ferguson, the general manager, and Mr. Ferguson said, "Yeah. I think we can." So that very evening they put me on the radio, doing ten minutes with just me and the guitar. Now, that's without the amplifier. And would you know, they was gonna start a competitive product to what Sonny Boy was advertising over in West Memphis.

Billy: Flour?

B.B.: *No, no. See, when he left Helena, that was the end of the* King Biscuit Time. *When he came to West Memphis, he was advertising for a tonic called Hadacol. Well, Mr. Ferguson was starting a new tonic called Pepticon. And that's what I was introducing.*

What exactly was it?

Billy: A little of everything.

B.B.: *Yeah. I never did really find out what Pepticon actually was until about eight years ago; somebody sent me a bottle of it. But I know we used to sell it like there wasn't gonna be no more. Come to find out it was 12 percent alcohol!* [Laughs.]

Billy: Somebody was feeling good!

B.B.: *Some of those church people were having a good time with it. I used to go out on the truck with the salesmen on the weekends, and man, they'd give me like $100, $150 sometimes, according to how much they sell. I'd be on the top of the truck singing* [sings the "Pepticon" theme]. *That's how it started, really.*

Billy: Going back to West Memphis, I had heard stories about the wildness. I mean, West Memphis was it, man.

B.B.: *Yeah, it was really good. I loved it. I really did.*

Billy: There are still guys today that talk about it. In fact, you can drive down that old main street, and it hasn't changed too much. You can pick up the feeling. There's still something about it.

B.B.: *Memphis was a bit conservative. They didn't believe in having racetracks and all that, so they put it right over in West Memphis, and all the money and everything would go over there on weekends. So they* had gambling and all that, as long as they had a particular sheriff that they kept in there for a long time.

Billy: Was there other live music?

B.B.: *Yeah. See, it wasn't just this particular little place. Anybody that was all right with the sheriff and the city government was okay, okay? That make sense? And there was a big white place out there where they really had good music all the time because they could afford to have the best—black, white, or any type of entertainment you could bring. What you have to remember, though, was that during this time it was still segregation, but when we went to that club, there was no segregation. You couldn't get out on the floor and dance, but you could have all the fun you could playing the music. Everybody get together and you talk, spin yarns as we usually did. The people out there was doing their thing, and we did ours in the back. But a few of the better clubs were black clubs where whites would come to them.*

Billy: That's so peculiar. Try as you might to keep a lid on a good time, you can't do it. When people want to have a good time . . .

B.B.: *They will have a good time.*

Billy: It's gonna be there.

B.B.: *And I'll tell you, had it not been for that, my life would have been very slow—very, very slow. I loved it.*

Billy: In fact, there is still a faction of people who, if they had their choices, would relive those times in West Memphis, particularly the '40s up to the '50s.

B.B.: *Oh, yeah.*

Was Beale Street similarly wild?

B.B.: *Not really. The guys would have what we called little turn-row crap games or something like that, but if a cop caught you, you were in big trouble! But it was always something going on. You had the One Minute*

Cafe where you could go in and eat for 15¢, man. I mean, really eat: bowl of chili, nickel's worth of crackers [laughs], and what we call a belly-wash—something like an Orange Crush drink. Man, you could live, I mean, really live. Sunbeam Mitchell's was one of the established places for music, so you'd have the best traveling musicians coming through. Let's assume that we were going through town: We'd go to Mitchell's, because we'd have a chance to see the best and find out what's goin' on in the city. That's where you get your information. Kind of like when I used to come to Houston, I'd go to the Fifth Ward and go to Club Matinee.

Well, Memphis was like that. You had several pawnshops. You used to keep a couple of good rings, a good tie pin, and a pair of good shoes, so if you got broke, you go down and pawn them. They know you coming back, because ain't nobody else gonna wear your shoes! Clothing and food and good music of all kinds. You had gospel, find a little spot over here where a guy's preachin', find another over here where some guy's sittin' on the stool playing his guitar, over further some guy's gambling. You may have a few pickpockets. You had some of everything going on in the area of three blocks.

Billy: Correct me if I'm wrong, but I've been told that in comparison to West Memphis, which was a different scene, Beale Street was wide open too, but in a stricter sense. There was a police department keeping everybody in line.

B.B.: Yeah.

Billy: You didn't want to act up. Beale Street was controlled.

Did old-time country blues mix with electric blues on Beale Street?

B.B.: Well, see, I didn't know the difference at that time. You had a chance to see people that you'd never seen before; you'd just hear about them. But on Beale Street, he was just another person. It's kind of like if we walked in a room now with Springsteen or the Beatles or U2 or the Rollin' Stones—we all people. You don't see them as if you're out there and don't get a chance to rub elbows with them. On Beale Street, guys like me was lookin' up, but the other guys were just, "Hey, there's old so-and-so. How you doin', man?" But it was a big thing for guys like myself that just came from Mississippi. I had a chance to see Muddy Waters, all the guys that was big then—Sonny Boy Williamson. And then you got a chance to see guys with big bands, like Duke Ellington coming through. Count Basie. And all these people would patronize or fool around on Beale Street.

During that time it was segregated, with the exception of certain places. Now, in the radio station where I worked at, there was no segregation. None. When you came in there, your title was whomever you were. If you was an elderly person, it was Mr. so-and-so or Mrs. so-and-so, but other than that, you were who you are and you was treated with respect. But when you walked out, it was like leaving the Embassy [laughs]. It was a different story.

Beale Street was similar, because everybody—white and black—that lived and worked there was accustomed and used to the people being there. Duke Ellington and Count Basie or Louis Armstrong was known not only to the blacks, but to the whites as well. They had the Hippodrome and a few other places where the slick black promoters would bring in one of the big artists, and they would play two shows— one for whites and one for blacks, and they made money. Those were the days, though, man. If you were a little entertainer, you could always stand in the background. Like when the big guys be on the stage, you'd be in the wings lookin'. So it was some beautiful moments, some moments that I'll cherish and forever love.

You think that you got drug problems today, but it was there too. Most of the people would say, "If you want to make it, don't do that there. See what that dude doin' on the corner? Leave it alone," like that. It was sort of controlled, but people did do it.

Some of the jug band musicians fell into that.

B.B.: *There was several great jug bands there. You know, in each society of music or whatever, you always got what I call the hierarchy, the people at the top that's the best at what they do, whether it be a boxer or a singer. So whenever one of these guys came around, like the great jug bands, everybody move over there where they can check that one out. I remember, for instance, Lightnin' Hopkins. When I first met Lightnin', it was in Memphis, met him there on Beale Street.*

Was there something called headcutting?

B.B.: *Well, you could call it that [laughs]. People do that now. When a great musician would come to town, like a jazz musician, well, all of the guys would be laying around him trying to cut his head. Well, we had* *some giant musicians there. The Newborn family was terrific. The old man, which was Phineas [pronounced fine-us] Newborn, played drums, and his son Phineas [pronounced fin-ee-us], they called him, played the keyboard. And he was bad—when I say bad, I mean terrific. And then he had a brother named Calvin, who's still around and plays back in Memphis. Terrible, man, I mean, he plays some guitar! And then you got Fred Ford, Bill Harvin, Herman Green—a lot of people that would be waitin' on you when you come to town. You supposed to be a musician, they want to get you on that stage up at Sunbeam's, and then they started calling Gershwin tunes and stuff like that.*

Billy: Oh, lord, look out! The tough stuff.

B.B.: *So if you wasn't trained or didn't know tunes pretty well, you'd see a guy start taking his horn down—something was wrong with his horn—and the other guy breaks a string on his guitar, and they move. A guy came to town named Charles Brown. I'm still crazy about Charles even today. The guy who made "Merry Christmas, Baby" is the one I'm talking about. Well, they knew Charles was a blues singer and a blues player, but they didn't know that Charles had been to college and majored in music. Nobody knew that.*

Billy: Whoa!

B.B.: *So Charles came to town. He had Wayne Bennett playing guitar, and a few other people. That night after the show they kept begging Charles to come up to Sunbeam's. They get him to get on the stage, and then they started calling "Lady Be Good" and any of the good jammin' Gershwin tunes, because those were the real jazz standards. That night when Charles Brown finally figured out what they was trying to do to him, he called "Body And Soul," which has got a lot of changes. When he called the tune, all the guys figured they really gonna cut him now. But then he started to modulate chromatically.*

Billy: Giving it to 'em!

B.B.: *So a guy done learned it in one key, and now Charles is taking them through it all chromatically. Then I started seeing guys who had something wrong with his horn and such. Finally it wound up with Charles Brown, the bass, and the drums [laughs]. That's the best example I ever seen, and it was really fun to see that happen.*

You recorded with some of the Newborns early on.

B.B.: *My very first record, the whole family was on it. I made my first record for Bullet Recording Company out of Nashville. I had old man Phineas on the drums, his son Phineas Newborn, Jr., was on keyboard, Calvin was on guitar, and a lady was playin' trombone—I can't think of her name right now. It had Ben Branch on tenor sax, Thomas Branch on the trumpet, and Tuff Green, bass. It was four sides, and we did them at the radio station in the largest studio, Studio A. "Take A Swing With Me," "How Do You Feel When Your Baby Packed Up To Go," "Miss Martha King," and "I Got The Blues"—the first four sides I ever recorded.*

Let's play another one of your early sides, "Mistreated Woman."

B.B.: *[Laughs.] That's on Modern Records—or RPM, really. That's me. [At this point the solo starts.] Yeah, that's the old guy.*

Billy: Gibson guitar?

B.B.: *Yeah. Crazy about T-Bone Walker. Crazy about Lowell Fulson.*

Charlie Christian?

B.B.: *Oh, yes. God, yeah. Well, Charlie Christian, Django Reinhardt— those are my jazz players. I don't know, this is going to sound a little weird to you, maybe, but I've always been conscious of being put down as a blues player. So I've had one thing that I always tried to keep in mind: It's always better to know and not need than to need and not know. I always like to know more than people think I know, so I practice hard trying to be able to do things that nobody would expect me to do. That's how I learned to fly airplanes; nobody ever thought that I could be a pilot, so I learned to be a pilot. I learned to do many other things simply because coming from Mississippi usually was the first downer, you know: "Yeah, man, this dude from Mississippi, still got clay mud on his shoes," stuff like that. It's still that way. So I started to say, "Yeah, I'm from Mississippi, and I'm proud of it." And today I'm very proud to be a Mississippian—very, very proud. Because I've been put down for trying to be something else. It wasn't a matter of just being something else—I just wanted to do what I did better than it had* *been done before. I felt that if I could do it there, I could do it at the White House, do it in New York, do it anyplace, and it could be thought of as being artistically well done.*

Billy: Through your graciousness over the years, you've become a cornerstone for so many people by knowing more than what people thought you knew.

B.B.: *Well, it was satisfactory to me, in a way of speaking. All right, I don't speak English well, but if I go to Spain, I'll try to learn a couple of words. Any different country, I'll try to learn a couple of words. So when I hear people talking in Japan and they say a few things, I'll pick it up. It's the same thing musically. If I hear you play [indicates Billy], I may not be able to play what I hear you play, but I'll know a little something about it because I'm* listening. *Got my ears on it. Same thing with him [indicates Jas] or whoever. Well, that is a peace of mind for B.B. King—maybe not to anybody else, but to me. And this is not something you do once in a while. Each day I've got my ears kind of cocked, learnin'. If I could do what you do or what somebody else do, I'd find myself saying, "You sound so good like that, but I wouldn't sound that good, so I better try it* this *way." But it's still your idea.*

Billy: Let me indulge in a little complimentary flattery by pointing to the single-string soloing on that track we just played. So many have cited the B.B. touch; so many people have made references to the B.B. King influence. I would say that it's your sound and approach to soloing that has made the guitar such a lead instrument. It's really inspired a lot of people to learn how to improvise and solo. Wouldn't you say that was just developing for the guitar around the time you recorded that track in '50?

B.B.: *It's a funny thing. During that time, guitars hadn't really come into being, if you will. Excuse the word, but it was a bitch to try to get a good guitar at that time—just to try and* get *one. And when you did get one, you better hold onto it—don't loan it to nobody. If you did, they didn't come back, most of 'em. So yes. Nobody had any idea that the guitar would become what it is today. Where I grew up at, there was no other instrument that was available to you, really, but maybe a harmonica. And everybody don't want to blow everybody's harmonica. In my area, they couldn't afford keyboards of any kind. You couldn't* *afford no pianos or organ. I guess I've only seen an organ in maybe three or four homes in an area of 150 homes, and those was what we called—an old word down there—uppity [laughs]. They had the uppity blacks as well as the whites, see. So very few people had those. Only time I ever seen a piano or organ was when I went to church. So when I would go over to somebody's house, there usually was an old guitar laying on the bed. And the only strings I ever knew about at that time, we bought them at a drugstore, and they was called Black Diamonds.*

Red packs.

Billy: Or the glass jar, if you really want to go back.

B.B.: *Yeah. And your E string, man, was about as big as my G string is today. I use a .010 for my E, a .013 for my B, and a .017 for my G string. And those E strings then had to be close to .014.*

Billy: At least. Somebody gave me a set of Black Diamonds, right out of the box—wires!

B.B.: *Now, when you break one of those strings, then you would take baling wire—the wire that you bale hay with—or the wire they used to wrap broomsticks, and we would use that for strings. You take that and tie it onto the string. Once you tie it on, you put that wire on your tuner, so from here to here [indicates from about the fifth fret to the bridge] you got string.*

Billy: You couldn't play down below that? Oh, man!

B.B.: *You could never play down low. But a lot of people didn't do it anyway—in fact, my friend Gatemouth still don't! So you take a clamp [capo]—when you could afford one—and put it on between the end of where the string is broke so you got good clear string. And if you couldn't do that—in most cases, we didn't—you get a pencil or a piece of stick that's straight across, and you put it on there, take some string, tie it down, and that's your clamp.*

A homemade capo.

B.B.: *Yeah. It's like the nut of your guitar.*

Billy: Hope that you sing real high for the rest of the week!

B.B.: *[Laughs.] Well, we learned to do things. We let [tuned] it down!*

As a child, did you ever make a one-string?

B.B.: *Yeah. We take the same cord from around that broom, and you put a big nail up there* [points about five feet up the wall]. *Take another one and put it down there* [about three-and-a-half feet lower], *and you put the string on the nails. Then you take something like a brick—we always found that a brick was really good for sustaining tones—put it in down there between the string and the wall, tighten it, put another brick up there on top, tighten it, and then you bang on it.*

Would you play with a slide?

B.B.: *I can't play slide on my guitar today!* [Laughs.] *Still can't. Another thing we used to do is take an inner tube—you don't find 'em often now, but most of the cars at that time had inner tubes inside of the tire. So when one of those would blow out, you'd take the rubber and stretch it. You'd make a board and put small bricks or pieces of wood on it, just like you do your guitar, and you could play that. You could also take a stick and wet it, put it across, and it sounds similar to a violin. You leave it to kids, boy—we'd find a way to make music!*

Was there a moment when it became clear that you were destined to play the blues?

B.B.: *Yeah. It was after I had been in the Army when I was 18. Working on the plantation where we lived, we was growing produce for the Armed Forces. You was compelled, you was drafted, as you became 18 during World War II. There wasn't no ifs and ands—you went and signed up for the Armed Forces. Well, in our area they claimed we was doing things for the Armed Forces, and they needed us there. So we went and took partial basic training, and then they reclassified you and sent you back home. You couldn't leave; you had to stay there. If you left, then you was reclassified again and went back in. But even if I die tomorrow, I couldn't get a flag, because we didn't complete the basic training. I came back home—I was driving a tractor at this time—and I* started to go on the street corners to sit and play on a Saturday evening after I got off work.

I would always try to sit on the corner of main streets, where we get blacks and whites coming right past us. I would sit and play; I didn't ask nobody for anything—I would hope! Now, I was singing gospel with a quartet; we were pretty good. We were like an opening act for groups like the Soul Stirrers, Spirit Of Memphis, and like that. But for some reason, the guys never seemed to want what I wanted. I wanted to move up a little bit with it, and everybody was very conscious of their families, which I can understand. But I guess I wasn't as family-oriented as they were. I kept thinking that we could go off and do like the Golden Gate Quartet and many of the other groups. Every autumn, after our crops was gathered, I would say, "Hey, now is the time to go," and we'd make plans to leave and go to Memphis or someplace where we could record. But every time that would happen, they'd say, "No. We didn't do too well. The crops don't . . . so we won't do it."

Anyway, while sitting on the street corners playing, people'd ask me to play a gospel song. And when I'd play it, they'd always pat me on the shoulder or something and compliment me very highly: "Son, you're good. If you keep it up, you're gonna be all right one day." But they never tip. But dudes who would ask me to play a blues song would always tip, man, give me a beer. Man, they'd yell at everybody else: "Don't you see this boy playin'? Give him something!" Instead of making my $22.50 a week on the plantation, I'd sometimes make, gosh, maybe $100—at least $50 or $60.

Billy: You're speaking of the war years now?

B.B.: *Yeah. So these people would always give me nice tips, man. That's when the motivation started. That's when I started deciding I would play the blues.*

What were the first blues 78s that knocked you out?

B.B.: *My aunt used to buy records like the kids do today, and some of her collection was Blind Lemon, Lonnie Johnson. She had Robert Johnson, Bumble Bee Slim, and Charley Patton. I could just go on and name so many she had. But my favorites turned out to be Blind Lemon Jefferson and Lonnie Johnson. I liked Robert and all the rest of them, but those were my favorites.*

What's the appeal of Blind Lemon?

B.B.: I wished I could tell you, because if I could, I'd do it! [Laughs.]
*He had something in his phrasing that's so funny. He had a way of
double-time playing. Say, like, one-two-three-four, and then he'd go*
[in double-time] *one-two-three-four, one-two-three-four. And the time
was still right there, but double-time. And he could come out of it so
easy. And then when he would resolve something, it was done so well.
I've got some of his records now—I keep them on cassette with me.
But he'd come out of it so smooth. His touch is different from anybody on the guitar—still is. I've practiced, I tried, I did everything,
and still I could never come out with the sound as he did. He was
majestic, and he played just a regular little 6-string guitar with a little
round hole. It was unbelievable to hear him play. And the way he
played with his rhythm patterns, he was way before his time, in my
opinion.*

Which of his songs would you recommend for guitarists?

B.B.: [Sings in a gentle voice]

"See that my grave be kept clean,
See that my grave be kept clean,
See that my grave be kept clean,
See da-da-da-da-da-da"

*That's one of them. Lightnin' Hopkins did it, and many people have
done it since. But that's where it came from.* [Resumes singing]

"It's a long road ain't got no end,
Long road ain't got no end,
Long road ain't . . ."

Oh, one other part:

"Three white horses in a line,
Three white horses in a line,
Three white horses in a line,
Gonna take me to my burying ground"

Something like that.

Billy: Since this interview is centered around Memphis and the early years, I'd like to cite a personal favorite vision that has recently come out. The two B.B. King albums that come over from England that have the picture of you . . .

B.B.: *Wearing shorts, huh?* [Laughs heartily.] *Well, you know, I used to think that I was kind of hot stuff. My cousin Bukka White told me something that has stayed with me over all these years. I mentioned how we used to be put down as blues singers. I've quite often said if you was a black person singing the blues, you black twice. And if you a white person, you black once. Because people usually will put you down. Like, if you from the country, people was, "Aw, look at the little country dude." And if you from the city, country people won't talk so much about it, but they say, "Well, he from the city, he think he's something." Well, my cousin Bukka White used to say, "You see how I dress?* [Tugs lapels of his suit.] *When you dress like this, it's like you're going to try to borrow some money. The banker don't know who are, and the people that you're talkin' to don't know what you are. So you always dress like that, and people don't know, because you look clean and neat, and they may loan you the money. But if you come up and you're not dressed nice, you look like you're a beggar. But dressed up, the white people see you, and you look like a preacher or something like that, so you get by a little easier." I started to do it, and I started to notice that made a difference—always. After that I started a trend for my own band, and we sort of set a pace like that. I got used to doing it, and I like it. Anyway, there was something else I started to tell you a little while ago . . .*

Billy: About the Bermuda shorts.

B.B.: *Yeah! Thank you. Well, I thought at that time that this was kind of slick, you know.*

Billy: It was slick. To this day.

B.B.: *Yeah, but if I had realized what my legs looked like then, I probably wouldn't have done it. I had seen guys from Australia wearing short pants, and I thought it was cool.*

Billy: In fact, in that photo you're playing a Gibson—it could have been a Switchmaster or the ES-5. Big-bodied.

B.B.: *Yeah, I think I had what they called the 400.*

Billy: Did the big bodies give you much trouble with feedback?

B.B.: *I didn't think of it so much at that time. T-Bone Walker had one that had three pickups, and I was crazy about it. Crazy about him. Well, as I said, during that time it was hard to get and keep a good guitar, so the early '50s is when the Fenders first came out. So I had one of the early Fenders. I had the Gretsch, I even had a Silvertone from Sears, Roebuck. So I had any kind of guitar you can probably think of. But when I found that little Gibson with the long neck, that did it. That's like finding you wife forever. This is she! I've stayed with it from then on. Now, a lot of times you may buy a guitar just to keep at home, but to play—for me, that was it. They had the ES-335, and then they had a new idea for the 355, and I've been crazy again. So that's the one I've held onto. But I've tried guitars through the years—you name them, I've probably had one.*

Billy: You've been credited with starting so many fads, trends, crazes, and things that have gone way beyond that now because they're carved in stone as just the way to do it. And people keep digging up relics of the past: Just recently a friend of mine sent me a postcard that's a reprint of a publicity shot of the B.B. King Orchestra. The band members are lined up, and you're leading the pack, standing in front of the bus. Everybody is just natty, neat as a pin. It's the definitive vision of the way an outfit should look. And it's coming back around to this.

B.B.: *Yeah, I remember that. We took that picture in front of my first old bus. That was a pretty big band then, about 12 or 13 pieces. I thought myself big stuff because we could play the blues like I thought we should, and then we could venture into other little things from time to time. This was '55.*

Billy: Well, you had the strength to be that leader.

B.B.: *I've enjoyed doing what I've done. I've had so much happiness from so many people.*

Billy: It shows.

B.B.: If you'd ask me 40 years ago—this is 41 years I'm into it now—would I even be living today, I would have bet you odds no. But so many good things have happened. I'm happier today, this very day, than I've ever been in my life. I've had so many wonderful things happen. And I'll tell you what, you've made me happy just sitting here talking with you. This is a real treat. I never dreamed this would ever happen. I really thank you. I've been asked before if there was anything I would do differently if I had this life to start again. And there are only two things I can think of that I would change: I would finish high school and go to college and try to learn more about the music, and I wouldn't marry until after 40!

ANALYSIS OF B.B. KING'S GUITAR STYLE (1987)
JERRY RICHARDSON

All the discussion about guitar technique culminates in Jerry Richardson's awesome research—based on literally years of listening to King's records, attending his concerts, and emulating his style. Based on his unpublished doctoral dissertation, this detailed exposition is a textbook course on how to play like King and, if possible, surpass him. What is unfortunately missing from this reprint of a chapter of his doctoral dissertation thesis (Memphis State, 1987) is elaborately annotated musical examples.

B.B. King's Guitar Technique

The development of B.B. King's guitar techniques has been gradual yet continuous and deliberate. In fact, the artist has always been motivated toward self-improvement, which accounts for his great penchant for listening to a variety of musical styles. Also, his early reluctance to use his instrument as an accompanying medium has only served to increase his capacity for inventiveness and creativity in effecting single string solos. This reluctance is borne out in his statement: "I've never been able to actually accompany myself with chords like a guitarist would do."[1]

It can be shown that King's guitar technique has advanced in the following areas: dexterity and facility and the gradual acquisition and devel-

---

1. B.B. King, interview with author, 7 June 1986. [Reprinted on pp. 107–127.]

opment of certain idiomatic or stylistic devices such as note sliding, position shifts, note embellishments, tremolo, pull-offs, octaves, and string bending.

B.B. King had not developed an impressive guitar technique by the time he did his first recording sessions for the Bullet label in 1949. In these earliest recordings (four altogether) King can be seen as a crude unrefined soloist relying on a limited guitar technique. This is manifested by his adherence and confinement to a single guitar position and by playing only descending blues scales. These early recording sessions displayed loose arrangements without much continuity or direction. Also at this time King gravitated toward the key of C major, as all four sides bear out this fact.

B.B. King did two separate sessions for Bullet in 1949: one in July and one in November. In the July session he recorded "Miss Martha King" (Bullet 309) and "When Your Baby Packs Up and Goes" (Bullet 309), both up-tempo boogie woogie jump tunes. His only solo work on both songs was confined to the introduction, which in the former was manifested by two short descending blues scales and a brief statement of a "T-Bone" Walker–derived motif. In fact, this motif was to become one of King's signature "licks" during his early style development and is still identifiable in a few cases in more recent examples.

He begins the introduction to "When Your Baby Packs Up and Goes" with the same descending scale, only differing from the former in his contracting the eighth note triplet ♩♩♩ to the triplet figure ♩ ♪ . In both the previously mentioned songs we find short solo choruses by both the tenor saxophonist and the trombonist. One outstanding characteristic of a novice guitar improviser is his confinement to a single key and a single position. This is the case in both Bullet sessions.

On the November, 1949, session King recorded two sides, a fast boogie woogie entitled "Take a Swing with Me" (Bullet 315) and a slower 12-bar blues called "I Got the Blues" (Bullet 315). In both renditions very little guitar is heard. In fact, one has to listen very carefully to detect a few disjointed guitar responses to several vocal lines. Thus we can conclude that in these earliest King sessions the artist possessed minimal dexterity for soloing, limiting himself to several memorized blues scale patterns in one position (the 8th fret) and a "lick" or motif borrowed from his idol, "T-Bone" Walker.

Upon entering the modest studio of Sam Phillips in the early part of 1950, it appears that B.B. King had made some strides as a soloist. Prior to his sessions for Phillips in the early 1950s King apparently devoted much of his time to practice and to the scrutiny of his guitar idols. Many of his early recordings for Phillips reflect a strong influence from "T-Bone" Walker, in fact, almost an imitation. A prime example of this influence can be detected by comparing Walker's solo in "I Got a Break Baby" (Capitol 10033, 1942) with B.B. King's "Questionnaire Blues" (KST-9011) recorded in January, 1951.

It is also interesting to note that in a few of his early sessions for Phillips King merely functions as a blues vocalist as is evidenced by the overlapping guitar lines. The side musicians in these sessions consisted of several young Memphis jazz musicians, including Phineas Newborn on piano, Hank Crawford on tenor saxophone, and apparently Calvin Newborn on lead guitar. Upon first hearing "B.B.'s Boogie" (RPM 304), one might mistakenly attribute the guitar solo to B.B. King, as there is no clear documentation on the sidemen used on this session. However, given the fact that King's solo development hadn't reached the inventiveness and jazz-like quality elicited in this rendition, the guitarist would have to be Phineas' brother Calvin, who did play on several of King's early sessions.

One of the first stylistic elements contributing to B.B. King's developing technique was his repetition of the same pitch consecutively played on an adjacent string. "T-Bone" Walker as well as many rockabilly guitarists utilized this same technique. This was probably done as a means of tonal contrast. This specific technique is effected by playing a given note on a higher string, then immediately sliding on the next lower adjacent string up to the same pitch. It is also an effective method of going from a lower to a higher position. This technique is evident in many of King's recordings of the early 1950s. A case in point can be found in the ninth bar of his improvised guitar solo in "She Don't Move Me No More" (US-7788, 1950). Another example can be detected in his first national hit, "Three O'Clock Blues" (RPM 339), which was released in 1951.

It is significant to point out that both repetitions occur on the dominant harmony and in the same measure of this 12-bar blues song. This repetitive note sliding technique can be found in "T-Bone" Walker's solos as well as in Chuck Berry's guitar solos of the mid to late 1950s. A most representative example can be heard in the latter's introduction to "Johnny B. Goode" (Chess 1691, 1958). King has continued to use this technique throughout his career, although not in the same manner as has been already demonstrated. In the mid-1950s and later he contracted the technique into one single repetition. We can find an example of this in King's guitar solo in "Boogie Rock" (RPM 435), a 1955 instrumental. This technique occurs in both the second and seventh measures.

As can be seen in the preceding examples, King bends up to the first note on a lower string, then plays the same note on the adjacent higher string. This same technique is continued in "Gambler's Blues" (BL-6001 and reissued later on MCA 27010 and ABC 509, 1966) in measure eight of King's guitar introduction. Other examples can be found in "Don't Answer the Door" (MCA-27010, 1966) and in "Sweet Little Angel" (ABC-509, 1965).

This technique not only gave King a tonal contrast but also helped him extend his range on the instrument. There is a tendency for the beginning improviser on the guitar to solo in one position, usually because of a lack of expertise and the confidence to venture away from a comfortable point of reference.

In the mid to late 1950s, B.B. King confined his soloing range to one or two close positions, only moving on occasion into distant positions with some uncertainty and uneasiness. In listening to King's second twelve-bar solo chorus in "Days of Old" (1958, Kent 307), one can detect a certain amount of apprehension and awkwardness in his attempt to go from the fourth position to the sixteenth fret to play an A-flat. To do this, he slides on the first string to the sixteenth fret. He barely executes the note intended in a muddled fashion; then he quickly returns to the fourth position where he regains his security. By the mid to late 1960s King became more proficient in moving into and out of various positions on his guitar, a technique acquired through much experience and practice. This is evident in his live recording, "My Mood" (1969, Bluesway 6031), an instrumental using the same chord progression as Claude Gray's "Night Life" (Decca, 1968). In his second solo chorus he is able to go from the seventh to the fourteenth position within four measures, a procedure which takes considerable dexterity.

A technique which gradually appears in King's guitar solos in the mid-fifties is his use of embellishments. This technique stems from his initial listening to Lonnie Johnson and later to such jazz guitarists as Charlie Christian, Django Reinhardt, and Bill Jennings, who played guitar in Louis Jordan's Tympany Five. An early example of embellishment can be seen in measure 5 of a recording previously mentioned, "Boogie Rock" (RPM-435). This can be compared to Lonnie Johnson's "Stompin' 'Em Along Slow" (OKEH 8558, 1928) in measure 6 of the third chorus and again in measures 8 and 9.

One of B.B. King's favorite jump bands of the 1940's was Louis Jordan's Tympany Five whose song "Salt Pork, West Virginia" (Decca

18762, 1946) left a strong impression on him.[2] In Bill Jennings' guitar solo one can hear a similar usage of embellishment at the end of measure 10 of this 12-bar blues.

This example is a reversal of the embellishment found in King's "Boogie Rock." However, it can also be compared with King's "Days of Old" (1958, Kent 307). King's entire solo here is based on a similar embellishment figure.

During the time B.B. King was living in Indianola, Mississippi, in the mid-1940s, a close friend, Willie Dotson, brought him several of Django Reinhardt's records he had picked up in Paris on leave from the Army during World War II.[3] King was immediately intrigued with the gypsy guitarist's innovative technique and mode of phrasing. It is obvious that B.B. King may have absorbed some of these techniques, especially in his note bending and use of embellishments.

B.B. King was also quite impressed with Charlie Christian's style. He had first heard Christian on a moviola located at Jones' Night Spot in Indianola.[4] It is difficult to trace semblances of Christian's style in King's solos, especially in regard to embellishments. However, in the tune "Wholly Cats" (Columbia, CL642) the jazz guitarist employs an embellishing figure in the sixth bar of his second solo break which resembles several of King's.

It must be pointed out that considerable practice over a period of time is required to effect a good grasp of embellishment technique on any instrument. Embellishments such as mordents present extenuating problems of executing on the guitar because of having to use a pull-off technique to sound the upper neighboring tone before returning to the original note.

King's use of embellishing notes diminishes somewhat after the 1950s, at which time a noticeable development of other techniques is apparent, especially the refinement of his left-hand finger tremolo. King fancies the bottleneck style of Delta blues guitarists, notably that of his cousin Bukka White. However, he wasn't sure how to transfer White's idiomatic vibrato sound to his own instrument. In fact, he can be seen to have taken approximately a decade to develop fully the technique. It appears to enter King's guitar improvisations between 1958 and 1960. In a previously mentioned song, "Days of Old," a slight amount of tremolo is utilized on notes held longer than a quarter in duration, but

---

2. B.B. King, as told to Jim Crockett, "My Ten Favorites," p. 45.

3. Sawyer, *The Arrival of B.B. King*, p.157.

4. Sawyer, p. 53.

the frequency of oscillation is much slower compared to his solos of the mid-1960s where his tremolo speed is increased considerably. In his guitar solo choruses found in "Please Love Me" (Kent-336, 1960) and "Crying Won't Help You" (Kent-336, 1960) we see this tremolo development manifested both in the speed and in the frequency of usage. His employment of the technique is fully developed in his solos found in "Sweet Little Angel" (1964) and "Gambler's Blues" (1966), both on the album *B.B. King: Back in the Alley* (MCA-27010).

It is significant that both of these songs are slower in tempo than the previously mentioned "Please Love Me." In King's playing there is a more frequent usage of the tremolo technique in slower 12-bar blues tunes. In a faster King shuffle tune like "Paying the Cost to Be the Boss" (MCA 27010, 1967) we find King's tremolo employed on most quarter notes and those of longer duration.

B.B. King employs his fully developed tremolo technique with the utmost speed and agility. He accomplishes this speed by lifting his left hand thumb completely off the back of the neck while "fanning" his index finger as fast as possible. Most jazz guitarists play their vibrato with the thumb supported behind the neck using slower motion. The "fanning" technique of B.B. King is both revolutionary and unique. One can see the continuation of King's tremolo technique into the 1980s.

Still another technique which B.B. King employs, though in moderation, is the pull-off, a technique usually reserved for jazz guitarists and some folk blues guitarists. There are two types of pull-offs, the single string pull-off and the chord pull-off. The former can be diatonic or chromatic. It is played by initially putting down from two to four left-hand fingers on a single string on consecutive frets. The highest note is sounded with the pick and the remaining notes are sounded consecutively by pulling (plucking) off the remaining fingers. The second type is played by placing 3 or 4 fingers on a given chord position and beginning with the lowest notes (lowest string) playing each string consecutively, picking in one direction, and lifting each finger off the chord position after playing each note. This gives the aural illusion of a virtuosic picking technique to the uninitiated listener.

Both types are very difficult to master. B.B. King plays the second type only from a lower string to a higher, whereas some jazz guitarists like Barney Kessel or George Benson (both of whom King acknowledges and respects) will play from a higher to a lower string. This technique necessitates putting the chord fingers down and then immediately releasing them after they have been played. This device requires extreme dexterity and diligent practice.

B.B. King incorporated the single string pull-off into his solos early in his career. In the song "Bad Luck" (RPM 468), recorded in 1956, he employs a repeated pull-off riff starting on the flatted seventh of the tonic. In another song entitled "Time to Say Goodbye" (Kent 327, 1958) he employs a pull-off on the third beat of the seventh bar of his 8-bar solo. In his introductory solo to the song "Sweet Sixteen" (Kent 330, 1960), he employs several repeated pull-offs in a single measure on bar two. King also uses pull-offs effectively in the same song in his guitar responses to his vocal lines.

B.B. King employs the chord type pull-off on more limited occasions, as it is more difficult to play and perhaps too jazzy sounding to employ very often in a blues framework. A representative example of this type can best be distinguished in "Gambler's Blues" (Bluesway 6001, 1966). This pull-off riff sounds very virtuosic and impressive, occurring on the upbeat of four.

In a later album entitled *Live and Well* (Bluesway 6031, 1969) King plays a three-chorus introduction to "Sweet Little Angel," where he displays an exorbitant use of pull-offs, mainly of the first type. However, in the eighth and ninth bar of the first solo chorus he employs both types. In this solo, King sounds amazingly like the gypsy master Django Reinhardt by straying from his normal blues style in utilizing more chromaticism and also in his creative jazz-like lyrical lines.

Pull-offs are exemplified in his later recordings, such as "Three O'Clock Blues" from his album *Together For the First Time* (MCA2-4160, 1974), "Don't You Lie to Me" from the album *King Size* (ABC-977, 1977), and in "Big Boss Man" from his album *Six Silver Strings* (MCA-5616, 1985).

A technique which King begins to employ in the late 1970s is his use of octaves. This technique generally consists of strumming three adjacent strings but muting the middle one. B.B. King's usage of this technique is somewhat limited, as was also the case with the pull-off technique. King often employs this technique toward the end of a solo passage.

It has been established that King is an eclectic guitarist drawing on many sources in forming his style and technique. He has no doubt incorporated nuances into his playing technique through his constant listening to other musicians over the course of his career. His octave technique was probably derived through his listening initially to Django Reinhardt and jazz guitarists like Wes Montgomery, whose solos were completely based on octave playing, and to George Benson, who has continued that same tradition in many of his solo choruses.

B.B. King's octave technique is first evident in his album *King Size* (ABC-977, 1977) on a song entitled "I Just Want to Make Love to You." He builds his guitar solo around the rhythmic motif for an extended period of repetitions. The entire song is a funky type of tune based on an A-flat seventh chord endlessly repeated. His solo consists of playing many melodic riffs based on this rhythmic motif. His octave usage begins at measure four and is stated several times using the rhythm mentioned above. In ending the song and his solo he alters the above octave riff by adding the dominant seventh of the chordal harmony—a G-flat directly below the tonic note A-flat.

B.B. King continues his octave technique up to the present time. In his song "The Victim" from the album *There Must Be a Better World Somewhere* (MCA-27034, 1981) he ends his twelve-bar blues solo with an octave figure, the last note falling off into a glissando. In the song "Broken Heart" from the album *Blues 'N Jazz* (MCA-5413, 1983) King employs a similar octave technique at the end of the tenth bar of his twelve-bar solo in almost the same manner as the preceding example. One can also find octave usage in B.B. King's album *Six Silver Strings* (MCA-5616, 1985). In the song "Big Boss Man" he plays octaves at measures 10 and 11 and again at measures 21 and 22. This is an interesting song in that the harmonic scheme is similar to Michael Jackson's "Billy Jean" (Epic 03509, 1982). King's song utilizes the repeated chord formula Ami - Bmi C6 - Bmi which repeats every two measures. On the same album, in a twelve-bar blues-rock tune entitled "My Lucille" King plays an octave figure in his second solo chorus at measure 10, glissing off the final octave B-flat.

Another technique, which is characteristic and fundamental to all blues guitarists and employed in a rather unique way by B.B. King, is that of string bending. In the first place, King's string bending technique is unusual in that it developed out of his insecurity and inability early in his career to hit accurately notes outside a given position on the instrument. This insecurity necessitated finding a compensatory approach. He found that by hitting the note a fret lower and bending up to it a half step he could sound bluesy and at the same time gain a sense of security in his soloing. King explains his unparalleled technique this way:

—I'd never heard anybody do it the way I do it. My reason was that my ears don't always hear like they should. I'm always afraid that I might miss a note if I try to hit it right on the head, so if I hit down and slide (or bend) up to it, my ears tell me when I get there. But also its more like violin or a voice; you just gliss up to it.[5]

Any B.B. King guitar solo is rife with this technique, although it has become more intense and more dramatic as his style has developed.

During the early stages of his style development he mixed glissandos and string bending proportionately, obviously because of the insecurity he alluded to earlier. One can notice this mixture of sliding and string bending in his early hit "Three O'Clock Blues" (RPM-339, 1951) in measures three through six.

In later solos King favors his tremolo and string bending technique over sliding as he has become more accurate in going in and out of positions. For example, in the song "My Lucille" (MCA-5616, 1985), King's solo displays a string-bending and tremolo technique which out-weighs any other technical or idiomatic devices. Besides being initially influenced by "T-Bone" Walker and other Delta guitarists, King also acknowledges saxophonist Louis Jordan has having given him the inclination to stretch notes up or down a half step.

In string or note bending King often plays these notes sharp or flat, especially if he is going to play the note twice, which occurs when he is returning to the original note a half-step lower. Often, when he bends up and holds a note out, his intonation tends to fluctuate. When changing from a minor third to a major third he may play the major third flat.

Development of Motifs in Guitar Solos

Charles Sawyer contends that B.B. King uses no more than two signature motifs in his guitar improvisations.[6] However, upon making a thorough perusal of his improvised guitar solos spanning his entire career, one finds at least three pervasive motifs which comprise a sort of musical grammar unique to King's guitar style. In analyzing these melodic fragments one can see a kind of evolution and style development of the guitarist in this respect.

In the beginning, King is somewhat confined to a very limited "bag" of motifs, ostensibly because of his inexperience as a soloist. We can see, though, in his development a gradual inclination either to vary or discontinue some of these melodic fragments in favor of others. However, it can be noticed that now, when performing songs from his earlier repertoire, he

---

5. Wheeler, "B.B. King," *Guitar Player Magazine*, September 1980, p. 64.
6. Sawyer, p. 172.

reverts back to some of his earlier motifs. The reason perhaps is that his older audience expects to hear a validation of their former conception of B.B. King and the artist obviously recognizes this and is very comfortable with his earlier repertoire himself. This also seems to be the case with other professional entertainers who do this as a means of continuing their identity and uniqueness.

One of the first motifs significant to B.B. King's style development can be compared to a similar motif of "T-Bone" Walker, as heard in King's "She Don't Move Me No More" (US 7788, 1949–50) and "T-Bone" Walker's "I Got A Break Baby." "T-Bone" Walker was the first and foremost contributor to B.B. King's melodic style development. This same signature motif can be found in many of King's guitar solos throughout the 1950s. He also employed the motif in his guitar responses to his vocal lines during the same time span. B.B. King hasn't abandoned this motif entirely, as it is found in his guitar solo in "Broken Heart" (MCA 5413, 1983) at measure 8. It is nonetheless rare to hear him employ it now.

A second motif which King himself invented and began employing in the mid-1960s is a triplet figure beginning on the fifth of the chord going up a whole step and leaping to the tonic note. It then ascends to the third, descending to either the tonic or the fifth on the first measure. Charles Sawyer briefly discusses this motif in his biography of the bluesman but without documentation of its occurrence.[7]

King generally reserves this triplet motif for introductions to slow 12-bar blues songs, although there are occasional exceptions where he will employ a four-note variation on a faster song like "Gambler's Blues" (MCA 27010, 1966). In his hit song "Paying the Cost to Be the Boss," an up-tempo blues, he remains on the third of the tonic chord on measure one which resolves to the tonic notes on measure two. In the introductory solo to "Gambler's Blues" King repeats a variation of this motif two times with several permutations. He begins the motif by sliding up to the sixth "B." Then, skipping to the tonic "D" and on to the second "E," he arrives as usual to the third, this time a minor third. King continues the use of this basic motif up to the present time, especially when playing older hits in live performances. In his live album, *B.B. King and Bobby Bland: Together For the First Time* (MCA 2 4160, 1974), he utilizes the motif to introduce his classic "Three O'Clock Blues." In observing the artist perform an engagement in Memphis, Tennessee, in 1985, this author witnessed

---

7. Sawyer, p. 172.

usages of this same motif to introduce "Lucille" and "Paying the Cost to Be the Boss."

A third motif employed consistently in B.B. King's guitar solos is one which begins on a note bend up a half step to the lowered seventh of the tonic chord. The motif is most often played against the I^7 harmony although it may fit any of the three chords employed in a traditional 12-bar blues framework. In the song "The Victim" (MCA 27034, 1981) King begins the motif on the fourth bar of this 12-bar blues. The underlying harmony at this point is a I^7 ready to move to a IV^7 at measure five.

The basic motif itself can be analyzed in several ways. It is fundamentally a descending A-minor pentatonic scale starting on "G," or it could be seen as an implied "A" blues scale without the flatted fifth E flat. A jazz musician might see the motif or "lick" as part of a dominant seventh (Mixolydian) scale or arpeggio. We might also say that it is a tonic minor seventh motif pitted against the underlying secondary dominant harmony. The C natural gives it the bluesy dissonant effect. King employs this motif characteristically at times just before a chord change to IV^7 to create tension and climactic building. Therefore, it is seen as a building device to arrive at the second "A" section or the "B" section of the typical three part blues form—AAB. This motif is first evident in King's solos around the mid-1960s. He uses it very effectively in his second solo chorus in the song "Worry, Worry" (*B.B. King: Live at the Regal,* MCA 27006, 1964). He employs the motif here repeatedly as a building device in the first four measures to arrive at the IV^7 at the fifth measure.

As can be seen, he alters the motif slightly on the third repetition at measure three. The harmony does briefly change to the IV^7 chord at measure two, but this is a common variation from the traditional harmony I - I - I - 17 for the first four measures.

In the second improvised chorus from his introduction to "Gambler's Blues" (MCA 27010, 1966), he essentially employs the motif in the same manner preceding the IV^7 chord change at measure five. He continues this same modus operandi in his second chorus of "Sweet Sixteen" (MCS 27074, 1971).

In his solo in "Three O'Clock Blues" (MCA2 4160, 1974) he again plays the motif several times, first at the end of the third measure, which seems premature to set up the IV^7 chord on measure, and then again at the end of the sixth bar to announce the arrival of the I^7 (tonic 7) again in measures seven and eight. We notice at this point that King deliberately ends up on an F sharp to coincide with the tonic "D" chord at measure seven. In the song "Don't You Lie to Me" (ABC 977, 1977) he employs the motif in the same manner to arrive at the I^7 coming up in measure seven.

B.B. King also uses this motif outside the traditional 12-bar blues framework in tunes like "My Lucille" and "Big Boss Man" from his latest album *Six Silver Strings* (MCA 5616, 1985). His solo chorus in the former is built around a harmonic progression based on suspended I^7 + 4 (sus 4) chords. He employs the motif twice in his solo chorus, both times on a B-flat (sus 4) harmony just before a subsequent B flat 7 harmonic change. The motif, however, is played identically in both cases.

King's song "Big Boss Man" (MCA 5616, 1985) is essentially a 12-bar blues with a double-time feel, making the overall form 24 bars. It also has a moving harmonic structure within each bar thus making the song rather unusual. The underlying harmony is taken from Michael Jackson's "Billy Jean" (Epic 03509, 1982), which was immensely popular. This progression gives King a new slant on his otherwise sometimes monotonous three-chord blues framework. This borrowed harmonic accompaniment or formula is utilized only on measures that would regularly employ a tonic harmony in a traditional 12-bar blues. Again, predictably, King plays the motif in the measure preceding the change to the IV^7 harmony (minor). In this case, it occurs on the eighth measure because the song has a double-time feel.

In his song "Broken Heart" (MCA 5413, 1983), a regular 12-bar blues, he digresses slightly from his normal usage in employing the motif. It is permutated rhythmically, on the second measure, and again on the fourth. As usual King utilizes the motif for dynamic contrast and expression in building his solo. This motif can be seen as an intrinsic part of B.B. King's musical grammar, unequivocally defining his style. We can see that he has continued its usage up to the present time and almost always in the same harmonic context.

Motifs Developed in Guitar Responses

One of the main style characteristics of blues artists is the instrumental response following their vocal lines, especially in the 12-bar blues format. Examples of these responses can be found throughout the recorded history of the blues, from the early recordings of Louis Armstrong, Bessie Smith, Blind Lemon Jefferson, the Delta blues singers, and right up through to the post World War II urban bluesmen like Muddy Waters, "T-Bone" Walker, and Howlin' Wolf. Of course, B.B. King is no exception. Historically instrumental responses have taken the following directions: (1) orchestral accompaniment providing the responses (Bessie Smith and other female blues singers), (2) soloists in the background playing responses, (3) the blues singer himself providing the response. B.B. King has incorporated all three types, but for the majority of his recordings he chooses to play his own, especially in smaller group contexts.

King considers his guitar responses very important in communicating the totality of this thoughts. He asserts that these short melodic fragments following his vocal lines are merely a continuation of his vocal statements. He confirms this in stating, "When the serious part comes after the melodic (vocal) line leaves the lips, then the serious part starts on the guitar."[8]

In other words, we might perceive his vocal lines as being punctuated by short series of notes that could be seen as musical statements serving to enhance his vocal statements.

An interesting phenomenon unique to King's style, which can be observed occurring simultaneously with his guitar responses, is his facial expressions. He denotes these as taking the place of his strumming:

> —then I'm hearing, after I stop singing, the guitar. I am singing through the guitar (by means of the guitar response). Then my facial expression (which he has observed on video tape) and all that is like the tempo of the strumming on the guitar that goes along with the melodic line on the guitar.[9]

As was mentioned in a earlier chapter, one of the main incentives for King to develop responses on the guitar came out of his own insecurity as an accompanist. He had the choice of becoming a blues singer like Bobby Bland or Joe Williams, who rely on their backup groups to play their responses, or to utilize his guitar in creating his own responses. King's guitar responses have also come to define the artist and his unique style.

These responses have basically taken on the same motivic shapes as his extended improvisations, though over the course of his career they have developed into shorter motifs limited to tonic clarification or emphasis.

His earlier responses consisted of longer melodic fragments paralleling

---

8. B.B. King, interview with author, p. 113.
9. Ibid.

and limited to those found in his improvised solos. For example, in the song "She Don't Move Me No More" (US 7788, 1949–1950) he employs a similar melodic fragment to one found in his 12-bar solos during the same tune.

As we follow the development of King's guitar responses during the 1950's, we find that they continue to be almost identical to the motifs observed in his extended solos. In comparing several motifs found in his guitar solo in "Three O'Clock Blues" (RPM 339, 1951) with his guitar responses in the same song, we see an amazing similarity. In examining a recording of the same song made almost 25 years later we see that King draws on a mixture of earlier motifs while developing newer ones.

Depending on the makeup of his accompanying group, King may play his own responses, or he may play them against a riffing ensemble background. He may also simply choose to have his back-up soloists play the responses entirely. In several early songs he chose to play his own responses for a few verses. Then in succeeding verses his sidemen took over. His 1950 recording, "Questionaire Blues" (KST 9011, 1951), is a prime example. Many times King will play responses in a free-for-all context, everyone competing for the spotlight. This occurs in early songs like "My Own Fault Darlin'" (RPM 335, 1950) and "B.B.'s Blues" (RPM-323, 1950). He still follows this trend in many of his live recordings where he is not confined to a strict time factor. Such albums as *Live at the Regal* (MCA-27006, 1964), *B.B. King: Live and Well* (Bluesway-6031, 1969), and *Blues Is King* (BL-6001, 1966), are exemplary. A specific example of the bluesman playing responses against a riffing ensemble background is found in his recording "I've Got a Right to Love My Baby" (Kent-333, 1960). This piece is also an excellent illustration of King's usage of earlier motifs in his guitar responses.

During the 1960s B.B. King continued to play several identifiable signature motifs in his guitar responses. This is clearly demonstrated in his song "Wee Baby Blues" (MCA 2-4124, 1966). These responses occur consecutively. The first follows the textual line—"It was early one Monday morning, I was on my way to school." The second response, a pull-off, is employed at the end of the vocal phrase "and that was the Monday morning that I broke my teacher's rule."

In the late 1960s, B.B. King's responses began to take the shape of several shorter fragments accentuating the tonic note of the key, sometimes isolated or followed by longer melodic fragments. This trend can be seen in examining his responses from approximately 1968 up to the present time. In the song "Having My Say" (MCA 2-4124, 1968) his response begins with a statement of the tonic note "C," which is an upward bend, followed in the succeeding measure by a short melodic fragment, both defining the tonal center. The next response begins with a similar "C," also bent upward, then followed by a longer melodic fragment. In another of King's songs from the same time period, "Worried Dream" (MCA 2-4124), his first response is a concise motif beginning on the tonic note with E-flat, F, and G to follow, thus alluding to the C-minor tonality. The ensuing response consists of a typical statement of the tonic note "C," an upward bend, followed by a longer melodic fragment.

By the early 1970's, King's responses continued to become shorter and compressed, mostly beginning on the tonic and only occasionally followed by longer melodic fragments. In his song "Sweet Sixteen" (MCA-27074, 1971) his first response begins with a tonic statement on "D" accented. The rest of the response diminishes in sound, seeming to imply a lesser significance.

From the mid-1970's to the present time we see a trend toward very short motifs, usually employing the tonic note on a fast "trill" (vibrato). These are often followed by notes of a shorter rhythmical value, which usually include the third or the sixth note of the key. In the song "Don't Answer the Door" (MCA2-4160, 1974) we find two consecutive responses, each concise and going to the third or the sixth note of the key. One finds a similar usage in "Never Make a Move Too Soon" (MCA-27011, 1978). The first response consists of a long "trilled" note followed by the sixth of the key, a shorter note. The second response is simply a trilled tonic G note. Most of King's other response motifs since 1978 have been limited to a range of a fifth. Exceptions to this can be found in motifs originating on the flatted seventh of the key. In the song "Heed My Warning" (MCA 5413, 1983) we see the use of the dominant seventh motif as well as the shorter "trilled" tonic motif. Other examples of King's usage of flatted seventh motifs occur in several of his songs on a more recent album, *Six Silver Strings* (MCA 5616, 1985). In the second response in the song "The Midnight Hour" he bends up to the flatted seventh, B-flat, then bends up to third, "E," finally sounding the tonic note "C" with a finger vibrato (trill). In the song "My Guitar Sings the Blues" (MCA 5616, 1985) a more typical flatted seventh motif is executed in the second response. This can be compared to measure two of his 12-bar solo in "Broken Heart" (MCA 5413, 1983).

Through developing numerous motifs during his career, B.B. King has been able to become more of a spontaneous improviser, possibly playing more from his "head" rather than contriving his solos or responses in a more predictable manner as manifested in his earlier works. It often takes many years of on-the-job experience to develop the expertise in conceiving and inventing musical lines spontaneously. King has begun to approach this ideal in the span of approximately 35 years.

The Relationship of King's Guitar Responses to His Vocal Lines

It has already been pointed out that B.B. King perceives his guitar lines as a continuation of his vocal phrases. It is apparent, however, that King's vocal phrases are more closely related to his vocal sources as represented in the works of Roy Brown, Wynonie Harris, Joe Williams, and Louis Jordan, to name a few. Many of King's vocals have not been original manifestations, although to be certain he has affixed his own individual stamp on each song. His first commercial success came with "3 O'Clock Blues" (RPM 339, 1951) recorded two years earlier by Lowell Fulson, its composer. "Every Day I Have the Blues" (RPM 421, 1955) was recorded earlier by Joe Williams, Lowell Fulson, and Memphis Slim. "Sweet Sixteen" (Kent 330, 1960) came from Joe Turner via Walter Davis, and "Sweet Little Angel" (Kent 340, 1960), one of King's most identifiable hits, had been previously recorded by Tampa Red and later by Robert Nighthawk. B.B. King's greatest hit, "The Thrill Is Gone" (BL-61032, 1970), was recorded earlier by Roy Hawkins.

King's guitar ideas, on the other hand, do not draw so specifically from a particular recording but more from a set "bag" or reservoir of licks, melodic fragments, or preconceived melodic lines—sort of a defined repertoire. In other words, King's instrumental improvisations as well as his guitar responses are somewhat set and predictable in an ad lib context. Earlier recordings of several vocalists serve as sources for songs, not for arrangements. His guitar responses thus can be seen as internal refrains, an instrumental extension of the vocal text drawn from a previously mentioned readily available collection of musical material.

B.B. King's Jazz Guitar Style

To be certain, King's overwhelming style characteristics place him in the blues idiom. However, it must be pointed out that on rare occasions his guitar sound and use of certain idiomatic devices may have momentarily positioned him in the realm of a jazz guitar style. King performs most of the time in a three-chord 12-bar blues framework. To be sure he has recorded with a plethora of jazz musicians, whose influence has had a substantial impact on his musical thinking. Nevertheless, he has confined his playing to the B.B. King blues style for the most part. This can be confirmed in listening to such jazz session albums as *King Size* (ABC-977, 1977), *There Must Be a Better World Somewhere* (MCA-5162, 1981), and *Blues 'N Jazz* (MCA-5413, 1983). Therefore, King's jazz guitar style has only been evident on a few live performance recordings and at his after-hours jam sessions. It is on these rare occasions that we may hear a jazzier guitar style emanate from the veteran bluesman. He obviously feels most at home performing in his own blues context, even when other musicians may take liberties. He always puts his audience first, desirous to play what they want to hear, not wanting to betray their image of who B.B. King is:

> —but what makes identity, what makes a person be themselves, is being what they are continually, as far as I am concerned, — There are certain licks that you are going to hit because that is me. I have to do that. That is kind of like trying to talk to you— you say the cliches or something to try to get my point over. I think the same way when I am on stage. To me I am carrying on a rapport with my audience— in other words, I am trying to say something so to identify to me— I feel like I am on stage with long rubber arms with a dancing partner which is the audience, and I like to be able to reach.[10]

It is easy to see why King is reluctant to change his image and the blues-infected style he is most noted for.

What then distinguishes King's blues style from his jazz style? King's jazz style evolved very slowly to be sure. He began by inserting jazzy nuances and "licks" into his pervasive blues style, therefore, on occasion offering a unique or peculiar sound.

King began to acquire a few jazz guitar techniques in the early 1960s. This is evident in his recording of "Mr. Pawnbroker" (Crown 5188, 1960). In this rendition he transcends the blues idiom by incorporating a pull-off into his more lyrically conceived jazz sounding solo and at the same time using fewer bluesy effects. Even his vocal lines hint more towards a Joe Williams sound rife with jazzy embellishment.

While "Mr. Pawnbroker" demonstrates King's growing awareness and predisposition for utilizing a few jazz guitar sounds, we do not hear a more fully developed jazzy guitar inclination until his album *Live and Well* (Bluesway 6031) produced in 1969. A most exemplary jazz-conceived solo

---

10. B.B. King, interview with author, pp. 122–23.

occurs in King's introduction to "Sweet Little Angel," where he displays a phenomenal use of jazz guitar technique and novel devices in a few of his guitar lines. He begins his solo with a signature motif in measures one and two, continuing to play in a typical King blues style up to the third measure. At this point he slides into several double-stopped notes on beat two. Sliding into thirds is more common in the jazz guitar idiom, as evidenced in the solos of Barney Kessel, Kenny Burrell, and a host of other jazz guitarists. In measure five King sets up a jazzy sound by his employment of stark chromaticism and by his grace note usage. In measure six he portrays a jazz-like style in his slide to F sharp on beat three and in his glissando and pull-off on beat four. However, his inadeptness in fitting notes to the implied harmonic background stands out at this same point as he implies a "D" harmony against the G7 accompaniment. A common fault of amateur jazz soloists is to improvise ahead of an upcoming harmonic change. This is the case on beats three and four of measure six where King creates ambiguity and dissonance erroneously and prematurely. King gets back on track in measures seven and eight with his tasteful usage of note sliding an embellishment. The zenith of his jazz-like digression occurs in measures nine and ten. He begins measure nine with a flashy jazz pull-off on beat one. On beats two and three his tasty A7 scale, with its chromatic passing tone, compliments the implied harmony at that point. On beat four he again prematurely sets up the forthcoming IV harmony by playing an E minor chord arpeggio. However, these notes tend to sound consonant because they are really an extension of the present A7 harmony, thus making the end result an A9 sound. This can be seen as purely accidental, as King would not have purposely created this tension. In measure ten he continues his jazz sound by playing a G-major-seven arpeggio on the first beat, which is syncopated, then completes the measure emphasizing the sixth of the G chord - E. In measure eleven he brings us back home to the blues with his string bends from a minor to a major third.

This rendition shows us that King has purposely listened to jazz guitarists and other jazz instrumentalists in a quest to diversify his style, and while he is capable of showing some expertise in this remote area, his inexperience as an improviser is apparent. It also shows us that King is reluctant to perform in his jazz style except in a relaxed context.

As has been the case with many jazz aspirants, B.B. King showed great curiosity and interest in Charlie Christian's jazz guitar style. During King's formative years, which encompassed the mid-1940s, the only jazz guitarists of any notoriety were Charlie Christian, Django Reinhardt, and to a lesser degree, Bill Jennings. These as well as later guitarists motivated King to practice major and minor scales and some arpeggios at various times in his development. However, one of King's greatest attractions was for the diminished harmonies of Charlie Christian. This attraction is borne out in King's own statement:

—Charlie Christian was really known for what we call diminished chords, and, man, he could break them up so pretty.[11]

As has been previously demonstrated, most of King's studio recordings are devoid of the jazz guitar style alluded to in his live recordings or performances. In these few rare instances, King's knowledge and use of altered scales is apparent. This occurred specifically in his instrumental ballad "My Mood" (Bluesway 6031, 1969) from the album *Live and Well*. King demonstrated a style influence from both Charlie Christian, with his use of diminished runs, and Django Reinhardt with his use of embellishments and phrasing. This ballad is in a 32-bar A-A-B-A form with cycle-of-fourth harmonies resembling Claude Gray's early tune "Night Life" (Decca, 1968). King has followed this chord formula in many of his ballad songs throughout his career.

A sampling of this genre of ballads can be found in the following B.B. King repertory: "I'll Survive" (CST-195, 1958), "I'm King" (CST-195, 1958), "How Long How Long Blues" (MCA-2-4124, 1981), "There Must Be a Better World Somewhere" (MCA-5162, 1981). It is interesting that in these examples King never plays the guitar but functions solely as a vocalist. The probable reason for this is that the harmonic scheme does not lend itself to a downhome bluesy style but rather more to a jazzy popular vocal style. Since all of these are studio recordings, King chooses to focus on his lyrical vocal style rather than to risk making mistakes in his attempt to improvise over the more diverse harmonies. "My Mood," on the other hand, is the perfect vehicle for B.B. King to demonstrate his limited prowess in the jazz style he is moderately familiar with. He is also situated in a more relaxed atmosphere—the club or concert setting.

Up to the present time jazz musicians have enjoyed improvising to tunes which either change chords in every measure or every other measure, giving them the opportunity to play a diversity of scales, arpeggios and idiomatic motifs. This type of improvising occurred in small group

---

11. Ibid., p. 125.

settings beginning with bebop in the 1940's and continuing in the "Cool" era of the mid to late 1950's. The tunes played would be standards drawn from the 1930's and 1940's such as "I Got Rhythm," "Sweet Georgia Brown," and "Stardust." In the 1950's and 1960's jazz musicians liked to improvise to tunes like "Misty," "Satin Doll," "Early Autumn" and "Girl from Ipanema." All of these tunes have a harmonic scheme focusing on a cycle of fourth chord progressions. This same kind of progression is found in measures 4–8 in the "A" sections of "Night Life." Here each successive chord moves up by a fourth -B7-E7-A7-D.

"My Mood" demonstrates King's inventiveness and use of jazzy nuances, such as note sliding, pull-offs, embellishments, and glissandos. In several cases he uses altered chord scales, never distinguishable in any of his studio recordings.

B.B. King begins his second eight-bar solo chorus (the A section repeated) with several slides which serve to get to a higher position while exhibiting both a jazzy and bluesy effect. In measure 2 he employs double stopped thirds, which he slides into twice. On the upbeats of "three" and "four" he plays the melody slightly altered by whole step note bends which are uncharacteristic of his straight blues solos. He also hints at the melody on the first two beats of bar 3. However, on the third and fourth beat King surprises us with a premature G sharp diminished seventh run, as the organist does not sound the harmony until the beginning of the following measure. As we have seen before, this is not out of line with King's thinking or background. Fortunately, his diminished seventh run doesn't sound too bad with the exception of the G-sharp which is dissonant with the accompanying G-natural. Finally arriving at measure 4 he plays a series of G-sharp diminished seventh chord pull-offs which are very jazz-like, fully complimenting the underlying harmony at that point. Then, at measure 5, King returns to a bluesy feel with half-step note bends to several F-sharps and an A-natural. He brings us back to a jazzy style in measure 6 with a glissando from "E" down to "A," a technique he reserves mostly for his jazz style. On beat "three" of the same measure we are once more surprised at his rare end employment of an augmented run against a dominant harmony. On beat "four" he returns again to a more bluesy affect by bending up and back on the eighth notes which move toward the tonic harmony in measure 7. In bar 8 he adequately sets up the sub-dominant harmony of the forthcoming "B" section by playing a tonic-7 (D7) scale lick which includes several chromatic triplet figures on the upbeat of "two" and on the down-beat of "three."

In the ensuing "B" section (refrain) he returns to his typical blues style with a riffing horn section in the background. In this section he does nothing extraordinary. However, in the final "A" section he again reminds us of Charlie Christian with his descending G-sharp diminished seventh melodic structure, the first three notes bent upward in measure 4.

Finally, we can conjecture that B.B. King sees himself primarily as a blues guitarist with a diversity of musical interests, and an occasional inclination to get away from a strict three-chord blues framework. He accomplishes this by showing off his somewhat limited jazz technique in situations where he feels most relaxed—the live performing context. We must keep in mind that his 300-plus nights-per-year performing schedule allows him at least some flexibility to perform in other style mediums.

As evidenced, B.B. King is not an expert jazz soloist, but he does exhibit enough knowledge and technique to impress the average blues enthusiast and is perhaps poor enough to sow the seeds of doubt in the minds of a few schooled jazz musicians or jazz critics.

In summary, B.B. King has gradually incorporated a variety of technical devices—some original—into his playing style. These advances in technique have served to distinguish him as a unique soloist capable of improvising in an electric blues guitar style and occasionally in a more jazzy mode of expression. Thus, over the period of his entire career he has become a consummate soloist drawing upon a reservoir of predetermined motifs and melodic fragments, enabling him to appear as a spontaneous and creative musician.

CHRONOLOGY OF B.B. KING'S DEVELOPING GUITAR STYLE

1935	Receives instruction on guitar from Archie Fair.
1943	Plays and sings on Indianola street corners (frailing style).
1945	Absorbs note bending & embellishment techniques from recordings of C. Christian & D. Reinhardt. Scrutinizes T-Bone Walker's guitar style. Copies Walker's melodic motifs.
1946	Lives with cousin Bukka White who tutors him on guitar.
1949	Begins recording career. Begins note sliding technique.
1950	Introduces repeated notes on adjacent strings.
1951	Records "Three O'Clock Blues," his first hit.
1955	Two-note repetitions employed (first note bent up, second note repeated on higher adjacent string). Range confined to close positions.
1956	Pull-off technique first employed.

1958	Tremolo technique first discernible.
1960	Jazz guitar style begins to emerge.
1964	Range expanded to higher playing positions. Introduces triplet motif in introductions. First employment of descending Dom 7 motifs. Tremolo technique fully developed.
1968	Begins to employ shorter response motifs following vocal lines.
1969	Mature jazz guitar style. Diminished 7th runs first discernible in recordings.
1977	Octave technique first employed.
1985	Use of novel chord progressions (montunos).

PART FOUR

Paying the
Cost to Be
the Boss

E PLURIBUS BLUESMAN (1991)
GENE SANTORO

Santoro is a prolific critic of jazz and popular music. Even in this
brief review he reveals he has thought long and hard about King.

Blues revivals, starting with the first big one of the mid- to late 1960s,
have been good to Riley B. King. Though the sixty-six year-old is still on
the road an average of 275 days a year—much more than his more famous
devoted students—he's looking fat and prosperous. And why not? He's
been collecting awards and playing high-ticket venues like Las Vegas and
Lincoln Center as well as lounges in Alaska; opening his own club, the
Blues Bar, on the famed Beale Street of Memphis, where the Blues Boy got
his radio nickname and his start; donating his collection of 20,000-plus
rare recordings to the University of Mississippi; continuing to work for the
Foundation for the Advancement of Inmate Recreation and Rehabilitation
(FAIRR), which he co-founded with F. Lee Bailey, and the John F. Kennedy
Performing Arts Center, of which he's a founding member; pulling in
Grammies and making the talk-show rounds; playing for the U.K.'s Queen
Elizabeth and at the White House for George Bush's 1989 inaugural; pop-
ping up on documentaries aired over PBS and HBO. No matter how you
look at it, B.B.'s been staying very visible.

So in the midst of this latest blues revival, which finds Jeff Beck and
Eric Clapton jamming with Buddy Guy and Bonnie Raitt sitting in with
John Lee Hooker, it's not surprising that his time has come—again.
Sometime this summer, MCA is planning to release a four-CD boxed set
that spans his legacy from his first 1951 hit, "The Three O'Clock Blues,"

on up to today. And what a set it should be. After all, King not only helped to further insinuate diverse strains like gospel and swing into the blues via his smoothly crying vocals, but also helped shape the sound of single-string blues guitar playing by mixing an eclectic array of sources.

According to B.B., eclecticism has been his musical game from the get-go. "I grew up liking people like Johnny Moore and the Three Blazers, and his brother Oscar Moore, who played with Nat Cole," he intones in the same gospel-inflected cadences that power his singing. "In fact, Robert Jr. Lockwood, who was in one of my earliest bands, brought that same jazzy influence into it. I also liked Jimmie Rodgers and Hank Williams; Jimmie Rodgers was one of the first white country singers to sing blues that black people liked. Believe it or not, Gene Autry did some things with that feeling too. Lonnie Johnson. I was crazy about Louis Armstrong, the big-band sounds of Duke Ellington and Count Basie and Woody Herman and Benny Goodman and Charlie Christian.

"This is long before I was a disc jockey. They used to have these video jukebox setups where you'd see a short film of the performers; each of them was about three to five minutes long. That's how I was introduced to the big bands and people like Ella Fitzgerald and Nat Cole and Cab Calloway. And then when I was a dj I discovered Django Reinhardt: I loved his vibrato and sense of melody, especially when he recorded with just a regular rhythm section." Given this list, maybe it's not surprising that B.B. shares heroes like Cole and Louis Jordan with Ray Charles, another towering African American artist who's blithely sailed over externally imposed categories to commercial success.

King sees his musical broad-mindedness as the key to outings like his sharing a stage with U2 for that band's concert film and album *Rattle And Hum,* or his own synth-laden *King Of The Blues: 1989.* "None of this has changed my way of working," he insists. "It's just given me more to think about while trying to perform. When I first started to play, the audience was my age and older, and it kept being that way until the late 1960s. Then we got a new following, all the white teenagers who heard about the blues from their idols, like Eric Clapton.

"The audience now is a much wider range of people, from the very young on up: two-thirds of my audience ranges between eight and thirty years old. My association with U2 has brought even really young kids in to hear what I do. So I will do things now I probably wouldn't have done years ago, because I didn't know to do these things then. For instance, I survey each audience and see musically as well as visually how they take certain tunes. So if I do a couple of tunes that get no real reaction—I'm talking about it in terms of having an apple and seeing a kid who wants it—I shift to different lines. I've got to try and be a pleaser."

The self-contradictions—and the suppressed anger behind some of them—indicate clearly B.B. King's sense of defensiveness about his current sounds. There are those, including me, who dispute his contention about exactly how deep his commercial need to please any crowd may be. The way he responds, with some modulated irritation in his voice, runs like this: "It's really strange that the same folks who support you when you're struggling turn their backs on you or start running you down when you've gotten somewhere. They think it's some kind of betrayal, but I'm the one who feels betrayed. That just doesn't seem like a good reason. It's not fair to me. Why would you support somebody only when they're struggling and not be happy for them when they've made it? You can't stand still."

There's more than a touch of truth in what he says, of course. Devotees of older, so-called folk forms like the blues tend to get nasty when they see their notions of a genre's "purity" or "integrity" messed with. It's a misplaced sense of possessiveness rooted in some good intentions, like the idea that these forms have their own very real value that shouldn't be condescended to, and some not-so-good, like the idea that the older forms were more "spontaneous" or "natural." That stance too often stems from or covers an unsettling brand of implicit racism—a nostalgic picture of them happy darkies out back of the massa's house whilin' the hours away with their untutored but earthy and immediate sounds, plucked from the union with Nature that childlike innocence brings. This brand of misshapen Romanticism implicitly, if sometimes inadvertently, denies its subjects the benefit of artistic consciousness. After all, what allowed kidnapped Africans to adapt strange instruments and musical formats to their own forbidden music to produce peculiarly American strains like the blues and jazz? It also denies them the possibility of continuing growth. If these sounds are "natural," how can they possibly be tampered with, never mind improved? And yet . . .

In my case, at least, my reaction to B.B.'s recent albums—which I see as a series of aesthetically unchallenging efforts to recast his already-hybridized blues, via ubiquitous synthesizers, for the MTV crowd—is based on an artistic difference of opinion, not misplaced blues purism. Just to take one set of examples to illustrate by way of contrast, it strikes me that his late 1960s/early 1970s shift of emphasis to soul-style charts, meshing his stinging, vocalic guitar with the Atlantic soul-music house rhythm section, produced chartbusting and aesthetically satisfying albums like *Live And Well* and *Completely Well*, as well as his big crossover single,

"The Thrill Is Gone." His latest recordings haven't served up anything that challenging and rewarding.

Continuing his defense of his latest directions, B.B. reaches for a revealing comparison. "I don't want to compare myself to President Bush," he begins. "But in my own small way, doing what I do, I have to make some of the same kinds of decisions he does. He has so many different constituencies to please—so many more than I do, of course. But he has to walk a fine line about what they want. In my way, so do I." Again, true enough—as far as it goes. But it seems to me that this analogy sidesteps some key issues.

Let's start from the top. George Bush is an elected politician. His job depends on feeding the people he (and his group of advisers) think support him most consistently, or who can be weaned away from political opponents. There's an adversarial relationship at work in this arena, then, that doesn't really apply all that clearly in a hybridized industry like the music biz, which attempts—at least in theory—to mate art and commerce. Artists aren't competing head-to-head about the levels of quality of their work. Most of them are competing for listeners, though, trying to expand their corners of the market. Take it a step further: there's some sort of lesson behind Bush's own precipitous slide in the public opinion polls he follows so slavishly, even to the point of ignoring or overturning positions he'd previously presented as convictions.

This points to what is most troublesome to a fan about B.B.'s attitude toward his music today. Asked about why he's doing what he's doing, he doesn't provide an artistic rationale, as he could and did with those great breakthrough albums of two decades ago, or as a similarly beleaguered Miles Davis could and did when disgruntled critics blasted pioneering efforts like *Bitches Brew* or *On The Corner*. Instead, he draws up the circular logic of a demographic justification. (More on demographics later.) If you want to watch the circle break down, go back and reread the quote where he explains how he hasn't really changed what he does, then explains why he's changed what he does.

Then, too, there's the simple and undeniable fact that, with his Grammies and TV-talk-show appearances and so on, B.B. King is hardly an unknown. If anything, he's become—rightly—a kind of icon. In other words, the portions of his audiences who are coming to see him via his U2 connection, say, are coming to see him; you might guess they're there to learn more about him and celebrate what he does, not to walk out. So why, then, does he feel so skittish about their loyalty?

For a partial answer, it helps if we dolly back. In a real sense, the musical dilemma of latter-day B.B. King and his music points up the underlying conundrum facing successful American artists caught between the often falsely separated notions of art and commerce. Too many people mistake commercial success for artistic success, and too many critics read commercial success as artistic failure. Will I be an artistic hero or a commercial goat? It's a misleading dichotomy that collapses the vast gray areas it houses, a Romantic leftover that deems Art-with-a-capital-A as a pseudo-religious form somehow above mundane trivia like survival and money and the desire to share what you've created with as many sympathetic ears as you can conjure. Nevertheless, it's a dichotomy that the press, especially the music press, has traditionally overplayed, with the usual and necessary backlash from its targets.

Then, too, the sweep of King's influences points up some of the funny ways in which blues history has been misunderstood—funny ways that may throw some light on B.B.'s current activities. Bluesmen like Charlie Patton and The Mississippi Sheiks usually boasted wide-ranging repertories that included everything from spirituals to rags to current hits; since they played street corners and juke-joint dances (and some, like the Sheiks, did white dances as well), their livelihoods depended on being able to please their audiences, who weren't at all shy about shouting out requests. As B.B. himself rightly says, "The blues has never been just one big thing. In fact, it's always been a lot of different things. You can't really compare Blind Lemon with Muddy or Skip James or Son House; they're individuals."

But when recording began to document blues in a big, if haphazard and unwitting, way during the early '30s, it relegated the results to a marketing niche—race records aimed at rural black listeners. That had two historical effects. First, it limited what parts of their musical bags the artists reached into for recording: the white label owners and field producers reasoned that the black record-buying public would want to hear "downhome" sounds above all others, and until the war the 78s they issued sold well enough to keep them feeling justified. As a result, we've gotten a somewhat distorted picture of blues as a collection of relatively isolated regional forms.

So a figure like Robert Johnson seems even more astounding partly because of the sheer reach of his stylistic tastes. Johnson's was the first generation where music in rural areas became available on jukeboxes and radio, and he apparently drank in whatever came his way. It was the most natural thing in the world. Two of his outstanding contemporaries, T-Bone Walker and Charlie Christian, both descendants of Blind Lemon

Jefferson's Texas-blues guitar, played in popular swing bands and blues combos alike. Given that historical context, it shouldn't surprise that B.B. and Albert King, among others, began to explore soul-music crossovers during the '60s.

Second, the division of taste by race perpetuated an approach to selling sounds that began with Jim Crow and is still too prevalent in the modern recording industry. Take album-oriented radio (AOR), which Living Colour founder/guitarist Vernon Reid (who this year co-produced a couple of tracks for B.B. that may surface on the blues great's next effort) dubbed Apartheid-Oriented Radio when he cofounded the Black Rock Coalition, a cooperative group of artists dedicated to getting African American artists an unbiased break in the record biz. Reid coined the term for that subset of demographically-driven radio because of its near-totally white playlists. The sad reality, though, is that AOR is just one facet of the all-too-typical racially-bounded marketing strategies still found, despite their denials, at many major labels. "If you're this color," the argument goes, "you should play this kind of music for this kind of audience. That's the only way we can sell you."

In the years since the formation of the BRC, thanks to bands like Reid's and Fishbone and the crossover success of rap, that bleak picture has brightened to some extent within record companies. But it's still largely true that, as far as radio and its advertisers are concerned, every musical genre should have its own specialty niche and target demographic. Since radio is how most folks turn on to things they haven't already heard, it's become an aesthetic chokepoint. So despite the synths and contempo dancebeats of his latest recordings, it's no picnic dialing around trying to find some station that's playing the newest B.B. King release.

Notes B.B. from his more personal perspective, "Blues has always been a stepchild in the music business. People often put it down, and put you down if you played it. I've worked to change that. You've got to look and behave a certain way. My cousin Bukka White told me years ago, 'When you're going to perform, dress like you're going to the bank to borrow some money.' I tried to incorporate that attitude into my music as a whole. I've sacrificed for that. I missed out on my children growing up, didn't take them to the movies much. Both of my wives quit me simply because my head has been involved in that.

"So I've never been the father or the husband I should have been, and those moments are gone. I spend more time with my grandchildren than I did with my children—which I get talked about for (laughs). But that's the way it is most times when you're living a public life. And I've been lucky;

my music has been accepted by more kinds of people and been heard in more kinds of places than any other blues."

B.B. King at work today.

B.B. King has the indefinable majesty befitting his name. He sits on a chair, acoustic baffles on either side of him, and a microphone suspended in front of his face. His legs are apart, and his guitar is held in an almost classical posture on his lap. Even partially obscured by recording paraphernalia, he is a commanding presence.

B.B. is here to learn four songs, then overdub his vocal and guitar parts. It has been years since he went into the studio with a band behind him and the songs rehearsed. These days he goes in by himself to overdub his parts. Only an aide accompanies him to make milky hot tea for his throat and guard Lucille. First B.B. listens to the guide vocals and follows the lyrics on a printout. The co-producer, Jon Tiven, stands in front of him, cueing him with hand signals. B.B.'s job is to master the lyrics, pay attention to the cues, then try to sound like every word is drawn from his personal experience. Inevitably, he messes up at first. "Get the ladies out of here, I'm fixing to cuss," he says as he fails to navigate some stops.

By the fifth or sixth take, it's beginning to gel. Co-producer Vernon Reid (coming off a multi-platinum Living Color album) tells the engineer to start saving the vocals in case there's something usable. After half-an-hour, they have at least two good vocal performances, and can probably edit the vocal together from those two tracks. By contemporary standards, this borders on spontaneity.

Now B.B. must do his guitar part. Michael Hill is one of the onlookers in the control room. He played rhythm guitar on the backing track; a huge, gentle man, he saw B.B. at Humber College in 1969 and wanted to come back to watch the overdubs. By the second take, B.B. is electrifying the control room. The usual glassy-eyed studio torpor has gone, and everyone is crowded around the glass. Michael Hill is in front, jittery with excitement, looking at B.B. with a blissful, open-mouthed smile. He comes back to the couch with tears in his eyes. Vernon Reid uses his favorite verb: "Slammin! Slammin!"

B.B. knows he's nailed it, and, after the fade, he takes off the headphones and walks into the control room to a round of applause. His modesty may be a little false, but it's affecting nonetheless. Everyone listens to the playback; B.B. in particular has reason to be satisfied. Everyone's loose, so now he holds court before getting down to the next song. He hands out stick pins, and starts telling stories. He recalls a time in Chicago when he had supper with comedian Pigmeat Markham, one of the sourest men he has ever met. During supper, Pigmeat sat with his arms crossed over the front of his overcoat. B.B. says he asked him why he still had his coat on, and was acting like he was protecting it. Pigmeat replied, "'Cause I just saw yours walkin' out the door." Everyone laughs. It's impossible not feel warmed by the presence of the man.

Things come unglued during the second song. It has been custom-written by Reid and Tiven, but it's too wordy for B.B. to navigate with ease. Sid Seidenberg, who has been more-or-less silent to this point, suggests that the word-count be trimmed, but B.B. seems to regard it as a point of honor to get the original lyrics right. Talking to the control room from the studio floor he complains that he can't get his feeling into the song, and asks to do it once the way he feels it. It's a strange paradox *lost on virtually everyone in the room* that this song, "Many Miles Traveled" (only available on the boxed set *King Of The Blues*), has been written *about* B.B. King, but he doesn't feel comfortable singing it because it's not in his voice. These aren't the words he would have used.

Finally, B.B. gets it to the point where Reid and Tiven are pleased. The tension eases; someone says it's good enough for the next single. B.B. comes back into the control room and appears well pleased. When he started recording 42 years earlier, three or four inputs were mixed through a radio console onto an acetate. Now he is surrounded by all the accoutrements of a modern studio; the walls are crammed with outboard devices, aglow with LEDs. "I never expected to be here," he says, clearly reflecting on the long, strange trip, and those who perished along the way. "There'll be a hell of a band up there," he says, casting his eyes toward Heaven. Then, surprisingly, he starts talking about Jimi Hendrix, and about a tape of the two of them recorded at a club one night that Hendrix always meant to give him.

Between songs, Sid Seidenberg conducts a little business. He hands over some checks to sign, and runs down the arrangements for the tour that begins in D.C. the following day.

The third and fourth songs are recorded quite easily. After listening to the playback of the fourth song, B.B. slumps in a chair in front of the console, and exhibits his legendary ability to sleep anywhere. He'd caught the red-eye in from Vegas that morning, and now he's working off his sleep deficit. The background singers arrive from Jersey. They come in with a blaze of energy. One of them has just come off a tour with the Rolling Stones; another is talking about her last-minute babysitting difficulties. Their arrival makes B.B. sit up and take notice for a few minutes, but he's soon asleep again, and leaves just as the vocal overdubbing begins.

IT'S GOOD TO BE THE KING (1995)
SCOTT JORDAN

Scott Jordan's interview, from the New Orleans magazine *Offbeat,* is the most recent, for instance, acknowledging that the man who looks as though he has eaten too many fried chickens is now a vegetarian who annually spends weeks at a "spa"; that the man who lamented his incapacities in reading music is now using a computer to make arrangements; and that the sometime sharecropper who heard music only rarely now hears it all the time, whether from his extensive private collection that accompanies him on tours or at the live venues surrounding his Las Vegas home.

The King Of The Blues needs no introduction. Like the voice of Billie Holiday or the saxophone of John Coltrane, B.B. King's unmistakable guitar tone transcends age, race, gender, and religious barriers to appeal to the most mysterious listener of all: the human heart. Riley "Blues Boy" King has been spreading his message of salvation in blues for almost half a century now, and considers retirement a four-letter-word. But while his stylistic link to fellow legends such as T-Bone Walker and Robert Jr. Lockwood can be quickly distinguished, understanding B.B. King the man is a more daunting task.

Over the course of a 40 minute conversation, the personal side of B.B. King came to light. In the following interview, the blues' greatest ambassador—a perennial favorite at Jazz Fest—speaks of the hardships of the road, confesses a few guilty pleasures, and acknowledges a surprising musical hero—Louis Armstrong. He also describes his precious time at home in Las Vegas, his relationship with his children, and his thoughts on his longevity in a notoriously fickle industry. As a man who's been lauded with countless honors, he humbly relays his continued quest for improving his musical identity.

And eligible females, take note: B.B. King is looking for a wife.

Do you remember the first year you played the Jazz And Heritage Festival?

No, I don't remember the first year, but I do know that every time I've played it, it's been really enjoyable.

Do you have any special memories that stick out in your years of playing Jazz Fest?

Food, music, pretty ladies, handsome gentlemen.

John Lee Hooker just retired from the road and is strictly making records. Do you ever envision yourself cutting back your touring schedule or retiring from the road?

No, I haven't envisioned myself doing that, I think as long as the people supports me, that is, by buying my records and coming to my concerts, and my health is good and I can still handle myself well, well, I'm gonna try to follow after George Burns.

Do you maintain any special exercise or diet program to keep yourself going strong?

Well, I exercise, yeah. I do walking a lot. Once a year I go to [a health spa] out in Santa Monica and stay out there a couple of weeks and exercise. I'm a vegetarian, so I don't eat a lot of the fattenin' foods that I used to; I've been a vegetarian for about seven, eight years. I eat fish, and I'll eat eggs, but other than that I don't eat any other meat. I think somebody put it this way: I eat nothing that has a mother—it has to be hatched.

I imagine growing up in the South you got spoiled with some good home cooking.

I still like it, it's just that I don't eat any of the meats. Chicken, pork, lamb, steaks or any of it. But I do eat all the greens and beans . . . and I love seafood, but that's it.

Is it hard with your new diet to find good food on the road, or do you have someone who cooks for you?

Well, I have a guy with me that does some cookin', but it's not as hard as it was six, seven years ago. The average city now has someplace that will feature some vegetarian food. And I'm from the country, I like peanuts and potatoes and all that.

When you're not on stage, doing interviews, or conducting business, how do you like to spend your time on tour? Do you have any hobbies you enjoy?

I'm a TV buff. I like watching television, and oh, I'm just kind of a homey, a down home country boy. They got the boy out of the country, but they never did get the country out of me!

Any current favorite TV shows?

Oh, you name 'em. I like actions things, the kind I guess I shouldn't. But those kind I like mostly, and geographical things, and wildlife, and that kind of stuff. I used to fly a lot, but now my manager and insurance company don't want me to fly after a lot of people were killed in private planes, so . . . it's the TV and the computer.

You have all that rigged up in your bus?

I have a computer in the bus, yes, but I have a little laptop that I carry around with me. You know, play games with it. But I like not a lot of games, I like to tutor myself on certain things. For the music, I've learned to arrange, and I use it for writing. And it's a big help along those lines, and it's fun: it's sort of like having a little rhythm section that you can pull out any time you want.

You donated your large record collection to the Center for Southern Culture a while back. Do you still collect records?

I probably have more now than when I donated to them!

How many records would you estimate you have now?

I really don't know, to be honest with you. I still have a lot of records, and you can't find records much anymore, it's all CDs. I must have at least 2,000 pieces.

There's some great record stores here in New Orleans. I don't know if you'll have time, but—

Oh, God yes. I can't wait.

Over the years you've worked with a who's who of the music business. Are there any special collaborations that really stand out in your memory?

Oh, yeah. I feel myself very lucky. I have toured with two of the No. 1 groups of the world, about twenty years apart. The first was The Rolling Stones, and then U2, and then I have recorded since then the Blues Summit, where I used a person from your area—Irma Thomas. And many of the other people on this CD, which was so enjoyable. And just recently I was in L.A., and Irma happened to be in the area, and she and her husband came by, and she sat in and played one of the tunes with me. I was so happy.

Any performers you haven't worked with you'd still like to record with?

Oh, God yeah. It's easier to ask me who I would not. I can't think of anyone I would not want to record with.

There's no one special person that—

All of them are special. I guess I don't see artists as some people do. I see them all as very special people. Some are better known than others, but to me they're all equally very special.

Your live shows seem to be tightly run affairs. Do you set guidelines or rules for your bandmembers to follow?

Yes, I think of that as General Motors would, or U.P.S. I like 'em to be in uniform, I like for them to be professional people at all times, whether it be man or woman. Be professional; what I mean by that is that certain little things that some people do, I wouldn't be happy if my band did them. Drugs is one. Drinking moderately is alright, as long as it's not on the stage. And one must remember who they are at all times—all times. That is, if they're going to work with B.B. King, 'cause I try to do that. I give respect, and I like to get it. And I want them to remember that—when we're on stage, it's all business.

Did you cultivate that philosophy yourself, or did you have an inspiration as far as your professionalism goes?

The bands I worked with was like that. So that's sort of a handed-down thing. Every band I ever worked with in the early years, that was their philosophy: do what you gotta do after, or before; don't come on the stage high and showin' it. That was an old thing. And they claim to us that the people walkin' the streets don't want to see you lookin' like them when you get on stage. Which means that you must wear something—if you have one suit, wash it. I'm from the old school, so I don't want the guys . . . new people, don't get me wrong, I have no kick about them doin' it. But the old school, you dress like you're goin' to the bank to borrow some money. I want 'em [bandmembers] all on stage lookin' like you wouldn't mind havin' 'em comin' to your house for dinner.

Do you have a method onstage you use to keep standards like "Let The Good Times Roll" sounding fresh every night?

Yeah, you play it as if you hadn't played it before. You play every thing, every night, even though you know the song, but you let go. Like jazz musicians play every night, they improvise, and they don't try to play what they played a few minutes ago. They may play the same song, but they're not trying to play what they did yesterday. Each day speak for itself. You have the chord changes, yes, but you play it as if you never played it before. That's the way I do it nightly, and that's the way I try and get my band to do—play free and open. We have like a map. You think of a road map leaving New Orleans going to Mobile. You know how to get there, but you may stop along the way. That's the reason why, playing "The Thrill Is Gone" since '69, it never gets old with me, 'cause each night I play it like I'm playin' it tonight.

And that's the way I did that night. I played it as I felt that night when we recorded it. So tonight I play it, I'll play it as I feel now. And usually, I think, most people . . . I don't add or take away, I just play it as I feel. And when you do that, I think, it's like anything—you're doin' it.

If music hadn't turned out to be your career, are there any other professions you'd be interested in? What can you see yourself doing besides playing?

Yeah, I was a pretty good disc jockey. I was pretty popular in Memphis. That's what really launched my musical career. I can see myself being a disc jockey. And I enjoyed being a farmer, I just didn't like the hours that I couldn't control. [laughs] A lot of people think that because you were a sharecropper and came up on a farm, that you hated it; I don't.

Do you tend a garden at your house?

I don't have a house that's out . . . I have a townhouse that you can't have a garden. I live in Las Vegas, and that's desert. But they do have some green out there. But if I ever get me what I'd like to have, a little place, two or three acres, yes, I would have a garden. And hopefully someday before the end, I'll still be able to do that. I'm looking forward to it.

Las Vegas seems like an odd choice for you. What is it about Vegas that made you decide to settle there?

Music! Nightlife. I am a musician, you know. [laughs] There are no places in the United States where they have more different kinds of music than Las Vegas.

Do you get out regularly when you're there and see shows?

Not too regular, but it's like, in your house if you drink sodas or Coca-Colas, you know you have it in the refrigerator and you can have it when you want it. When I'm home, I'm so glad to be home, but I know the music is all around me, there's a lot of popular people out, I could go out if I want to. The night is always open, and it's safe to go to the hotels.

Who's the last performer you saw?

I don't necessarily go to see the shows, as maybe one would who's coming there. I go to the hotels and the lounges to see people play. I was over at The Hilton, they had a group over there about a week ago when I was home. They had a group over there on one of the small stages, and you don't have to pay anything; you can just have a glass of juice and listen. I'm not a drinker, so I'll have me some orange juice or Evian water, and enjoy it.

Do you ever give the casinos a roll?

Yeah. Once in a while. But not like it was before I moved there. Before I moved there, I was like most people that visit there. "Give me this slot machine! That one's mine!"

How's your luck?

No. No. If it wasn't for bad luck, I wouldn't have any at all. No, I'm not lucky. But once in a while, there's a game called keno, I'll play it—that's one of my favorite games. Then I'll play twenty-one a little bit. But livin' there, you find quickly that it's not somethin' you want to do. You know, it's like, once in a while, if you married and you live in New Orleans, you may take your wife or your girlfriend out to dinner, but you don't do it every day. You know that there are nice places that you can go and have a good time, and once in a while you work yourself up to it and do it. I'm for the cities that want gamin'. I'm for it if . . . I don't think it shouldn't be simply because a few people think that people shouldn't gamble, is what I'm talkin' about. I think that's a personal choice. And anybody that gets [addicted] . . it's like becoming an alcoholic: go get treatment.

I hear that you have a love for the silver screen, and you've had some bit roles. Have you ever considered acting if a role came along that you liked?

I've had about eight or ten bit parts in movies. I'm in, offhand, there's one called Medicine Ball Caravan, *quite a few documentary-types, I'm in* Spies Like Us, *I'm in* Heart and Soul *with Robert Downey Jr., and I'm in* Amazon Woman On The Moon, *and there are others.*

If you got offered a leading role, would you give it a shot?

I would like that. That's one of the things that I hope for in the future.

You just opened your second music club in Los Angeles . . .

Yes, we're about to open a third now in Nashville, Tennessee.

What was the driving force behind that? Was that a dream of yours for some time?

All my life.

To open up first in Memphis must have been a big thrill.

Yes, that's home. I was born in Mississippi and raised in Mississippi, but Memphis is like my second home. When I left Indianola, I went straight to Memphis. A lot of the blues singers went to Chicago, but I didn't. I went to Memphis.

And you still consider Memphis the home of the blues.

Yes, I do.

How active are you in the clubs as far as running the business end of it?

Oh, no. I'm no businessman, I'm a musician. [laughs heartily] My manager is a businessperson, and so is our chairman of the board. Me, I'm just a guitar player playing Lucille, and it carries my name for some reason. The clubs are called The B.B. King Blues Clubs, but I'm just a little part in them. I don't really own them. I've got money in them, though.

Do you feel there are any common misperceptions that either your fans or critics might have about you? Do you ever read something or hear something about yourself that makes you say, "that's not true"?

That's happened quite often. But never had the scandals like I've seen some people, but I've quite often seen misquoted things; and somebody said something critical of me, but that's their opinion. How can you,

you know . . . I think of it this way: I remember once back, I recorded an album with Bobby Bland. One critic in one of the popular magazines said, whatever we was doin', we should go back and start to doin' it right again, because what we did there was nothin'. And that hurt me a little bit, because I felt that this person had never done what we did. So how could he say it was nothin'? But if this person had said, it was somethin' he didn't like, and thought the way we was doin' we shouldn't do it, and we should go back and do it . . . I would accept that, because every person has a reason to like or dislike somethin' if they want.

But if he critically says that it was nothin', we didn't do anything, and he doesn't play, then I figure he doesn't know what he's talkin' about. So, that part hurts me. But if a person criticizes me because of their thoughts about it, I've had that all my life, too. Sometimes it hurts, yeah, it hurt pretty deeply. But what can you say when a person . . . if everybody liked me, I'd be more popular than I am.

Do any of your children help out with your career?

Uh, no, not with me. One of my sons work with me at this time, and he drive on the buses. I've got two daughters that are into the business a bit. One of 'em seem to really be into it. I think a lot of times, children want to be impressive. And I always tell my children I love 'em anyway. I don't care if they dig ditches—I love 'em, [even] if they didn't do anything. But I wanted them to have a good education. But I love 'em all. But to make a long story short, I think what I'm trying to say is, I think this one is not tryin' to impress me. I think she's trying to really make it on her own.

You've never been a man with any vices, but you've always said that you're crazy about women.

Yes, I haven't found anything better.

Is it hard to find that "special" relationship with your busy lifestyle?

Well, that's been hard, because . . . I've been married twice, and divorced twice. So it's not always easy for a travelin' musician. Because usually the average lady would rather you didn't travel. They'll travel with you some, but when they get tired of it, they figure you ought to be tired of it, too. And, I guess we men think like men. And there are some of the women in the business now that also think like we do. I've had several friends like Bonnie Raitt and a few others, that are very popular, but they feel there are things they must do. And that's the way I feel, and a lot of the women disagree.

So, there are ladies, that I think, well, not do I think . . . I know Lawrence Welk and Count Basie and a lot of other people that I've known that was married all thirty years and stayed married. Benny Goodman, a lot of 'em. Lionel Hampton. So there are ladies that are supportive and will be there for you, and with you. And then there are a lot of the others, the life is no good.

What qualities might a future Mrs. B.B. King have? What do you look for in a woman?

Kind of bright, if you will. Uh, I think all women are good to look at. [Pauses then laughs]

I agree.

She don't have to be . . . I want her to be over 18, and she has to be less than 69. I'm 69. So she has to be between 18 and 68. Well, size, she can't be as large as I am, but then I don't want a twig, either. So she got to be 200 pounds or less, but over a hundred.

A few last questions. Since you are so associated with the blues, how do you approach a project like the Diane Schuur record or the recent country duets album?

I approach them the way that usually the producers approach me. They say, "B, be yourself. Do what you do." And that's what I've tried to do. You know, one of my mentors—God, I wish I could be more like him— was Louis Armstrong. And many people have never heard me mention it. Well, I would love to be just like him. I wish I could be the musician he was. But Louis did things with many, many people—but he always was Louis Armstrong; you knew it was him. Whatever he did, or how- ever he done it. And I remember when I first went with the agency that I'm with now, Louis was with 'em. This person was the manager of Louis, that was the president of Associated Booking Agency. And his name was Joe Glaser. And I'll never forget, I went to New York, my manager and I went over to see Mr. Glaser, and we got there, and he had a pile of checks. Checks that he had to sign, and it looked like it must have been half a million dollars worth of checks, that he was signing that day. And he looked at me with his reading glasses, and says, "Have you heard of Louis Armstrong?" And I said, "Yes sir." "You heard of Fats Domino?" And I said, "Yes, sir." He said, "Well, if you be like them, you'll do alright." And I've tried to be more like both of them every day. [laughs]

You have had a personal relationship with Fats, and he's given you some good—

Very good advice. He's one of the nicest men that I know in show business.

Do you still talk to him regularly?

Not that often. We never hardly talk, but he tells me whenever I'm down there, I'm always welcome to come have some red beans and rice, which he know I like. And he's a good cook, too.

Did you ever get to meet Louis Armstrong or play with him?

Oh, I met him, yes. I knew him pretty well. I didn't know him as well as a lot of people, but I knew him pretty well. Like I said, his manager was my agent, and I'm still with, believe it or not, that agency today.

I think that's impressive in this business. Same thing goes for your longstanding relationship with MCA. Is it just a matter of mutual respect?

Well, for me, they're the greatest for me. I don't know what they think of me, but, I think of them being the greatest company for me, because they're all around the world, and I travel around the world quite often. So any place I'm there, there's always a representative from the company, and some product. Ah, I never asked them what they thought of me. [laughs]

They must like you pretty well.

I hope so. We're not that big operation like a lot of the rap or rock or soul people would be. Our demands are small. In so many ways, we're not always in the red. So I guess that's another reason, meaning that, if I was demanding much, I imagine, being a blues singer, they'd probably would have cut me loose a long time ago. But our demands are small, and I guess there's a reason for that, because we're not like Simply Red or some of the big artists, The Rolling Stones, that can generate that monumental mound of success, if you will.

What do you see in the future for blues? Blues "revivals" seem to come and go, but do you foresee any changes or things you'd like to see?

It's startin' to be, but I sometimes take a little bit of issue with "resurgence," because I've been tryin' to play professionally for 45 years, and it's never been as popular as it is today. Never been, since I've been tryin' to play it. So, a lot of the people that started to play it maybe in the '50s and '60s like the rock players, wasn't blues players anyway; they just played some blues. And so to a lot of people that's like it's left and it's now comin' back. But it's just that some of the rock players, which was most popular anyway, sort of like when they played, what's that old sayin', when this company speak, people listen'. I forget the commercial . . .

E.F. Hutton.

Yeah. When they speak, people listen. So when the rock player spoke, people listen. But when they didn't, they thought it wasn't bein' played anymore. So today, some of them, maybe, there's a resurgence for some of them. But the blues has always been there.

I think, though, that what is happening is a lot of the young people are payin' attention to it today, and they're supportin' it. And they're not ashamed of it; they're not afraid to speak up for it and let it be known. But as popular as some of the blues players are, or as popular as some people credit me with being, we still don't have blues shows every day like you do rock, rap, and soul.

In your city, which is a big city, you may have one show now and then that plays some blues, but the average city don't have a blues show. So however popular we may seem to be, we're not until we can be recognized and have shows like everybody else.

In one hundred or two hundred years from now when people look back at your work and your career, how do you think you'd best like to be remembered?

Well, I would like to be remembered as a guy that tried, and did the best he could do, and liked to be thought of as a good neighbor—a friend next door. One you could trust.

THE LEGACY: KEEP THE HAMMER DOWN (1996)
CHARLES SAWYER

King's biographer considers his legacy.

You better not look down
If you want to keep on flying.
You can keep it movin'
If you don't look down.

You better not look back
Or you might just end up crying.
Put the hammer down
And keep it full speed ahead.

[From "Better Not Look Down" by Joe Sample and Will Jennings, Irving Music, Inc., Four Nights Music Company, BMI]

When I wrote "The Once and Future King," the chapter speculating on what the future held for B.B. King, the most tantalizing question was whether or not he would ascend to the level of stardom that transcends time, place, and generation, where the likes of Charlie Chaplin, Marlene Dietrich, Enrico Caruso, Charlie Parker, Elvis Presley, Josephine Baker, and Louis Armstrong dwell for all time. There was the prospect that he might assume the mantle of Louis Armstrong as America's Musical Goodwill Ambassador to the world. Would fate call on him to take up this role as America's cultural representative? Would he carry this part of our heritage to the world responsibly and with the dignity of a diplomat? There was a specter, too, the specter of self-doubt which had been the cornerstone of his art. Even if fate so called him, there was this ever-present gulch into which he could slip or even throw himself.

The answers are much clearer now, fifteen years later. As we watch him press on with no concession to his age, we are witnessing the concluding act of this drama. His every performance shows that he is ready and eager to accept Armstrong's mantle, his every new honor validates him as Armstrong's heir.

Since 1980, B.B. King has received many and diverse honors as his star has continued to rise—honors from academia, the recording industry, television, his home state of Mississippi, and the White House, with a tip of the hat from Hollywood. Some have descended on him predictably, while others have required strange turns of events, like the one that took him to the White House.

Now that he is a pop star, and not only a blues legend, the most popular television programs write him into their scripts. Fast food chains and international airlines compete for his endorsements. The first of the chain of blues clubs that bear his name opened in Memphis, in 1991. This helped spark the revival of the very Beale Street that nurtured his raw talent 50 years ago, launched him toward stardom, and now claims him as its icon. Memphis is now known as the hometown of *both* Elvis and B.B. King.

All this has been accomplished in spite of a conspicuous absence of hit records and sustained airplay—the chicken and egg riddle of the record business. A popular musician who becomes a transcendent star without a string of hit records is almost as improbable as a movie star with no hit movies. Imagine Humphrey Bogart without a box office bonanza, Eugene O'Neill without a Broadway hit, or Kurt Vonnegut without a single book that appeared near the top of the best seller list.

How has B.B. achieved the tremendous success and worldwide popularity he enjoys in 1995? What has he done with his celebrity? And, what, indeed, is the legacy of B.B. King? The answers to these questions all go back to his character, and his history.

The most important factor in B.B. King's success is that he has avoided giving in to self-doubt and falling victim to the consequent ruin that claims so many; and he has done so by remaining true to his character as it was formed by the time he left the Mississippi Delta. He has secured his self-esteem day after day through hard work and fidelity to the same values he has practiced all his life. Like planter Johnson Barrett he never lost sight of his responsibilities to his dependents and employees. Taking on the responsibilities of stardom, he has handled the extraordinary pressure of celebrity with grace and nerves of steel.

But he has also grown into his success. He has grown as an artist, collaborating with respected jazz, rock and country artists as well as other blues greats. He has become an entrepreneur, licensing franchises for B.B. King Blues Clubs. He has tried to return to society some of the good it has given him by continuing his program of prison concerts and embarking on visits to schools and colleges to talk about the blues and history. Most important, he has steadily broadened and deepened his following, winning them one-by-one, in person. He has relied on his most basic skill as an entertainer, the one he learned from the Sanctified Preacher Fair, leading his listeners through a personal catharsis that binds them to him for life. By playing an average of 250 engagements per year for 46 years, he has conducted roughly 11,500 such group purges. Such a sustained devotion to the music and the audience is with-out equal. Few celebrity performers manage this many appearances a year at their peak, and all, except B.B. King, take vacations. He has proved that you don't need hit records when you visit your constituents in person and touch them in their heart of hearts.

As to be expected, there is a dark side to B.B. King's success. He is now subject to griping, smallminded criticism from purists who fault him for becoming a pop star, instead of staying put as a "pure" blues artist. Also, he has realized with sadness that he will never get back the years of his children's youth, and recognizes the irony that as a father-figure to musicians around the world, he has not been a "good enough" father to his own children, because of his long and constant touring schedule. Though he won his audience with that schedule, he lost the chance to be there, physically, for his children when they were growing up.

How far has B.B. King come in the fifteen years since this book first appeared? Let's start with a sample of his activities in 1994–95. A profile of his schedule, and his recording activities will help to assess where his career stands today. The schedule in the summer of this, the 50th year of his career as an entertainer and the 70th year of his life, is only slightly less demanding than what he braved on the chit'lin' circuit just after "Three O'Clock Blues" reached #1 on the rhythm and blues charts, commonly referred to as the race record charts, in 1952.

July 4	Fraudenau	Vienna, Austria
July 5	Villa Celiomontana	Rome, Italy
July 7	Piazza Duomo	Pistoia, Italy
July 8	Giardini Reale	Torino, Italy
July 9	Palais des Congres	Vittel, France
July 11	Centre de Congres et D'Expos	Montreau, Switzerland
July 14	Contress Centre	The Hague, Holland
July 15	Royal Festival Hall	London, England
July 16	Falkoner Center	Copenhagen, Denmark
July 18	Marco Le Naiadi	Pescara, Italy
July 19	Palazzo Bellini Court	Comacchio, Italy
July 20	Philharmonic Hall	Munich, Germany
July 21	Kirjurinluoto	Pori, Finland
July 22	Stadtpark	Hamburg, Germany
July 23	La Finede Gould	Antibes, France
July 25	Plaza de la Trinidad	San Sebastian, Spain
July 27	Fem de Fond Robert	Chateau Arnoux, France
July 29	MareepoliceLa	Seyne Sur Mer, France
July 30	Theatre de la Nature	Cognac, France
Aug 4	Mt. Hood Jazz Festival	Gresham, Orgeon
Aug 5	The Gorge Amphitheater	George, Washington
Aug 6	The Greek Theatre	Los Angeles, California
Aug 7	Star of the Desert Area	Stateline, Nevada
Aug 9	New Mexico State University Practice Field	Cruces, New Mexico
Aug 11	Shoreline Amphitheater	Mountainview, California
Aug 12	Reno Hilton Amphitheater	Reno, Nevada
Aug 13	Concord Pavilion	Concord, California
Aug 15	Fiddler's Green Amphitheater	Denver, Colorado
Aug 17	Starlight Amphitheater	Kansas City, Missouri
Aug 18	Mark of the Quad Cities	Moline, Illinois
Aug 20	Great Woods	Boston, Massachusetts
Aug 21	Tanglewood Performing Arts	Tanglewood, Massachusetts
Aug 22	Wolftrap	Vienna, Virginia
Aug 23	Fox	Detroit, Michigan
Aug 24	Kingswood Music Theater	Toronto, Canada
Aug 25	Connecticut Center for Performing Arts	Hartford, Connecticut
Aug 27	Blockbuster Sony Music Entertainment Center	Camden, New Jersey
Aug 30	Paramount Theater	New York City
Sept 1	Fox	St. Louis, Missouri
Sept 2	Hawthorne Racetrack	Chicago, Illinois

Sept 3	Minnesota State Fair	St. Paul, Minnesota
Sept 7	Riverbend Music Center	Cincinnati, Ohio
Sept 8	Mud Island Amphitheater	Memphis, Tennessee
Sept 9	Riverfront Park	Nashville, Tennessee
Sept 10	Horse Park	Lexington, Kentucky
Sept 15	TBA	Raleigh, North Carolina
Sept 16	Chastine Park	Atlanta, Georgia

This slice of B.B. King's schedule, beginning in Vienna on July 4th and ending on September 16th in Atlanta, Georgia, on his 70th birthday—46 concerts over a 73-day period, covering 20 states and 11 countries—underscores two defining characteristics of his life as a professional musician: his extraordinary stamina, coupled with his sense of mission. Ever since he left Memphis B.B. King has lived by a motto in the words of a song Joe Sample and Will Jennings wrote for his 1979 album, "Take It Home." The song is "Better Not Look Down" and the motto is "Put the Hammer Down and Keep It Full Speed Ahead." [In slang the "hammer" is the throttle of an airplane or truck.]

Between Europe in July and America in August and September B.B. had a scant four days to recharge his batteries. The American tour, with three other major blues acts on the bill was known as "Blues Music Festival 95." Attendees began watching and listening in the hot sun and finished late in the evening under the stars. The lineup was formidable: Jimmy Vaughn, brother of the late Steve Ray Vaughn and guitarists of the Fabulous Thunderbirds; Etta James; and Blues Time, featuring J. Geils, Magic Dick and Elvin Bishop, guitarist in the original Paul Butterfield Band. This annual touring festival is the contemporary counterpart of the Rhythm and Blues tour of the 1950's that might have featured Willie Mae "Big Mama" Thornton, Lowell Fulson, Little Milton and Nappy Brown, just to mention a few. In those days the black neighborhoods would be festooned with yellow posters studded with photos of the artists for weeks in advance. The difference between the tours of those days and this modern version is the venues. Gone from the itinerary are the temples of black culture, the Howard, the Royal, and the Regal Theaters; gone are the large capacity nightclubs of the ghetto, places like the Burning Spear in Chicago, or the Flame Showbar of Detroit. In their places are Great Woods near Boston; Tanglewood, the summer home of the Boston Symphony; the Paramount Theater in Midtown Manhattan, and the Reno Hilton Amphitheater.

The change in his audience has left B.B. King feeling ambivalent. He has achieved his mission to bring blues into the mainstream, but young black listeners barely seem to notice this piece of their culture. When the black press asked him if he considered that blacks have deserted the blues, he replied that whatever you may call it, neglecting the blues and leaving it entirely to others to practice and appreciate amounts to just that.

When my book first appeared B.B. King's discography listed 65 albums. That number has grown. And today record producers for other artists know that the name "B.B. King" on their albums will boost sales. For instance, the 1995 Manhattan Transfer album, "Tonin'," (Atlantic) had B.B. playing guitar on "The Thrill Is Gone," with Ruth Brown and Janis Siegel singing lead vocals. On "Lifetimes" (Warner Brothers), by Peter, Paul and Mary, B.B. plays guitar and sings with Mary Travis on "House Of The Rising Sun." An all-star anthology devoted to the memory of songwriter Doc Pomus, "Till The Night Is Gone: A Tribute to Doc Pomus" (Forward/Rhino), includes B.B. King singing and playing guitar on "Blinded By Love."

The latest B.B. King recording, "Lucille and Friends," released in Europe in June, 1995, is a compilation of his collaboration with major artists from blues, jazz, and pop over the past 25 years. The list of artists and songs read like a Who's Who of the best known from each genre.

John Lee Hooker	"You Shook Me"
Bobby Bland	"Let The Good Times Roll"
Robert Cray	"Playin' With My Friends"
Albert Collins	"Frosty"
The Crusaders	"Better Not Look Down"
Dr. John, Gary Wright, Ringo Starr	"Ghetto Woman"
Leon Russell, Joe Walsh	"Hummingbird"
Mick Fleetwood, Stevie Nicks	"Can't Get Enough"
U2	"When Love Comes To Town"
Grover Washington Jr.	"Caught A Touch Of Your Love"
Gary Moore	"Since I Left You Baby"
Branford Marsalis	"B.B.'s Blues"
Vernon Reid	"All You Ever Gave Me Was The Blues"
Stevie Wonder	"To Know You Is To Love You"

1995 has been a good television year for B.B. King as well. He joined Jimmy Vaughn, Robert Cray, Eric Clapton, Bonnie Raitt, Dr. John, Buddy Guy and Art Neville in a special production of "Austin City Limits," a showcase for country and blues-rock artists, in tribute to Stevie Ray

Vaughn. At the 25th Essence Awards devoted to stars of color, broadcast on the Fox Network, he sang a duet of "Rock Me Baby" with Michael Bolton and led the finale of "Let The Good Times Roll" with the entire cast. On September 1, 1995, the Arts and Entertainment Network showed a one-hour concert shot during the recording of the B.B. King album "Blues Summit."

In other television action during 1995 B.B. King continued to be a reliable cameo character in the most popular sitcoms and action drama shows. Network producers have found over the years that B.B. King is a kind of uncle to all of America and that a television show can boost its ratings by writing B.B. King into their scripts. "Baywatch," America's most popular action-drama series, worked him into the scenario of an episode, as did "The Bill Cosby Show," "Blossom," and "General Hospital." These appearances, perhaps more than any other facet of B.B.'s career during the last decade, attest to the fact that B.B. King is more than a pop star. He has achieved a status that few entertainers can claim—to be part of the American family. He has become an icon that stands for something all Americans can relate to and claim for their own. This could be said not just for Americans but for the rest of the world as well.

B.B. King is, in the truest sense, a citizen of the world. In 1994 he ran the string of countries he has visited and played up to 58. A spring tour in Europe included a swing through the newly independent Baltic states of Lithuania and Latvia. Earlier in the year Brazilians flocked to see and hear him. He sold out the 3,000 capacity theater in Buenos Aires seven times for a total gate of 21,000. In Sao Paulo, he sold out the Bourbon Street Nightclub three times, and in Montevideo, Uruguay, he sold out the Plaza Theater and sent representatives of his record label scrambling when the stores ran out of stock of all his recordings.

The Spring 1994 Far Eastern Tour brought B.B. King to a place where the press customarily awaits photo opportunities with world leaders and statesmen. This time it was not a photo of an American President standing on the Great Wall of China that flashed around the world on Reuters wire service, it was a picture of B.B. King atop the ancient wall, cradling Lucille in his arms, waving triumphantly. The engagement that brought him to China was the official opening of the Beijing Hard Rock Cafe—an oxymoron if there ever was one. Ten or twenty years ago the idea of such a venue would have seemed as implausible as a date at the Whisky A Go

Go in Vatican City, or the Baghdad B'nai Brith. To add to the sense of the surreal, two nights before the Beijing gig B.B. played the Hard Rock Cafe in the capital of the "other China," Taiwan. But as Somerset Maugham put it so succinctly, "nothing is too rum [strange] to be true." Still, it is not surprising that one of the earliest commercial products to appear in the new markets of China would be American pop music. And the choice of B.B. King to open in Beijing confirms his stature as elder statesman for the blues, America's unofficial, but immensely important Musical Ambassador of Good Will, a post once held by Louis Armstrong but vacant since his death in 1971.

The dates in the two China's were part of a Far East tour that took him to four Australian cities, plus Hong Kong, Singapore, and seven cities in Japan—18 concerts in 26 days.

Most artists and performers have a special place in their trophy cases and in their hearts for awards given them by their peers. For musicians this is a Grammy. B.B. has seven of them, total, but one stands out above the rest, his Lifetime Achievement Grammy Award. The National Academy of Recording Arts and Sciences established the award in 1962 to recognize performers "who, during their lifetimes, have made creative contributions of outstanding artistic significance to the field of recording." It requires a two-thirds vote of the Board of Trustees. In 1987 when B.B. King received his gold and ebony plaque from the Academy, his fellow honorees were jazz saxophonist Benny Carter, Enrico Caruso, Ray Charles, Fats Domino, Woody Herman, Billie Holiday, Igor Stravinsky, Arturo Toscanini, and Hank Williams, Sr.

Among this impressive list of ten, two honorees, Fats Domino and Ray Charles, are musical peers of B.B. King. One thing sets him apart from these two, and that is the scarcity of his hit records. According to the best research volume on the subject of hit records, *Top 40 Hits (1955–1992)*, by Joel Whitburn (Billboard Books, New York, 1992) Fats Domino had 37 hit records, during his career, 21 of which reached the top 20, and Ray Charles had 33, 17 of which went to #20 or higher. Compare this with B.B. King's entry which lists six records, only one of which, "The Thrill Is Gone," reached the top-20 at #15 on the Pop Chart (#1 on the R&B Chart) in 1970. In the record industry hit records are the coin of the realm, and yet here is B.B. King, elevated alongside Fats, and Brother Ray, with only one Pop Chart hit among all the songs he has recorded, many, many of which were hits on the R&B Chart and some of which registered in the middle and lower tiers of the Pop Chart. This calls for an explanation.

Why hit records have eluded him so consistently is simple—blues records do not get the kind of steady airplay on large-market, commercial radio stations that is needed to make such hits. Of course you can hear blues music on the radio, but throughout most of B.B.'s career the blues listening audience has been neatly circumscribed on the airwaves. *Blues* radio programs play blues records, and those programs are not generally heard on the big commercial stations.

Although popular entertainers may regard the record charts as the show business equivalent of the Dow Jones Industrial Average, B.B. found other ways to reach the truly vast audiences that comprise the pop music market besides records sales and airplay. In the 70's he broadened his audience dramatically when he joined the Rolling Stones on their U.S. tour. This put him in front of audiences whose demographics gave new meaning to the term "crossover." The late 1980's brought two new opportunities comparably powerful in granting him access to new listeners, one a tour to rival the Stones tour of the 70's, the other a gig with the Prez, the one who lives at 1600 Pennsylvania Avenue, Washington, D.C. In both cases there was an element of luck, but the key ingredient was the reverence he inspired in the hearts of a few who could invite him to the party.

In 1987 the Irish rock group U2 was arguably the world's most popular rock and roll musical group. In the spring of that year they had two #1 hits. How they came to adopt B.B. as their musical spiritual father is the stuff of show biz legends. Just before B.B. King took the stage to play a concert in Dublin, Ireland, his manager, Sid Seidenberg, told him that U2 would be attending. "A group of the magnitude of U2! Oh God!" B.B. told *Melody Maker* (Jan. 29, 1990). "I was really, really nervous. I tried not to think about it on stage . . . When I go to the dressing room, I'm told U2 is here. 'Oh, God, they were here.' They seemed to be kind of in awe of me, and I was just as nervous, meeting them. We had a nice chat, and I said to Bono, 'Sometime when you're writing a song, will you think of me?'"

The result of that conversation was a song named "When Love Comes To Town," which B.B. King performed for the first time with U2 in Texas on the "Joshua Tree" tour. B.B. was then invited to join U2 for the closing concert of the tour in Arizona. This, in turn, lead to two big breaks for B.B.—he was featured in the documentary film about U2 on tour, "Rattle And Hum," and the accompanying album and video by the same name; and he was invited to join U2 as the opening act on a four-month world tour in the fall of 1989, which took them to Australia, New Zealand, Japan, Germany, Ireland, and Holland. During these four months B.B. King spread the gospel of blues to vast rock audiences ordinarily well beyond his reach. U2 introduced B.B. King to their fans in terms that made it clear that they were privileged to be in the presence of musical royalty.

U2 treated B.B. like royalty, too. Near the beginning of the tour in September they gave B.B. a surprise 64th birthday party on a luxury yacht in Sydney Harbor, Australia. He described his emotional response to this special honor to *Melody Maker* (op. cit.) this way. "Sid [B.B.'s manager] said, 'U2 is going fishing with me, would you like to come?' . . . We get there and they got this beautiful yacht, and they've invited people that was working with us, about 40, 50 people, I guess. So I get on the yacht, and I'm still thinking that we're just going fishing.

"Once we started to leave the dock, then they started letting out balloons and singing happy birthday. They hired a band to play for me, and we jammed and sang and had a lot of fun. And Bono sang a song he wrote for me, 'Happy Birthday BB King,' and it was so good, I cried. I couldn't hold back the tears.

"We came back in at sunset, and I thought it was all over. We'd had such a wonderful time. Then I saw one of greatest fireworks displays I've ever seen, and it was in my honor, so I cried some more." [*Melody Maker*, op. cit.]

The U2/BB King "package" consisted of four elements: a tour; a film, "Rattle And Hum," and an album by the same name; a single record, "When Love Comes To Town;" and a video which got extended airplay on MTV. Suddenly, all those years in recording studios searching for a song that would get the airplay that would make him a hit record were behind him. Suddenly, he had airplay of a kind that dwarfs the exposure offered by radio—he was a star on MTV. A single play of the video on MTV reached millions of viewers/listeners. In September, 1989, the video "When Love Comes To Town" won the MTV best-video-from-film award.

The packaging of U2 and B.B. King had an immediate impact on B.B.'s audience that could be seen at every concert. Now the crowds chanted "B B B B, B B B B, . . ." This chant was completely new. The ebb and flow of audience energy levels changed, too. B.B. King is the master of working the cycle of tension and release repeated to higher and higher peaks. As his audience grew to include more rock fans the troughs between the peaks became less dramatic. The new fans refused to let go so completely and willingly as the seasoned blues fans in the crowd.

How people in the far corners of the world learn about artists like B.B. King is a curious process. The *avant garde,* the *aficionados* of a genre, seem to learn about them despite the great odds. They find their sources through travelers, short wave broadcasts, friends in the diplomatic corps, airline employees, any way imaginable. But until a tidal wave of popularity lifts an artist up and carries him across borders and boundaries, the rest of the world waits. I had a chance to see, first hand, how this process worked in the case of B.B. King on two visits I made to Bulgaria—the first a few years before U2 adopted him, and the second, not long afterward.

In 1986 I visited Bulgarian National Television on the invitation of a television producer who had seen the English edition of this book. Over dinner we had hatched the idea for a fifteen minute program introducing B.B. King through commentary, photos from the book, and music from tape cassettes I carried with me. The music presented a problem, as there was no obvious way to feed the tracks from my Walkman onto the audio track in the control room. We set out in the sprawling complex to find the right hardware. Wherever we inquired, no one knew who B.B. King was and no one was interested to help, until we came to the studio where foreign language films were dubbed, where a bearded technician wondered aloud what we were doing there. When he understood our problem, he snapped into a posture of keen mobilization and declared "*B.B. King!* I'm going to stick to you like a postage stamp until you accomplish your mission." The technician, it turned out, was a devoted fan of B.B. King. He brought us into an equipment storage room and produced a Nagra cine sound recorder, which he connected to the Walkman with wires and alligator clips. Then he cranked up the volume and took a spot right in front of the speakers. A look of sublime pleasure came onto his face as he closed his eyes and drank in the sound of B.B. King.

Alas, the program was produced but never aired, for political reasons. The videotape was erased on orders from the department chief, who had been on vacation when the segment was shot. When she returned and found that one of her subordinates had produced a piece featuring an unknown American journalist reporting about an unknown American entertainer, she couldn't take the risk of broadcasting it. At that time and place things American were still suspect. Perhaps if it had been Kurt

Vonnegut, presenting a lesser known author, or if I had been commenting on Nat King Cole, the risk in running the piece would have been less because any challenge could have been answered by the world renown of one half of the combination. As it was she felt that just possibly she could lose her job, which would mean losing her career. I had seen talented and dedicated professionals lose everything when less obvious risks had been challenged by the authorities.

On a return trip to Bulgaria in 1989, I was sipping coffee in a Sofia household when I heard the unmistakable sound of Lucille floating up from the radio on the kitchen table. I was astonished! What had happened in the meantime, I wondered, to make B.B. King a safe addition to the local play list? Had the political climate really changed so much? No, The Berlin Wall was still standing and Todor Zhivkov, President of Bulgaria, was right where he had been for 35 years. As I listened the answer became apparent: this was "When Love Comes To Town," the new song by U2 *with* B.B. King. It was U2's universal popularity that explained the sound I heard, not any political development, nor change in B.B.'s recognition in this far corner of the globe.

During the decade and a half since 1980 B.B. King has added five Grammy Awards, not counting his Lifetime Achievement, to the Grammy he won in 1970 for "Thrill Is Gone" in the Best R&B Vocal (Male) category:

1981	Best Ethnic or Traditional Recording, "There Must Be A Better World Somewhere"
1983	Best Traditional Blues Recording, "Blues 'n' Jazz"
1985	Best Traditional Blues Recording, "My Guitar Sings The Blues" from "Six Silver Strings" album
1990	Best Traditional Blues Recording, "Live at San Quentin"
1991	Best Traditional Blues Album, "Live at the Apollo"

The evolution of Grammy categories shows the struggle of the Academy to adjust to changes in the musical terrain. The categories for Rhythm & Blues, Folk Music, and Ethnic Music went through many changes and blues floated between them, before distinct categories for blues, per se, were created, starting in 1982 when the Grammy for Best Traditional Blues was created. In the 1950's the Academy seemed confused even as to what comprised R&B. In 1958, for example, The Champs beat Harry Belafonte for Best R&B Performance with their recording of "Tequila." By 1960 R&B was a suitable for Muddy Waters to be nominated for an award in that category. In 1961 they added Gospel as a distinct category. In the mid-1960's R&B was a catch-all for artists like Aretha Franklin, Ray Charles, Lou Rawls, and Sam and Dave, and to accommodate the diverse talent the category was split into several categories, e.g. Best R&B Group, Best R&B Duo, Best R&B Vocal (Male and Female). In 1970, the year B.B. King won for Best Male R&B with "Thrill Is Gone," the new Ethnic or Traditional Recording category became a shibboleth for Urban Blues. The award for this category went to T-Bone Walker the first year and Muddy Waters the next two years. It was in this category that B.B. got his 1981 Grammy. Then, in 1982, the Academy created the Traditional Blues category, followed in 1988 by a further division into Best Traditional Blues Recording and Best Contemporary Blues Recording. At last the Academy had recognized blues as a distinct form and style with its traditional artists and its innovators. Many artists besides B.B. King helped to win this status—people like Robert Cray, Etta James, Stevie Ray Vaughn—but nobody's contribution exceeds his. In part, the Academy awarded the Lifetime Grammy to B.B. King for legitimating those categories.

Politics brought about the other great turn of events that gave B.B. King a visibility way beyond that of King of the Blues. Politicians often seek to boost their appeal to the public by rubbing shoulders with rock stars, movie actors and actresses, even the giants of classical music. And vice versa. Less common is the politician who uses high office to bring great and deserving artists further into the mainstream by showcasing their work at political gatherings. Yet one politician used the bully pulpit of the White House to do precisely this for B.B. King. Before 1989 if one tried to write a script placing B.B. King on-stage at the Kennedy Center for the Performing Arts to celebrate the end of a new President's first year in office, the role of President would surely have been cast as a liberal Democrat, probably from a Southern state. Perhaps he would have had a black vice president, as I postulated in 1980. The idea that the President might be from an aristocratic New England family and a conservative Republican would have been beyond belief.

Yet, real life drama often exceeds our wildest imagination. So it was that George Herbert Walker Bush, forty-first President of the United States, chose B.B. King to entertain the "Eagles," a group of 800 of his wealthiest supporters who gathered at the Kennedy Center to celebrate his first year in office. Seven months before, in June of 1989, B.B. had met and talked with President Bush in the Oval Office. A photo run by *Jet* magazine shows the two of them standing in front of a mantelpiece as B.B. presents President Bush with a Lucille model Gibson guitar.

Behind this improbable turn of events is the story of a southern white boy who loved rhythm and blues. This aggressive, ambitious boy, born in 1951 in Atlanta, Georgia, son of an insurance claims adjuster and a school teacher, grew up to be a man of widely recognized political skills, questionable campaign ethics, and unfettered admiration for his black musical heroes. His name was Lee Atwater.

As a teenager in Columbia, South Carolina, Atwater played guitar in his own rock band, The Upsetters Revue, and as an adult, kept on playing the music he loved. In 1974 he opened a business as a political consultant, advising candidates on how to win elections. In four years he helped 28 Republican candidates win election to local offices.

In 1978 Lee Atwater managed the successful re-election campaign of Strom Thurmond, U.S. Senator from South Carolina. Thurmond began political life as a Democrat, but bolted the party in 1948 when he led several southern delegations in a walk-out from the Democratic (presidential) nominating convention in protest over the party's position on civil rights. He founded his own party, The States' Rights Democratic Party, dedicated to preserving the political system of the segregationist South, then ran for President, and lost the election to Harry S Truman. Later he joined the Republicans. As director of Thurmond's senatorial campaign, Atwater gained a reputation as the master of negative campaigning—expert at discrediting his opponents by innuendo based on half-truths. His association with Thurmond was his stepping-stone into national politics.

In 1984 Atwater directed the Reagan/Bush campaign, and in 1987 George Bush chose him to run his campaign for President. Bush won the election and appointed Atwater chairman of the Republican National Committee, making him head political strategist for the party in control of the world's most powerful government.

Atwater wasted no time using his newly won power to showcase his musical idols. The most conspicuous of his efforts was a gala party for young Republicans campaigners, billed as a "Special Tribute to Rhythm And Blues Artists." The affair was held at the Washington, D.C., Convention Center, the night after Bush's inauguration, and featured Bo Diddley, Percy Sledge, Sam Moore (of "Sam And Dave"), Albert Collins, Eddie Floyd, Steve Cropper, Donald "Duck" Dunn, Dr. John, Delbert McClinton, Koko Taylor, Willie Dixon, William Bell, Jimmie and Stevie

Ray Vaughn, Joe Cocker, Billy Preston, Carla Thomas, and Chuck Jackson. When Bush arrived at the party Atwater took the stage and ripped into a version of "Hi-Heel Sneakers," backed up by Carla Thomas, Sam Moore, Percy Sledge, Chuck Jackson, Joe Cocker and Billy Preston. Later President Bush was called on stage to accept a white Fender Stratocaster embossed with "The Prez," presented to him by Sam Moore. The following morning readers of American newspapers saw a photo of their patrician President, wearing a goofy grin and holding his new Fender.

As a guitar player and blues lover Atwater naturally had a special admiration for B.B. King, for whom he saved the best honors he had to bestow, starting with a gig at one of the grand inauguration balls held the night the new President was installed in office, followed a few months later by lunch at the White House, and capped the next January by the Eagles' party at the Kennedy Center.

To be so honored fulfilled a lifetime dream for B.B. King. In American society there are few forms of respectability that can compare to a Presidential command performance and none that can exceed it, and, thus for B.B. King, who had waged a lifelong campaign to make blues music popular with the general public, and, above all, respected as an important part of our heritage, lunch at the White House represented everything he had struggled to achieve for his special piece of American culture, the blues.

The connection between B.B. King and Lee Atwater went far beyond these ceremonial events. They were friends and collaborators. Atwater took the bandstand to play beside his idol at every opportunity and B.B. welcomed him with enthusiasm. Atwater was representative of the legions of musicians who sooner or later drop the idea going professional, and choose another line of work, a "day job." Usually it's a less withering way of making a living, but in Atwater's case, it was just another form of show business—national politics.

This contingent of the music audience, the day job crowd, exerts an influence on popular tastes that should not be dismissed lightly. As the core of enthusiastic listeners, day-jobber musicians affect booking policy in clubs, and are very often to be found at the tables near the edge of the stage. They are a formidable presence at the bins in the record stores. Often they serve as freelance reviewers for newspapers and entertainment guides that cannot afford staff reviewers. Some continue to play on weekends and at jams. All such players continue living out their dreams in the imagination. Lee Atwater's day job happened to be in the White House, and his boss happened to be the chief executive. His power and notoriety gave him the chance to make those fantasies real. His brash style of politics was mirrored in his musical style. He struck outrageous poses, strutted like a bantam rooster, put every move he knew, and some he didn't know, into his playing.

If anyone doubted that Lee Atwater was serious about his music, those doubts vanished when he released an album called "Red, Hot And Blue" on Curb Records, featuring himself with Carla Thomas, Isaac Hayes, Sam Moore, Chuck Jackson, and, of course, B.B. King, who got co-billing with Atwater. The appearance of the President's political advisor on an R&B album was enough, in itself, to bring much attention to its release. As Robert Hilburn wrote in his review of the album for the *Los Angeles Times* (April 5, 1990, Sec. F, page 8) "The most entertaining thing about this ensemble salute to spicy Memphis-style '50s and '60s R&B is the way it lets you surprise your friends. Play a selection such as 'Knock on Wood' or 'Bad Boy' for someone without identifying the singer, then watch their eyes bulge when you reveal that it's the controversial national chairman of the Republican Party . . . Lee Atwater." The reviewer's summary critical judgment of Atwater, the musician, was, "Better than a singer in an average bar band . . . more convincing than such other celebrity pop figures as, say, the Blues Brothers." The two stars awarded to the album seemed to say *better than poor, not quite good.* [It should be said that getting two stars from the *L.A. Times* reviewer is far beyond the realistic expectations of most day-job musicians, should they ever get the chance to release an album.] About Atwater the musician B.B. is both honest and generous. He was careful to distinguish him from the average wannabe: Atwater could make a living as a musician, B.B. insisted, but instead music was his hobby. "Some people like to play tennis and some like to jog. He enjoys playing the blues. And he's very good." (*Jet*, March 17, 1989, page 57) The Grammy nominating committee thought the title track from the album worthy of a nomination.

Lee Atwater was not the sort of man to be content with one album of music, any more than he would have been content with a one-term presidency for his boss in the Oval Office, but fate had a harsh surprise in store for him. Just when all his ambitions had become realities and he was in his prime, he collapsed at the podium during a speaking engagement and was rushed to a hospital. Eventually he was diagnosed with a malignant brain tumor. He accepted the challenge of his illness with the same fierce, fighting spirit he brought to every political campaign he ever waged.

As the tumor grew he opted for the most hazardous radiation treatment available, in which pellets of radium were thrust into the affected part of his brain, making his brain tissue radioactive. But it wasn't enough to stop the growth. Finally, after a hard-fought battle he succumbed on March 29, 1991. He was 40 years old. B.B. spoke of his own loss in these strong terms: "I felt as if I lost a son when Stevie Ray Vaughn passed unexpectedly and I feel similarly on the passing of my friend, Lee Atwater." (*Jet,* March 15, 1991)

There is a darker side to the story of Lee Atwater, the hottest Republican hotshot, political hatchet man for the President, which is bound to raise conflicting feelings for anyone who loves B.B. King and who is also politically aware, and that is the role Atwater played in the presidential election campaign of 1988, when he was at his height.

The 1988 campaign was particularly venomous, especially on the topic of race. Throughout most of this century the Republican Party has had little constituency among black Americans. Republican candidates have rarely had to worry that their positions on issues of social policy might lose them black votes. Given the racism that has survived in white America long after the death of Jim Crow (the mythical character who symbolized racial bigotry in America), Republican strategists have often been tempted to play the "race card." The only risk in playing that card lies in alienating white voters who might object to the implied intolerance. Any politician who could find a way to appeal to racist sentiments, without offending liberal-minded voters, would gain support from bigoted white voters who would gladly turn the clock back to a time when Walter Doris, B.B.'s school chum, now deputy sheriff of Montgomery County, Mississippi, would be wearing bib overalls, instead of a badge and gun. American pundits call this the "Bubba vote," after the Southern nickname which is a corruption of the word "brother." It conjures up the image of a red-faced, middle-aged Southern white man driving a pickup truck with a gun-rack across the rear window, a hunting dog in the passenger seat, and a Confederate flag in place of the front license plate.

In the 1988 campaign for President the Republicans found a way to woo the Bubba vote, at little cost in support among more tolerant white voters. It was accomplished under the guise of a tough-on-crime issue. The Democratic candidate for President was Governor Michael Dukakis of Massachusetts, one of the New England states. During Dukakis' term as governor, Massachusetts had a prison furlough program that allowed prisoners, some of them serving long sentences for violent crimes, to leave prison for a few days at a time without supervision, based only on their promise to return. One such prisoner was a man named William Horton, who had been convicted of armed robbery and murder, and sentenced to

life without parole in 1974. Horton had been allowed nine previous fur-
loughs and had always returned, but on June 6, 1986, he left prison on his
tenth furlough and disappeared. Soon the FBI put him on its "Ten Most
Wanted List." Ten months after he "escaped" from prison in
Massachusetts, police in Maryland caught William Horton driving a
stolen car owned by Clifford Barnes, who, with his fiancee, Angela Miller,
had been kidnapped from his home. Barnes had been bound and
assaulted. Miller had been assaulted and raped. Horton was tried and convicted for these new crimes, and was returned to prison, this time at the
State Penitentiary in Maryland.

"Willie" Horton, as he came to be called, offered Republican strategists the chance to charge that Dukakis was so soft on crime that he had
released a violent offender into the community, with a result of assault,
kidnapping, and rape. Television advertisements, paid for by the Bush
campaign and aired across the country, featured a menacing Willie
Horton, hands cuffed behind his back, being led away by the police after
his capture. For any viewer with the slightest trace of racial bigotry,
Horton was their worst nightmare—the crazed, criminal black man who
invades your home, ties you up and rapes your loved one. Another campaign ad showed a line of mostly black prisoners walking near a guard
tower, passing outside the prison walls through a turnstile, suggesting that
leaving prison was as easy as entering the subway. To some voters the message was simple: Dukakis turned this beast loose, rather than keep him in
chains where he rightly belonged, and if you elect him he will turn all their
black asses loose.

The issue of crime in its various guises—"law and order," "safe
streets," "tough on crime"—has been a factor in national elections for
decades, and often it has been recognized as a thinly veiled appeal to the
racism which persists in spite of the great progress since the 1960's. But
never before had the association of crime and race been so conspicuous,
so blatant, so inflammatory as it was in 1988.

The architect of the Bush campaign was Lee Atwater. When political
commentators called the television campaign racist Atwater dismissed the
charges. He wore his combative stand, his win-at-any-cost approach to
waging politics, as a badge of pride. Indeed, he made Lee Atwater the
issue, a brilliant tactical move, since he, not the candidate, took all the
heat. In private he boasted that he had made Willie Horton into Dukakis'
Vice Presidential running mate. When the campaign was over and Bush
was President-elect, the country was more racially divided than it had
been since the days of the civil rights struggles of the 1960's. It seemed

unlikely that we would have the "kinder, gentler nation" that Bush had promised as the fruit of his presidency.

Black Americans were quick to express their feelings about Atwater and his effect on American politics. Soon after Bush took office, Atwater joined the Board of Trustees of Howard University, the country's leading black university in Washington, D.C. Atwater was genuinely enthusiastic about the appointment and was eager to use his fund-raising talents on behalf of the university, but his appointment was short-lived. The students were so angered by his selection to the Board that 200 of them occupied Howard's administration building in protest. Atwater resigned.

There is an odd coincidence in all this which seems to symbolize how race continues to plague American politics and how out-of-the-way places provide the political scene with its most influential characters. South Carolina's old segregationist warrior, Strom Thurmond, discovers South Carolina's new master of negative campaigning, Lee Atwater, who discovers the escaped murderer, Willie Horton, born in Chesterfield, South Carolina, just six months after his own birth, and converts him into the ideal instrument to appeal to racist sentiments in the quest for the highest office. Thurmond was among the political celebrities attending Atwater's gala inaugural celebration that featured his favorite soul singers. Thurmond's skin is like parchment, his dyed-red hairline is the obvious result of a transplant and his face is a mask. The sight of this octogenarian war-horse of the Old South applauding the National Chairman, who was doing splits on stage and singing "Diddy-wah-diddy," sitting among a throng of young politicos, most of whom were not yet born when he first took a seat in the U.S. Senate, was a testament to how very strange are the juxtapositions of American politics.

The public friendship between Lee Atwater and B.B. King is another strange juxtaposition that may cause discomfort to some of B.B.'s admirers. B.B.'s great achievement is a triumph over racism and his contribution to American culture is the preservation of the blues form and its elevation to a plateau of high respect alongside jazz as a unique American art form. But questions are bound to come up. Was it a compromise of his art and accomplishment to lend his prestige to a political figure known for his toxic effect on race relations? Did B.B. King, knowingly or not, seem to acquit his powerful admirer by inviting him on-stage to trade licks? Did Lee Atwater use B.B. King to distract attention from his role as the man who made race an issue in a presidential campaign?

These are troubling questions and very unpleasant at best, but they must be addressed in fairness to B.B. King. To dismiss them or never to raise them would be to taint any summary of his life achievement. A look back at how he has handled celebrity may shed some light on the subject. From the beginning when celebrity in the white world rushed upon him in the late 1960's he has carefully and skillfully avoided politics. For example, on his first real exposure to the white press in New York around 1968 he was asked "What do you think of Ronald Reagan and what do you think of the Black Panthers?" in one breath, no less. "Well, I hear the Panthers feed breakfast to poor children and anyone who does that can't be as bad as they are made out to be," he answered, "and I think that Reagan was a pretty good movie actor." So much for any attempt to push him into politics.

To B.B. King the idea that he might reject the friendship of anyone who is so obviously and sincerely devoted to R&B, soul and blues music because his political career is "seen by some to be antithetical to minority interests," as described in the *L.A. Times* (op. cit.), would be absurd. He is not one to let politics—or race—dictate his choice of friends. It would run contrary to his most basic values on friendship and music. Isaac Hayes, who co-produced six of the songs on the Atwater/King CD, "Red, Hot and Blue," was asked if he thought it was appropriate for Atwater to join the recording scene. He laughed at the notion that there was anything wrong.

"First of all, music should be for all people," Hayes told the *L.A. Times* (op cit). "It should be free: No one should put a tag on music and say who's to like what. If it suits your fancy, you embrace it, and that's what that little boy from South Carolina did. I don't see it having anything to do with party affiliation."

And what would be the result if B.B. King had rejected Atwater's friendship? Blues would not have gone to lunch at the White House. Blues would not have been honored at the Kennedy Center. Blues would not have been featured at the President's Inauguration. Blues would not have been featured at the 1992 Republican nominating convention when B.B. King played a concert in honor of Atwater's memory. In short, he would have lost a chance to bring the unique respect and recognition bestowed by 1600 Pennsylvania Avenue to the music he has campaigned for, for forty years, not to mention the friendship he would not have enjoyed had he chosen to spurn his young admirer because of his politics.

And finally, as for Lee Atwater, his devotion to the music rings true in every respect. Whatever political gain he might have realized from associating with B.B. King, it doesn't diminish his good deed in elevating soul, blues, and B.B. King to new heights of respectability, nor does it dilute his sincerity. And let it be said that in promoting soul, blues and B.B. King, in particular, Atwater, paradoxically, did something positive for race relations in America. Doubtless the friendly association of Atwater and many of the best black artists is strong testimony to the power of music to transcend all differences however great they may be.

In the end, long after history has forgotten Lee Atwater, B.B. King will be remembered as the greatest blues artist of his generation and blues will be celebrated along with jazz as an American original, and a great contribution to world culture.

A complete account of B.B. King's step by step ascent to the highest level of American idols would be incomplete without mentioning several lesser honors he accumulated during the decade and a half of the 1980's and 1990's.

- In November of 1991 the City Council of Jackson, Mississippi, named a stretch of Interstate 95 the "B.B. King Freeway." Now, every day in the state of Mississippi, whose flag still bears the stars and bars of the secessionist Confederate States of America, founded to preserve the institution of slavery, cars drive along a freeway highway named after a native son, B.B. King, grandson of the Mississippi slave, Pomp Davidson.
- The front page of the *New York Times* on June 11, 1983, carried an article describing a reception in honor of B.B. King, held in his home town of Indianola, Mississippi. The *Times* cited his contribution to improving race relations in a place where, fifty years before, the killing of a black man by a white might attract scant recognition from the authorities.
- Berklee College of Music, widely regarded as one of the country's leading conservatories of jazz, and Rhodes College in Memphis, Tennessee, gave honorary doctorate degrees to B.B. King in 1985 and 1990, respectively.
- On October 18, 1987, B.B. King was one of 15 new inductees into the Rock and Roll Hall of Fame. To qualify, an artist must have released a recording at least 25 years before becoming eligible. Inducted at the same ceremony were Big Joe Turner, memorialized by Doc Pomus; Muddy Waters, inducted by Paul Butterfield; Clyde McPhatter, lead singer of The Drifters, eulogized by Ben E. King; Jackie Wilson, who was remembered by his son; Marvin Gaye; Bill Haley, whose son, Pedro, dressed in the uniform of his military school, was introduced by Chuck Berry; Roy Orbison,

who sang a duet on "Pretty Woman," with his nominator, Bruce Springsteen; Carl Perkins, saluted by the man who discovered him for his Sun Records label, Sam Philips; and Bo Diddley; Smokey Robinson; and Aretha Franklin. Also honored in 1987 were non-performers: songwriters Mike Lieber and Jerry Stoller, and record producers Ahmet Ertegin, Jerry Wexler and Leonard Feather. Finally, among the honored artists were three "early influences" Louis Jordan, T-Bone Walker and Hank Williams.

• The NAACP (National Association for the Advancement of Colored People) honored him in 1993 with its Blues Image Award for the third time, 1975 and 1981 being the years of previous awards.

• The National Endowment for the Arts gave him a national Heritage Award, calling him one of "our national treasures." The honor was accompanied by a $5,000 award.

Besides an Oscar, Hollywood has one other tangible award that is universally recognized as a credential for stardom, and that is a star on the Walk of Fame. The political intrigues and pressure groups that come into play during selection for a star on the Walk rival those of the Oscars. The five-member selection committee is comprised of one representative each from the film, radio, recording, performing, and television industries, and whose identities are, in principal, secret. The chairman of this secret committee, Johnny Grant, also ceremonial mayor of Hollywood, represents the Walk of Fame Committee at awards ceremonies.

In September, 1990, when B.B. King was immortalized with his own star, two other musical artists, jazz singer Nancy Wilson and Marvin Gaye, were enshrined on the Walk in separate ceremonies. (It is worth noting that King and Gaye were inducted into the Rock and Roll Hall of Fame in the same year, 1987.) The entertainment press found the combination notable in that all three endured an unnecessarily long wait for this honor, especially in light of the committee's choice of Janet Jackson, youngest of the eight siblings of Michael Jackson, for the same honor five months before. Ms. Jackson is no show business lightweight with four #1 hits to her credit, and $32 million contract with Virgin Records [signed a year after her star was laid in the Walk], but she was born 27 years after the first B.B. King record was cut and seven years after Marvin Gaye made his first record.

The dedication of Gaye's star followed an intense 18-month campaign mounted by Motown Records and the Sheridan Broadcasting Corporation. The first time his name was proposed Gaye's nomination was passed over (for "insufficient public support," his backers were told).

His supporters collected 100,000 signatures, making it difficult for the committee to further defer the honor. As if by way of apology Chairman Grant told the press, "The Walk of Fame is such a big tourist attraction . . . [and] we like to honor some of the younger stars who show all the signs of having longevity in the business. . . . The committee goes through 200 to 300 applications per year." [*Billboard,* Oct. 20, 1990, page 24] B.B. King's name had been proposed three times over a three-year period. The exact timing of the award ceremony was chosen to coincide with the release of his album "Live At San Quentin," which won a Grammy that year.

When I read the schedule of a B.B. King tour invariably I imagine a map on which are marked the actual locations of each stage where he performs. Each stage, like the deck of an aircraft carrier, waits for him to touch down at the exact time specified by the contract. Like a carrier pilot, condemned to fly from flat-top to flat-top, he touches down, sings and plays for the throng gathered on the deck, refuels and is airborne again. That is his life, that is his choice. Can such a life hold anything else beyond the next landing? With such a schedule how can there be time for anything else?

In the 1980's he returned to radio as a disk jockey with his own weekly show, "B.B. King Blues Hour," syndicated on 112 stations—most, but not all black-oriented—around the U.S., as well as the Armed Forces Radio Network abroad. B.B. always carries enough music, even backstage in his briefcase, to make an excellent hour of listening, so recording programs was simply a matter of arranging periodic appointments in studios at participating radio stations in the cities where he played. This endeavor is B.B.'s answer to the young black audience's apparent indifference to their heritage. "'More than anything else it is important to study history, to know history,' he says. 'To be a Black person and sing the blues, you are Black twice,'" he told Ebony Magazine in February of 1992. (*Ebony* V 47 P45) "'Long after I'm gone, when [blues artist] Robert Cray is my age, I hope kids will know what this music is all about. . . .'" (*Ebony,* V 47 P48) To this end he played and talked about vintage blues, contemporary blues, and blues rock on the "B.B. King Blues Hour" which was broadcast every Sunday morning at 10:00 AM for several years—one of the few radio blues programs not aired in the middle of the night. In April of 1990, the syndicator canceled the program rather abruptly, to the dismay of the audience. Angry listeners embarked on a letter-writing campaign to "Bring Back B.B.," to no avail. But there will be, and are, other pulpits for B.B.

Besides returning to the airwaves B.B. King returned to Beale Street in Memphis during the 1990's. For many years after its decline as a center of black night life in the middle South, Beale Street looked like the main street of a ghost town. In the late 1970's there was not a single business open on the strip. All the storefronts and club entrances were covered up with sheets of plywood. On May 3, 1991, at the heart of a full-scale revival of Beale Street, B.B. King's Blues Club opened for business.

Three years later, in September of 1994, B.B. King played the opening of the 500-seat B.B. King's Blues Club in Universal City Walk, the sprawling entertainment and shopping complex in the Los Angeles suburb of Universal City. These two clubs on opposite sides of the continent are the vanguard of a projected chain of clubs licensed by KINGSID Ventures, Ltd. Plans are for new clubs to open in Nashville in November, 1995, followed by new franchises in Orlando (home of Universal Attractions and Disney World) in early 1996, then Seattle, Miami Beach, and Tokyo in 1996–97.

In strictly musical terms B.B. King has grown artistically in this time since 1980. As to be expected he has not diluted his devotion to the blues. At the core of his every concert is still classic blues, performed in the style he forged during the 1950's. Younger artists continue to relish every lick he plays and to find new depths in his playing. As Jerome Geils of the smash blues-rock band "J Geils" said on the eve of embarking on the Blues Music Festival tour with B.B. King, "no matter how long you listen to him, he always finds new and surprising ways to play."

But B.B. has not been content simply to stick with his stock in trade. In 1985 while on tour in the Far East, he met a young jazz singer named Diane Schuur when the two of them played a music festival in Tokyo. The fact that they admired each other's work was not surprising—she was a respected jazz singer and pianist, and he was King of the Blues. What was, to some, unexpected, was the urge to collaborate. But as much as B.B. loves the blues, he loves many other forms of music as well and yearns to express himself in other styles. Schuur's eagerness to work with B.B. is not surprising. Everyone from country singer Randy Travis, to Mary Travis, of Peter, Paul and Mary, is eager to merge his or her music with B.B.'s voice and guitar.

Reviewers were skeptical about the combination of B.B. King and Diane Schuur when their album, "Heart to Heart," was released on jazz-oriented GRP Records in May of 1994. Would B.B. King attempt to sing standards and ballads without resorting to his trademark grit? Would he, could he, croon? And would Schuur tone down the oversinging she was prone to when paired with a blues singer? The initial skepticism gave way for most reviewers, to praise and appreciation that they had taken the risk to perform together.

One critic, Geoffrey Himes, caught the sense of this risky combination of talents immediately when he compared it with the pairing of R&B artist Brook Benton with jazz singer Dinah Washington on the album, "The Two of Us," produced by Clyde Otis in 1959 for Mercury Records. That album yielded two top ten hits, "Baby (You Got What It Takes)" and "A Rockin' Good Way (To Mess Around And Fall In Love)," in 1960.

Phil Ramone, best known for his role as producer on the Sinatra duet albums and several albums of Billy Joel, produced "Heart To Heart." The production is so slick it gleams. The choice of material reveals an attempt to find an audience in several popular genres. There are two cuts that could be called country, "I Can't Stop Lovin' You," and "You Don't Know Me," which were back to back hits for Ray Charles in 1962, the first holding the #1 spot for five weeks, and the second, written by country crooner Eddy Arnold, reaching #2 on the Billboard Pop Chart. There are standards, "Glory of Love" and "Try a Little Tenderness"; a soul tune, Aretha Franklin's classic "Spirit in the Dark"; a taste of funk, "Freedom," which gave B.B. a chance to let Lucille do some talking in her classic "twingy string" mode; some jazz ballads, "No One Ever Tells You" and "At Last"; and a showtune by Irving Berlin, "I'm Putting All My Eggs in One Basket."

In the studio B.B. King presented himself with all the trepidation and humility that accompanies his every move into new dimensions. "'I've played pop tunes before, but I had never tried to sing them,'" B.B. told Billboard in July of 1994. "'Diane was like the teacher and I was the student. . . . She tried to show that I was there, and gave me confidence.'" (*Billboard,* July 9, 1994, P1) The collaboration turned out to be enormously satisfying to B.B. For him the move from blues to jazz/pop balladeer has a close parallel in the move of Nat King Cole from jazz pianist to popular balladeer. Whether or not it results in the kind of breakthrough Cole had, it has provided B.B. with a great sense of accomplishment and the prospect that he will be remembered not only for his blues.

The album was generally well received and held the #1 jazz album position for five weeks after its release—B.B.'s first #1 album ever. It produced one side effect that, by itself, might make the investment worthwhile for both artists. This was a television commercial for Northwest

Airlines which portrays a passenger relaxing in his reclining chair aboard a Northwest flight, and seeing/dreaming that the inflight entertainment is B.B. King and Diane Schuur, live! B.B. plays Lucille, Diane plays her electric piano, and they harmonize a few bars to the delight of the passenger. Such exposure, however fleeting, is tremendously important in establishing a performer's credentials as thoroughly mainstream. B.B. King's endorsements for products such as Kentucky Fried Chicken, Wendy's hamburgers, Pepsi, Budweiser beer, Amiga computers, and Panasonic have played an important part in making his image secure and robust across generational, cultural and racial boundaries.

In personal terms the 1980's and 90's brought changes for B.B. King. His family life, never normal by ordinary standards, changed with the loss of his father in the early 1980's and the addition of five children by adoption. His grandchildren number fourteen. Until recently B.B. has been protective of his scattered family. He specifically requested that his authorized biography should not identify his children by name, except for those in show business, Shirley, a dancer, and Leonard and Willie, who work for him on the road. In 1993 he made an important exception to that policy when he played a free concert at a Florida prison where his daughter, Patty, was serving a term for trafficking in drugs. Perhaps he saw an opportunity to show young people the pain that drugs can inflict by bringing prominent attention to his daughter's case. Whatever the reason, he arrived at the Gainesville Community Correction Center in Gainesville, Florida, with an entourage of journalists from one of the three major television broadcast networks, CBS, and *People Magazine,* America's major popular celebrity magazine. The reunion between father and daughter was, predictably, emotional. Courageously and tearfully, B.B. and his daughter went before the television cameras of CBS's "Street Stories," held hands, and answered questions by Ed Bradley, America's leading black television journalist/interviewer. When Bradley asked B.B. what kind of father he had been, B.B. answered, "Not nearly good enough." When asked how she came to be imprisoned there, Patty answered, "By making a lot of bad decisions."

The details of the story which they gave to *People* (March 23, 1993) offer a glimpse of what it meant to be one of B.B. King's children.

In the 1950's B.B. King made Gainesville's Blue Note nightclub a regular stop on his periodic swings through the deep South. Essie Williams, the club's owner, and B.B. became lovers. In 1956 Essie, who had two children from a previous marriage, gave birth to Patty. B.B. and Essie never married, nor did Essie ever remarry. Patty described growing up as B.B.'s daughter by recounting how she and her mother anticipated his visits. "When I was 5 years old and my daddy was coming in [to visit], my mother dressed me in this beautiful crinoline dress," she told *People* (op cit). "She would allow me to stand in front of the big picture window. And I would wait and wait. And then I would hear the bus coming. And I would get so excited, my little heart would just pound because I hadn't seen him for a while. He'd come maybe four or five times a year, whenever he was performing in the area."

In 1974 after graduating from high school, Patty moved west to work for her father as a receptionist in his Las Vegas office, By 1982 she was back in Gainesville, a single mother of two daughters. She married a man, Leroy Walton, and discovered "too late" that he had a criminal record. That same year her mother, Essie, died, and Patty and her husband were convicted of forging $857 worth of checks. Her life began to unravel from there. She received probation for the forgery charge, but she violated her probation status when she was charged with possession of marijuana. She was sentenced to two consecutive five year terms, of which she served four years. She and Walton were divorced in 1984. Patty remarried in 1988 to a convicted felon, Alvin McHellon. They had two children, Alvin, Jr., and Alton. In 1990 they were arrested for cocaine trafficking. She was convicted and sentenced to nine years. She becomes eligible for parole in 1995.

The reunion between B.B. and Patty King in the Gainesville prison, like all their meetings, was fleeting. After the concert and taping B.B. spent just an hour visiting with Patty and her four children, ages 3 to 20. Then he returned to the road to make that evening's gig in a concert hall.

How long will B.B. King keep the hammer down? This question is frequently on the lips of interviewers and B.B.'s answer is always the same: so long as his health permits him to continue meeting his public, and his public still wants him, he'll be there. His attitude toward his career late in life is reminiscent of the answer given by jazz great Red Mitchell, when asked what plans he had for retirement: "I plan to be cremated my first day of retirement," said Mitchell.

B.B.'s health continues to be a testimony to human endurance. He has two chronic conditions, diabetes and high blood pressure, both aggravated by obesity, which he monitors and controls with daily oral medication. In April, 1990, he collapsed on tour and was hospitalized. It was then that he was diagnosed as diabetic. He resumed his tour schedule in a matter of days. With attention to diet and medication his diabetes is well in check. The 1995 European tour was marked by a rare event that demonstrated the limits of his stamina. In Italy he ate a tuna fish sandwich which had not been properly refrigerated. A few hours later he was hospitalized with violent vomiting. The toxins he ingested with the sandwich destabilized his diabetes and he was barely conscious until the medical team understood the diabetic complication and gave him an injection of insulin. One Italian performance was cancelled, the first time he had ever missed a show on a European tour.

His weight has been a problem for the last twenty years. The diagnosis of diabetes made it even more imperative that he lose weight, and with that goal he checked into the Pritikin Institute, a weight-loss clinic, in 1994 for a two-week stay. Weight loss for the seriously over-weight must, necessarily, be achieved gradually and by a systematic approach. He now makes a two-week stay at Pritikin an annual part of his schedule. The Pritikin visits seem to have had a beneficial effect, for B.B.'s bulk is shrinking.

In 1995 a B.B. King performance has every bit as much energy as one from the 50's or 60's. His only concession to age is a chair, placed at center stage by his nephew and musical director, Walter King, in the middle portion of every performance. Nephew and uncle, by their ceremonial air turn a simple folding chair into a throne for the king. As B.B. takes his throne the horn section quits the stage, leaving him with a small combo, little more than a rhythm section, that purrs along behind him as he stretches out his legs, and relieves his mind. The mood becomes relaxed and conversational. The king is holding court. He talks about old times, jealous lovers and whatever else seems to come to mind. During this part of the performance he plays extended guitar solos and sings, emphasizing the gentler, more reflective songs of his repertoire. After, perhaps, twenty minutes in this mode, the horns return, the chair is removed, B.B. stands and delivers the climactic conclusion. This soft interlude brings an element of sustained, quiet intimacy that had been absent until the 1980's when he slipped on an icy sidewalk and injured his knee. Forty-five minutes' performing on his feet was no longer an option and the chair was the solution.

In the mid-1980's B.B. developed a persistent hoarseness that became progressively worse. He had always treated his voice with great care, avoiding air conditioning, even in the hottest weather, drinking tea with honey and lemon in the dressing room, and downing a tumbler of water moments before taking the stage. He always took care to keep his fatigue levels from dropping below the threshold where his larynx became an exhaustion meter. But these troubles were different. None of his usual measures could relieve the discomfort he felt or the rasp in his voice. Eventually he sought the help of a specialist, who examined his larynx with a lapriscope, a tiny camera on a flexible probe, which the doctor maneuvered up B.B.'s nostril and down his throat. The view from the lapriscope was projected on a screen. In the dim light of the examination room, B.B. gazed at the two pairs of folds of mucous membranes with which he had made his living for thirty-five years. The doctor saw no polyps, the great fear of all professional singers. What he observed was severe inflammation of one side of the larynx caused by over-singing on that side to compensate for a weakness on the other side. No surgery was required but a prolonged period of total silence was prescribed for the patient, lest he do permanent damage to his voice.

B.B. King canceled all engagements for six weeks and retreated to his Las Vegas condominium. [He had sold his grand house in favor of a smaller, more manageable dwelling.] Once a day his secretary would call in person to deliver his mail and messages to him and to take any instruction he might have prepared for her in writing. Most days it was simply "Here's your mail Mr. King," to which B.B. would bow gratefully. "Can I get you anything special today?" she would ask, to which B.B. would smile and shake his head in a silent No, thank you. "Then I'll call by tomorrow around the same time," she would say in parting.

The regimen of silence was a complete success. When he returned to his concert schedule B.B. King was in the best voice he had enjoyed in many years. No problems have occurred since then.

This interlude was completely without precedent in B.B.'s life and career. It gave him a chance to reflect on what lay behind and what might lie ahead. If ever there was a time when he might decide to ease the pace or substantially cut back his appearances to use his creative powers in other ways, this forced vacation was such a time. But to do so would have been to violate all the lessons he learned from Planter Barrett and to desert his flock. Preacher Fair had shown him how to move the bodies and levitate the souls of the congregation. Every great preacher believes he has a duty to preach and the greater the gift the greater the duty. When the doctors pronounced that it was safe for him to resume singing B.B. put the hammer down. B.B. King belongs to the Red Mitchell school of retirement plans—cremation on day one of retirement.

How will history remember B.B. King? This is the most difficult question of all to answer. His place in history is assured and yet such achievements, both personal and musical, as described in this chapter, are usually relegated to the status of footnotes when it comes time to write the history of an epoch. Put another way, history will remember Charlie Parker, large as life, and will, less vividly, remember Django Reinhardt, but it has already forgotten Paul Butterfield.

First, history might well have forgotten B.B. King were it not for the events of 1965–66, beginning with the performance of Paul Butterfield at the 1965 Newport Folk Festival, when urban blues was exported from the ghetto into the mainstream. Quite possibly, urban blues would have been lost to the collective consciousness of the decade that followed, and B.B. King would have remained unknown beyond the racial enclave that patronized his music. Blues music would have been a historical curiosity, despite its already substantial role in our culture. B.B. King was the principal beneficiary of those events, Yet, without his force of character, his tenacity and ambition to make his music widely known, the recognition of this music as a distinct form would have been much less pervasive. His dedication and devotion to winning the widest possible recognition for this music is the single most important reason our culture has embraced this form as something more enduring than the mere predecessor to rock and roll which would otherwise have been its likely destiny.

B.B. King's contribution is properly compared with that of Duke Ellington and Louis Armstrong. Ellington brought jazz from the nightclub and dance hall into the concert hall and the cathedral. Armstrong, before him, brought ensemble jazz from the saloon to the silver screen and onto the diplomatic circuit where it became a symbol of America in the 20th century. Our cultural center of gravity was shifted by their contributions. The same can be said for B.B. King. His penetration into the mainstream has given blues a distinct place and a clearly defined identity as a result of his success.

The second legacy of B.B. King is his contribution to racial tolerance. By bringing the chit'lin' circuit to Middle America, B.B. King allows white America and the wider world to experience the musical culture of black America undiluted. The wider the exposure between the two cultures, the greater the interface between the races, and the deeper is the liberalizing influence on race relations. When B.B. King, an orphaned sharecropper, who witnessed the body of a black man on public display on the courthouse steps after his electrocution, is hosted at the White House, our society has changed for the better. When he, who ran in fear from the white hoods of the Ku Klux Klan, bows his head to accept the crimson hood of Doctor of Arts from Yale University, our values are confirmed in a way that marks progress.

Every generation considers its successor to be its legacy, good or bad. B.B. King, as the one artist who, more than any other, defined the guitar as the primary instrument of blues music, leaves as his legacy a generation of younger players whose debt to him is evident every time one of them picks up the instrument to play. Indeed, it is not uncommon to hear younger players quote entire B.B. King solos, note for note, in their performances and recordings.

Finally, there is a legacy embodied in his recorded music. Many generations from today, when people want to hear the music of the 20th century known as *blues* they will listen to the records of B.B. King and hear that music played at its very best.

Discography

JIM KEREKES and DENNIS O'NEILL

Album Releases

The albums listed below are grouped by record label and listed sequentially by their release numbers. In most cases, the sequential release numbers correspond to chronological order. Shown beginning on page 260 is the (approximate) year of the release (albums listed below don't have certain release dates); throughout Discography is record label along with the release number, album title (not available on some of the earlier releases), and the album song titles. There have been various compilations and foreign releases drawing on B.B. King's early recordings which are not noted here. Some of these albums are now available on compact disc; current catalog numbers are given when known.

Late 1940s–Early 1950s

Crown 5020 Singin' the Blues
(Reissued as United 7726; with The Blues, issued on CD as Flair 86296/Ace 320)

Three O'Clock Blues
You Know I Love You
Woke Up This Morning
You Upset Me, Baby
Please Love Me
Blind Love
Every Day I Have the Blues
Ten Long Years (I Had a Woman)
Did You Ever Love a Woman
Sweet Little Angel
That Ain't the Way to Do It
Cryin' Won't Help You
Bad Luck

Crown 5063 **The Blues**
(Reissued as United 7732; with Singin' the Blues, *issued on CD as Flair 86296/Ace 320)*

Boogie Woogie Woman
Don't You Want a Man Like Me
What Can I Do (Just Sing the Blues)
Ten Long Years (I Had a Woman)
Ruby Lee
Early in the Morning
I Want to Get Married
Why Do Everything Happen to Me
You Know I Go for You
Past Day
When My Heart Beats Like a Hammer
Troubles, Troubles, Troubles

Crown 5115 **B.B. King Wails**
(Reissued as Crown 152; reissued again under new title I Love You So *as United 7711/Custom 1049)*

The Fool
Time to Say Good-bye
Sweet Thing
I've Got Papers on You, Baby
Tomorrow Is Another Day
I Love You So
We Can't Make It
Treat Me Right
The Woman I Love

Crown 5119 **B.B. King Sings Spirituals**
(Reissued as Crown 152; United 7723; Custom 1059)

Precious Lord
Army of the Lord
Save a Seat for Me
Ole Time Religion
Sweet Chariot
Servant's Prayer
Jesus Gave Me Water
I Never Heard a Man

I'm Willing to Run All the Way
I'm Working on the Building

Crown 5143 The Great B.B. King
(Reissued as United 7728)

Sneaking Around
What Can I Do (Just Sing the Blues)
Ten Long Years (I Had a Woman)
(I'm Gonna) Quit My Baby
Be Careful with a Fool
Days of Old
Sweet Sixteen—Part 1
Sweet Sixteen—Part 2
I Was Blind
Whole Lot of Lovin'
Someday Baby
I Had a Woman

Crown 5157 King of the Blues
(Reissued as Crown 195; United 7730)

(I've) Got a Right to Love My Baby
Good Man Gone Bad
Partin' Time
What Way to Go
Long Nights
Feel Like a Million
I'll Survive
If I Lost You
You're on Top
I'm King

Crown 5188 My Kind of Blues
(Reissued as United 7724)

You Done Lost Your Good Thing Now
Walking Dr. Bill
Hold That Train
Understand
Someday Baby
Mr. Pawnbroker

Driving Wheel
My Own Fault Baby
Catfish Blues
Please Set a Date

Crown 5230 Blues for Me
(Reissued as United 7708; Custom 1046)

Bad Luck Soul
Get Out of Here
Bad Case of Love
You're Breaking My Heart
My Reward
Shut Your Mouth
I'm in Love
Blues for Me
Just Like a Woman
Baby Look at You

Crown 5286 Easy Listening Blues
(Reissued as United 7705)

Easy Listening (Blues)
Blues for Me
Night Long
Confessin'
Don't Touch
Slow Walk
Walkin'
Shoutin' the Blues
Rambler
Hully Gully (Twist)

Crown 5309 Blues in My Heart
(Reissued as Custom 1040)

Your Letter
You're Gonna Miss Me
Let Me Love You
I Can't Explain
Troubles Don't Last
Got 'Em Bad
I Need You, Baby

So Many Days
Downhearted
Strange Things
The Wrong Road

Crown 5359 The Soul of B.B. King
(Reissued as United 7714; Custom 1052; Kent 539)

Going Home
You Never Know
Please Remember Me
Come Back, Baby
You Won't Listen
Sundown
You Shouldn't Have Left
House Rocker
Shake Yours
The Letter

Kent 5012

Three O'Clock Blues
You Know I Love You
Woke Up This Morning
When My Heart Beats Like a Hammer
You Upset Me, Baby
Sneaking Around
Ten Long Years (I Had a Woman)
Sweet Little Angel
Why Do Everything Happen to Me
Every Day I Have the Blues
Sweet Sixteen—Part I & II
Bad Case of Love
Rock Me, Baby
Please Love Me
Just a Dream
Did You Ever Love a Woman

Kent 5013

Whole Lot of Love
(I'm Gonna) Quit My Baby
You're Gonna Miss Me

Let Me Love You
I Can't Explain
Troubles Don't Last
Walking Doctor Bill
Hold That Train

United 7742/Kent 5021 **The Jungle**

Blue Shadows
Eyesight to the Blind
Five Long Years
Ain't Nobody's Business
The Jungle
It's a Mean World
Long Gone Baby
Beautician Blues
I Can Hear My Name
The Worst Thing in My Life
Got 'Em Bad

KST 533 **From the Beginning**

Please Love Me
Rock Me, Baby
Everyday I Have the Blues
Woke Up This Morning
My Own Fault
Five Long Years
You Upset Me
Blue Shadows
The Woman I Love
You Know I Love You
Sweet Little Angel
Treat Me Right
Sweet Sixteen
Eyesight to the Blind
Beautician Blues
Bad Luck
Troubles, Troubles, Troubles
Sneakin' Around
Sweet Thing

Three O'Clock Blues
The Jungle
Let Me Love You
The Worst Thing in My Life
Shotgun Blues

United 7756 **The Incredible Soul of B.B. King**

A New Way of Driving
The Other Night Blues
B.B.'s Boogie
Walkin' and Cryin'
Everything I Do Is Wrong
She Don't Love Me No More
I Gotta Find My Baby
My Own Fault Darling
That Ain't the Way to Do It
B.B.'s Blues
She's Dynamite
Questionnaire Blues

United 7763 **Turn On with B.B. King**

Looking the World Over
Worried Life
Bad Luck Soul
Goin' Down Slow
Please Set a Date
Shut Your Mouth
Baby Look at You
You Done Lost Your Good Thing Now
Walkin' Dr. Bill
Recession Blues

KST 561 **B.B. King: Better Than Ever**

I've Got a Right to Love My Baby
Partin' Time
Feel Like a Million
If I Lost You
Good Man Gone Bad

I'll Survive
Long Nights
What a Way to Go
That Evil Child
You're on Top
I'm King

KST 9011 Anthology of the Blues: B.B. King 1949–1950

I've Got Papers on You, Baby
Tomorrow Is Another Day
A Fool Too Long
Come By Here
The Woman I Love
My Silent Prayer
I Love You So
Sweet Thing
We Can't Make It
Treat Me Right
Time to Say Good-bye
I'm Cracking Up over You

United 7736/KST 515 Live! B.B. King on Stage

Please Love Me
Everyday I Have the Blues
Sweet Sixteen
Three O'Clock Blues
Rock Me Baby
Sweet Little Angel
Baby Look at You
Woke Up This Morning
You Upset Me Baby
I've Got a Right to Love My Baby
Let Me Love You

1962

ABC 456 Mr. Blues

Young Dreamers
By Myself
Chains of Love

Another Love
Blues at Midnight
Sneaking Around
On My Word of Honor
Tomorrow Night
My Baby's Comin' Home
Guess Who
You Ask Me
I'm Gonna Sit in 'til You Give In

1965

ABC 509 Live at the Regal
(Reissued by ABC/Dunhill on ABCS-724;
now MCAD 31106)

Every Day I Have the Blues
Sweet Little Angel
It's My Own Fault
How Blue Can You Get
Please Love Me
You Upset Me, Baby
Worry, Worry
Woke Up This Morning
You Done Lost Your Good Thing Now
Help the Poor

1966

ABC 528 Confessin' the Blues

I'd Rather Drink Muddy Water
Goin' to Chicago Blues
See See Rider
Do You Call That a Buddy
Wee Baby Blues
In the Dark
Confessin' the Blues
I'm Gonna Move to the Outskirts of Town
How Long, How Long Blues
Cherry Red
Please Send Me Someone to Love

Bluesway BL 6001 Blues Is King
(Now MCAD 31368)

Waitin' on You
Gambler's Blues
Tired of Your Love
Night Life
Buzz Me
Don't Answer the Door
Blind Love
I Know What You're Putting Down
Baby, Get Lost
Gonna Keep on Loving You

Bluesway BL 6011 Blues on Top of Blues

Heartbreaker
Losing Faith in You
Dance with Me
That's Wrong, Little Mama
Having My Say
I'm Not Wanted Anymore
Worried Dream
Paying the Cost to Be the Boss
Until I Found You
I'm Gonna Do What They Do to Me
Raining in My Heart
Now That You've Lost Me

Bluesway BL 6016 Lucille
(Now MCAD 10518)

Lucille
You Move Me So
Country Girl
No Money, No Luck Blues
I Need Your Love
Rainin' All the Time
I'm with You

Stop Puttin' the Hurt on Me
Watch Yourself

Bluesway BLS 6022 **His Best—The Electric B.B. King**
(Now MCAD 27007)

Tired of Your Jive
Don't Answer the Door
The B.B. Jones
All Over Again
Paying the Cost to Be the Boss
Think It Over
I Done Got Wise
Meet My Happiness
Sweet Sixteen
You Put It on Me
I Don't Want You Cuttin' Off Your Hair

1969

Bluesway BL 6031 **Live and Well**
(Now MCAD 31191)

I Want You So Bad
Friends
Get Off My Back, Woman
Let's Get Down to Business
Why I Sing the Blues
Don't Answer the Door
Just a Little Love
My Mood
Sweet Little Angel
Please Accept My Love

Bluesway BL 6037 **Completely Well**
(Now MCAD 31309)

So Excited
No Good
You're Losin' Me
What Happened
Confessin' the Blues

Key to My Kingdom
Cryin' Won't Help You Now
You're Mean
The Thrill Is Gone

ABC 713 Indianola Mississippi Seeds
(Now MCAD 31343)

Nobody Loves Me But My Mother
You're Still My Woman
Ask Me No Questions
Until I'm Dead and Cold
King's Special
Ain't Gonna Worry My Life
Chains and Things
Go Underground
Hummingbird

ABC 723 B.B. King Live in Cook County Jail
(Now MCAD 30180)

Introduction
Every Day I Have the Blues
How Blue Can You Get
Worry, Worry, Worry
Medley: Three O'clock Blues
Darlin', You Know I Love You
Sweet Sixteen
The Thrill Is Gone
Please Accept My Love

ABC 730 B.B. King in London
(Now MCAD 10843)

Caldonia
Blue Shadows
Alex's Boogie
We Can't Agree
Ghetto Woman

Wet Haystack
Part-Time Love
Power of the Blues
Ain't Nobody Home

1972

ABC 734 **L. A. Midnight**

I Got Some Help I Don't Need
Help the Poor
Can't You Hear Me Talking to You?
Midnight
Sweet Sixteen
(I Believe) I've Been Blue Too Long
Lucille's Granny

ABC 759 **Guess Who**
(Now MCAD 10351)

Summer in the City
Just Can't Please You
Any Other Way
You Don't Know Nothin' about Love
Found What I Need
Neighborhood Affair
I Takes a Young Girl
Better Lovin' Man
Guess Who
Shouldn't Have Left Me
Five Long Years

ABC 794 **To Know You Is to Love You**
(Now MCAD 10414)

I Like to Live the Love
Respect Yourself
Who Are You
Love
I Can't Leave
To Know You Is to Love You
Oh to Me
Thank You for Loving the Blues

ABC 878 Back in the Alley—The Classic Blues of B.B. King
(Previously issued on Bluesway BLS 6050, now MCAD 27010)

Sweet Little Angel
Watch Yourself
Don't Answer the Door
Paying the Cost to Be the Boss
Sweet Sixteen
Gambler's Blues
I'm Gonna Do What They Do to Me
Lucille
Please Love Me

ABC 767 The Best of B.B. King
(Now Chess/MCAD 19099)

Hummingbird
Cook County Jail Introduction
How Blue Can You Get
Caldonia
Sweet Sixteen
Ain't Nobody Home
Why I Sing the Blues
The Thrill Is Gone
Nobody Loves Me But My Mother

ABC 898 Lucille Talks Back
(Now MCAD 22023 [different order of tracks])

Lucille Talks Back
Breaking Up Somebody's Home
Reconsider Baby
Don't Make Me Pay for His Mistakes
When I'm Wrong
I Know the Price
Have Faith
Everybody Lies a Little

1976

Dunhill DHL 6-50190 Bobby Bland and B.B. King: Together for the First Time
(Now MCA 2-4160)

Three O'Clock Blues
It's My Own Fault
Don't Cry No More
Driftin' Blues
I'm Sorry
Why I Sing the Blues
I'll Take Care of You
I Like to Live the Love
Don't Answer the Door
Goin' Down Slow
That's the Way Love Is
Medley

Impulse ASD 9317 *Bobby Bland and B.B. King: Together Again . . .*
Live
(Now MCAD 27012)

Let the Good Times Roll
Medley: Stormy Monday Blues
Strange Things Happen
Feel So Bad
Medley: Mother-in-Law Blues
Mean Old World
Everyday
Medley: The Thrill Is Gone
I Ain't Gonna Be the First to Cry

1977

ABC 977 King Size

Don't You Lie to Me
I Wonder Why
Medley: I Just Want to Make Love to You
Your Lovin' Turned Me On
Slow and Easy
Got My Mojo Working
Walkin' in the Sun
Mother for Ya
The Same Love That Made Me Laugh
It's Just a Matter of Time

MCA AA 1061 **Midnight Believer**
(Now MCAD 27011)

When It All Comes Down
Midnight Believer
I Just Can't Leave Your Love Alone
Hold On
Never Make Your Move Too Soon
A World Full of Strangers
Let Me Make You Cry a Little Longer

MCA 3151 **Take It Home**

Better Not Look Down
Same Old Story
Happy Birthday Blues
I've Always Been Lonely
Secondhand Woman
Tonight I'm Gonna Make You a Star
Story Everybody Knows
Take It Home

MCA2-8016 **B.B. King Now Appearing at Ole Miss**
Intro—B.B. King Blues Theme
Caldonia
Medley: Don't Answer the Door
You Done Lost Your Good Thing Now
I Need Your Love So Bad
Nobody Loves Me But My Mother
Hold On
I Got Some Outside Help (I Don't Really Need)
Darlin' You Know I Love You
When I'm Waiting
The Thrill Is Gone
Never Make Your Move Too Soon
Three O'Clock in the Morning
Rock Me Baby

Guess Who
I Just Can't Leave Your Love Alone

MCA 5162 There Must Be a Better World Somewhere
(Now MCA 27034)

Life Ain't Nothing But a Party
Born Again Human
There Must Be a Better World Somewhere
The Victim
More, More, More
You're Going With Me

MCA 5307 Love Me Tender
(Now MCAD 886)

One of Those Nights
Love Me Tender
Don't Change on Me
(I'd Be) A Legend in My Time
You've Always Got the Blues
Nightlife, Please Send Me Someone to Love
You and Me, Me and You
Since I Met You Baby
Time Is a Thief
A World I Never Made

MCAD 2-4124 Great Moments with B.B. King

Waitin' on You
Gambler's Blues
Tired of Your Jive
Night Life
Buzz Me
Blind Love
See See Rider
Wee Baby Blues
I'd Rather Drink Muddy Water

I'm Gonna Move to the Outskirts of Town
How Long, How Long Blues
Cherry Red
Baby Get Lost
Gonna Keep on Loving You
I Know What You're Puttin' Down
Heartbreaker
Dance with Me
That's Wrong Little Mama
Paying the Cost to Be the Boss
Until I Found You
I'm Gonna Do What They Do to Me
Having My Say
I'm Not Wanted Anymore
Worried Dream

1985

MCA 5616 Six Silver Strings

Six Silver Strings
Big Boss Man
In the Midnight Hour
Into the Night
My Lucille
Memory Lane
My Guitar Sings the Blues
Double Trouble

1986

VIRGIN 86231 Spotlight on Lucille

Slidin' and Glidin'
Blues with B.B.
King of Guitar
Jump with B.B.
38th Street Blues
Feedin' the Rock
Just Like a Woman
Step It Up
Calypso Jazz

Easy Listening Blues
Shoutin' the Blues
Powerhouse

MCAD 27119 Blues 'N' Jazz

Inflation Blues
Broken Heart
Sell My Monkey
Heed My Warning
Teardrops from My Eyes
Rainbow Riot
Darlin' You Know I Love You
Make Love to Me
I Can't Let You Go

1988
MCAD 42183 King of the Blues: 1989

(You've Become a) Habit to Me
Drowning in the Sea of Love
Can't Get Enough
Standing on the Edge
Go On
Let's Straighten It Out
Change in Your Lovin'
Undercover Man
Lay Another Log on the Fire
Business with My Baby Tonight
Take Off Your Shoes

1989
SCD 4931 Live at "Newport in New York"

Little Red Rooster—"Big Mama" Thorton
Ball and Chain—"Big Mama" Thorton
Confessin' the Blues—Jay McShann
They Call Me Mr. Cleanhead—Eddie Vinson
Hold It Right There—Eddie Vinson
Kidney Stew—Eddie Vinson

That's Alright Now Mama—Arthur "Big Boy" Crudup
Long Distance Call—Muddy Waters
Where's My Woman Been—Muddy Waters
Got My Mojo Workin'—Muddy Waters
Outside Help—B.B. King

This album was recorded live at the Philharmonic Hall on June 29, 1973. Only a major event like Newport in New York could have brought so many masters of the blues together under one roof for just a night's work, and only B.B. King—the night's master of ceremonies and host—could have kept things moving as smoothly as they did.

1990

MCAD 6455 Live at San Quentin

B.B. King Intro
Let the Good Times Roll
Everyday I Have the Blues
Whole Lotta Loving
Sweet Little Angel
Never Make a Move Too Soon
Into the Night
Ain't Nobody's Bizness
The Thrill Is Gone
Peace to the World
Nobody Loves Me But My Mother
Sweet Sixteen
Rock Me Baby

1991

VIRGIN 29653 The Fabulous B.B. King

Three O'Clock Blues
You Know I Love You
Please Love Me
You Upset Me Baby
Bad Luck
On My Word of Honor
Everyday I Have the Blues

Woke Up This Morning (My Baby's Gone)
When My Heart Beats Like a Hammer
Sweet Little Angel
Ten Long Years
Whole Lotta Love

MCAD 10295 There Is Always One More Time

I'm Moving On
Back in L. A.
The Blues Come over Me
Fool Me Once
The Low Down
Mean and Evil
I've Got Something up My Sleeve
Roll, Roll, Roll
There Is Always One More Time

TSD 3507 Everyday I Have the Blues

Sweet Sixteen
The Other Night Blues
It's My Own Fault Baby
Long Nights
Mr. Pawnbroker
You Done Lost Your Good Thing Now
Catfish Blues
Paying the Cost to Be the Boss
Everyday I Have the Blues
B.B. Boogie
A New Way of Driving
Walkin' and Cryin'
How Blue Can You Get
The Letter

GRD 9637 Live at the Apollo

When Love Comes to Town
Sweet Sixteen
The Thrill Is Gone
Ain't Nobody's Bizness
Paying the Cost to Be the Boss

All Over Again
Nightlife
Since I Met You Baby
Guess Who
Peace to the World

1992

MCAD 20256 Why I Sing the Blues

The Thrill Is Gone
Ghetto Woman
Why I Sing the Blues
Ain't Nobody Home
Hummingbird
To Know You Is to Love You
How Blue Can You Get?
Sweet Sixteen
So Excited
Chains and Things

VIRGIN 39013 My Sweet Little Angel

Sweet Little Angel
Crying Won't Help You Now
Ten Long Years
Quit My Baby
Don't Look Now But I've Got the Blues
You Know I Go for You
Why Do Everything Happen to Me
Worry, Worry
Shake Yours
Please Accept My Love
Treat Me Right
Going Down Slow
Ain't That Just Like a Woman
Time to Say Good-bye
Early Every Morning
You've Been an Angel
Growing Old

The B.B. King Companion
274

In the Middle of an Island
String Bean
Recession Blues
You Shouldn't Have Left

VIRGIN 40072 Heart and Soul

Lonely and Blue
Sneakin' Around (with You)
You Can't Fool My Heart
Story from My Heart and Soul
Don't Get Around Much Anymore
You Know I Love You
I'm King
A Lonely Lover's Plea
My Heart Belongs to You
Don't Cry Anymore
Please Accept My Love
Peace of Mind
I Was Blind
On My Word of Honor
I'll Survive
If I Lost You
My Reward
I Am
I Love You So
Key to My Kingdom

MCA 4-10677 King of the Blues *(4 Disc Box Set)*

Disc 1: 1949–1966
Miss Martha King
She's Dynamite
Three O'clock Blues
Please Love Me
You Upset Me Baby
Everyday I Have the Blues
Rock Me Baby
Recession Blues
Don't Get Around Much Anymore
I'm Gonna Sit in 'til You Give In

Blues at Midnight
Sneakin' Around
My Baby's Comin' Home
Slowly Losing My Mind
How Blue Can You Get
Rockin' Awhile
Help the Poor
Stop Leadin' Me On
Sweet Little Angel
All Over Again
Sloppy Drunk
Don't Answer the Door, Parts One and Two
I Done Got Wise
Think It Over
Gambler's Blues

Disc 2: 1966–1969
Goin' Down Slow
Tired of Your Jive
Sweet Sixteen, Parts One and Two
Paying the Cost to Be the Boss
I'm Gonna Do What They Do to Me
Lucille
Watch Yourself
You Put It on Me
Get Myself Somebody
I Want You So Bad
Why I Sing the Blues
Get Off My Back Woman
Please Accept My Love
Fools Get Wise
No Good
So Excited

Disc 3: 1969–1975
The Thrill Is Gone
Confessin' the Blues
Nobody Loves Me But My Mother
Hummingbird
Ask Me No Questions

Chains and Things
Eyesight to the Blind
Niji Baby
Blue Shadows
Ghetto Woman
Ain't Nobody Home
I Get Some Help I Don't Need
Five Long Years
To Know You Is to Love You
I Like to Live the Love
Don't Make Me Pay for His Mistakes

Disc 4: 1976–1991
Let the Good Times Roll
Don't You Lie to Me
Mother Fuyer
Never Make a Move Too Soon
While It All Comes Down (I'll Still Be Around)
Better Not Look Down
Caldonia
There Must Be a Better World Somewhere
Play with Your Poodle
Darlin' You Know I Love You
Inflation Blues
Make Love to Me
Into the Night
Six Silver Strings
When Love Comes to Town
Right Time, Wrong Place
Many Miles Traveled
I'm Moving On
Since I Met You Baby

1993

MCAD 10710 **Blues Summit**
(with various other players)

Playin' with My Friends
Since I Met You Baby
I Pity the Fool

You Shook Me
Something You Got
There's Something on Your Mind
Little by Little
Call It Stormy Monday
You're the Boss
We're Gonna Make It
I Gotta Move Out of This Neighborhood/
Nobody Loves Me But My Mother
Everybody's Had the Blues

MCAD 20379 I Like to Live the Love *(with Bobby 'Blue' Bland)*

Three O'Clock Blues
It's My Own Fault
That's the Way Love Is
I'm Sorry
Don't Cry No More
Don't Answer the Door
Goin' Down Slow
I Like to Live the Love
Driftin' Blues
Let the Good Times Roll

1994

GRD 9767 Heart to Heart *(with Diane Schuur)*

No One Ever Tells You
I Can't Stop Loving You
You Don't Know Me
It Had to Be You
I'm Putting All My Eggs in One Basket
Glory of Love
Try a Little Tenderness
Spirit in the Dark
Freedom
At Last

1996

MCAD2 11443 How Blue Can You Get? Classic Live Performances 1964 to 1994 *(Double CD Set)*

Disc 1: 1964 to 1971
Every Day I Have the Blues
Sweet Little Angel
Please Love Me
You Upset Me Baby
Gambler's Blues
Buzz Me
Baby Get Lost
Blind Love
Don't Answer the Door
Please Accept My Love
Worry, Worry
How Blue Can You Get?
Eyesight to the Blind
Chains and Things
Sweet Sixteen
The Thrill Is Gone

Disc 2: 1976 to 1994
Let the Good Times Roll (with Bobby Bland)
I Got Some Help I Don't Need
Caldonia
Night Life (with The Crusaders)
Never Make a Move Too Soon (with The Crusaders)
All Over Again
Please Send Me Someone to Love (with Gladys Knight)
Nobody Loves Me But My Mother
When Love Comes to Town
Paying the Cost to Be the Boss
Ain't Nobody's Business (with Ruth Brown)
T-Bone Shuffle (with Joe Louis Walker)
Rock Me Baby

Single Releases

The recordings listed below are grouped by record label and listed sequentially by their release numbers. In most cases, the sequential release numbers correspond to chronological order. Shown on pages 280–285 is the year of the release (approximate), the record label along with the release number, and the song titles (both sides).

Modern 1 Please Love Me/Cryin' Won't Help You
Modern 3 Woke Up This Morning/Bad Case of Love
Modern 11 When My Heart Beats Like a Hammer/You Upset Me
Modern 19 You Know I Love You/Ten Long Years (I Had a Woman)

1949

Bullet 309 Miss Martha King/When Your Baby Packs Up and Goes
Bullet 315 Got the Blues/Take a Swing with Me

1950–51

RPM 304 Mistreated Woman/B.B. Boogie
RPM 311 The Other Might Blues/Walkin' and Cryin'
RPM 317 I Am/Worry, Worry
RPM 318 My Baby's Gone/Don't You Want a Man Like Me
RPM 323 B.B. Blues/She's Dynamite
RPM 330 She's a Mean Woman/Hard-Working Woman
RPM 339 Three O'Clock Blues/That Ain't the Way to Do It

1952

RPM 348 Fine-Looking Woman/She Don't Love Me No More
RPM 355 Shake It Up and Go/My Own Fault, Darling
RPM 360 Someday, Somewhere/Gotta Find My Baby
RPM 363 You Didn't Want Me/You Know I Love You
RPM 374 Story from My Heart and Soul/Boogie Woogie Woman

1953

RPM 380 Woke Up This Morning/Don't Have to Cry
RPM 386 Please Love Me/Highway Bound
RPM 391 Neighborhood Affair/Please Hurry Home
RPM 395 Why Did You Leave Me/Blind Love
RPM 403 Praying to the Lord/Please Help Me

1954

RPM 408 Love You Baby/The Woman I Love
RPM 411 Everything I Do Is Wrong/Don't You Want a Man Like Me

RPM 412 When My Heart Beats Like a Hammer/Bye! Bye! Baby
RPM 416 You Upset Me Baby/Whole Lot of Love

1955

RPM 421 Sneaking Around/Everyday I Have the Blues
RPM 425 Lonely and Blue/Jump with You, Baby
RPM 430 Shut Your Mouth/I'm in Love
RPM 435 Talkin' the Blues/Boogie Rock
RPM 437 What Can I Do (Just Sing the Blues)/Ten Long Years (I Had a Woman)

1956

RPM 450 I'm Cracking Up over You/Ruby Lee
RPM 451 Crying Won't Help You/Sixteen Tons*
RPM 451 Cryin' Won't Help You Baby/Can't We Talk It Over*
RPM 457 Did You Ever Love a Woman/Let's Do the Boogie
RPM 459 Dark Is the Night—Part 1/Dark Is the Night—Part 2
RPM 468 Sweet Little Angel/Bad Luck
RPM 479 On My Word of Honor/Bim Bam Boom

1957

RPM 486 Early in the Morning/You Don't Know
RPM 490 How Do I Love You/You Can't Fool My Heart
RPM 492 I Want to Get Married/Troubles, Troubles, Troubles
RPM 494 (I'm Gonna) Quit My Baby/Be Careful with a Fool
RPM 498 I Wonder/I Need You So Bad
RPM 501 The Key to My Kingdom/My Heart Belongs to You

1958–59

Kent 301 Why Do Everything Happen to Me/You Know I Go for You
Kent 307 Don't Look Now, But You Got the Blues/Days of Old
Kent 315 Please Accept My Love/You've Been an Angel
Kent 319 The Fool/Come By Here
Kent 325 A Lonely Lover's Plea/The Woman I Love
Kent 327 Time to Say Good-bye/Every Day I Have the Blues
Kent 329 Sugar Mama/Mean Old Frisco

---

*RPM 451 issued in two versions.

Kent 330 Sweet Sixteen—Part 1/Sweet Sixteen—Part 2
Kent 333 (I've) Got a Right to Love My Baby/My Fault
Kent 336 Please Love Me/Crying Won't Help You
Kent 337 Blind Love/You Upset Me Baby
Kent 338 Ten Long Years (I Had a Woman)/Every Day I Have the Blues
Kent 339 Did You Ever Love a Woman/Ten Long Years (I Had a Woman)
Kent 340 Woke Up This Morning/Sweet Little Angel
Kent 346 Good Man Gone Bad/Partin' Time*
Kent 350 You Done Lost Your Good Thing Now/Walking Doctor Bill
Kent 351 Things Are Not the Same/Fishin' After Me
Kent 353 Bad Luck Soul/Get Out of Here
Kent 358 Hold That Train/Understand

1961

Kent 360 Someday Baby/Peace of Mind
Kent 362 Bad Case of Love/You're Breaking My Heart

1962

Kent 365 Lonely/My Sometimes Baby
Kent 372 Hully Gully (Twist)/Gonna Miss You Around Here
Kent 373 Mashed Potato Twist/Three O'Clock Stomp
Kent 381 Mashing the Popeye/Tell Me Baby
Kent 383 Going Down Slow/When My Heart Beats Like a Hammer
Kent 386 Three O'Clock Blues/Your Letter
Kent 387 Christmas Celebration/Easy Listening (Blues)**
Kent 388 Down Now/Whole Lot of Love
Kent 389 Trouble in Mind/Long Nights
Kent 390 The Road I Travel/My Reward
Kent 391 The Letter/You Better Know
Kent 392 Precious Lord/Army of the Lord
Kent 393 Rock Me Baby/I Can't Lose
Kent 396 You're Gonna Miss Me/Let Me Love You
Kent 403 Beautician Blues/I Can Hear My Name
Kent 415 The Worst Thing in My Life/Got 'Em Bad

---

*Kent 346 has also been listed as Sweet Little Angel/Did You Ever Love a Woman.
**Has also been listed as Kent 412.

Kent 421 Please Love Me/Look at You

ABC 10316 I'm Gonna Sit in Till You Give In/You Ask Me
ABC 10334 My Baby's Coming Home/Blues at Midnight
ABC 10361 Sneakin' Around/Chains of Love
ABC 10367 Tomorrow Night/Mother's Love
ABC 10390 Guess Who/By Myself
ABC 10455 Young Dreams/On My Word of Honor
ABC 10486 Slowly Losing My Mind/How Do I Love You

1963
ABC 10527 How Blue Can You Get/Please Accept My Love

1964–65
ABC 10552 Help the Poor/I Wouldn't Have It Any Other Way
ABC 10576 The Hurt/Whole Lot of Lovin'
ABC 10599 Never Trust a Woman/Worryin' Blues
ABC 10616 Please Send Me Someone to Love/Stop Leading Me On
ABC 10634 Every Day I Have the Blues/It's My Own Fault
ABC 10675 Night Owl/Tired of Your Jive
ABC 10710 I Need You/Never Could Be You
ABC 10724 All Over Again/The Things You Put Me Through
ABC 10754 I'd Rather Drink Muddy Water/Goin' to Chicago Blues
ABC 10766 You're Still a Square/Tormented

1965
Kent 426 Blue Shadows/And Like That
Kent 429 Just a Dream/Why Do Everything Happen to Me
Kent 435 Broken Promise/Have Mercy Baby

1966
Kent 441 Eyesight to the Blind/Just Like a Woman
Kent 445 Five Long Years/Love, Honor and Obey
Kent 447 Ain't Nobody's Business/I Wonder
Kent 450 I Stay in the Mood/Every Day I Have the Blues

ABC 10856 Don't Answer the Door—Part 1/Don't Answer the Door—Part 2

ABC 10889 Waitin' for You/Night Life

Bluesway BL 61004 I Don't Want You Cuttin' Off Your Hair*

1967

Kent 458 Blues Stay Away/It's a Mean World
Kent 462 The Jungle/Long Gone Baby
Kent 467 Growing Old/Bad Breaks

1968

Kent 492 Blues for Me/The Woman I Love
Kent 510 Shoutin' the Blues/The Fool

Bluesway BL 61015 Payin' the Cost to Be the Boss
Bluesway BL 61018 Losing Faith in You/I'm Gonna Do What They Do to Me
Bluesway BL 61019 The B.B. Jones/You Put It on Me**
Bluesway BL 61022 Get Myself Somebody/Don't Waste My Time
Bluesway BL 61026 I Want You So Bad/Get Off My Back, Woman

1969

Bluesway BL 61029 Why I Sing the Blues/Friends

1970

Bluesway BL 61032 The Thrill Is Gone/You're Mean
Bluesway BL 61035 So Excited/Confessin' the Blues
ABC 11268 Ask Me No Questions/Go Underground
ABC 11280 Chains and Things/King's Special

1971

ABC 11290 Nobody Loves Me But My Mother/Ask Me No Questions
ABC 11302 Help the Poor/Lucille's Granny
ABC 11310 Ghetto Woman/Seven Minutes
ABC 11313 Sweet Sixteen/(I Believe) I've Been Blue Too Long

---

*Bluesway BL was the designation for "Bluesway," the ABC label devoted to blues music.
**Has also been issued with "Stop Putting the Hurt on Me" on the B-side.

ABC 11321 I Got Some Help I Don't Need/Lucille's Granny
ABC 11339 Summer in the City/Shouldn't Have Left Me
ABC 11433 Who Are You/On to Me
ABC 12029 Philadelphia/Up at 5 A.M.
ABC 12053 My Song/Friends

Bibliography

Barlow, William. *Looking Up at Down: The Emergence of Blues Culture*. Philadelphia, PA: Temple University Press, 1990.

Cohn, Lawrence, et al. *Nothing but the Blues: The Music and the Musicians*. New York: Abbeville Press, 1993.

Cook, Bruce. *Listen to the Blues*. New York: Scribner's, 1973.

Cowdery, Charles K. *Blues Legends*. Salt Lake City, UT: Gibbs Smith, 1995.

Dance, Helen Oakley. *Stormy Monday: The T-Bone Walker Story*. Foreword by B.B. King. Baton Rouge, LA: Louisiana State University, 1987.

Dickerson, James. *Goin' Back to Memphis: A Century of Blues, Rock 'n' Roll, and Glorious Soul*. New York: Schirmer Books, 1996.

Ferris, William. *Blues from the Delta*. Garden City, NY: Doubleday Anchor, 1978.

Govenar, Alan. *Meeting the Blues*. Dallas, TX: Taylor, 1988.

Harris, Sheldon. *Blue's Who's Who*. Amended edition. New York: Da Capo, 1989.

Herzhaft, Gerard. *Encyclopedia of the Blues*. Fayetteville, AR: University of Arkansas, 1992.

Hyman, Stanley Edgar. *The Critic's Credentials*. New York: Atheneum, 1978.

Keil, Charles. *Urban Blues*. Chicago: University of Chicago Press, 1966.

King, B.B. and David Ritz. *Blues All Around Me: The Autobiography of B.B. King*. New York: Avon, 1996.

Lomax, Alan. *The Land Where the Blues Began*. New York: Delta, 1995.

Murray, Albert. *The Hero and the Blues*. Columbia, MO: University of Missouri, 1973.

Oliver, Paul. *Blues Off the Record: Thirty Years of Blues Commentary*. New York: Da Capo, 1988.

Palmer, Robert. *Deep Blues*. New York: Viking, 1981.

Rowe, Mike. *Chicago Blues: The City and the Music*. New York: Da Capo, 1988.

Sawyer, Charles. *The Arrival of B.B. King*. Garden City, New York: Doubleday, 1980.

Scott, Frank. *The Down Home Guide to the Blues*. Pennington, NJ: a cappella books, 1991.

Welding, Pete, and Toby Byron. *Bluesland*. New York: Dutton, 1991.

Notes on the Contributors

Rob Bowman is an authority on the history of Stax records and is the author of the forthcoming *The Stax Records Story* (Schirmer Books, 1997). He teaches at the University of Toronto.

Stanley Dance, born in Braintree, England, was first attracted to jazz in 1926. First coming to the U.S. in 1937, he has produced many jazz records and written several books, including *The World of Duke Ellington* and *The World of Earl Hines*.

Colin Escott, residing currently in Toronto, has authored *The Sun Records Story* (1991), *Hank Williams* (1994), and *Tatooed on Their Tongues* (1996).

Nothing is known of Tam Fiofori.

Barret Hansen has written books, and produced audio tapes, records, and videos under the pseudonym of "Dr. Demento."

Scott Jordan is a New Orleans–based journalist.

Jim Kerekes and Dennis O'Neill maintain the web site, http://www.worldblues.com.

Michael Lydon is a writer and musician who lives in New York City. A founding editor of *Rolling Stone,* Lydon is the author of four books, *Rock Folk, Boogie Lightning, How to Succeed in Show Business by Really Trying,* and *Writing and Life.* He is currently writing a biography of Ray Charles and has just released his second album, *Love at First Sight.*

Richard Middleton is a Reader in Music and Cultural Studies at the Open University in Great Britain. He has authored several books on popular music, including *Pop Music and the Blues* (1972) and *Studying Popular Music* (1990), in addition to editing since the late 1980s the annual *Popular Music* for Cambridge University Press.

Jas Obrecht is a regular contributor to *Guitar Player* and other magazines on guitar.

Jerry Richardson is a professor of Musicology and Guitar Studies at Southeast Missouri State University, Cape Girardeau, Missouri. He writes that, prior to completing his doctorate at Memphis State University, for over 25 years he backed up "such artists as Ed Shaughnessy, the Drifters, the Shirelles, Bob Hope, and others."

Jim Roberts was a columnist with *The Tri-State Defender*.

Gene Santoro, a prolific writer on rock, jazz, blues, and pop, is the author of *Dancing in Your Head: Jazz, Blues, Rock, and Beyond*.

Charles Sawyer wrote the first biography of B.B. King. He is a Boston-based music critic who writes on blues and jazz.

Harold Steinblatt has long been an editor at *Guitar World* magazine.

Tom Wheeler has written several books on guitar history, including *The Guitar Book*.

Permissions

Stanley Dance: "Interview (1967)," reprinted from *Jazz* by permission of the author.

Colin Escott: "B.B. King: Guitar Strumming Realizes Ambition to Cut Original Platters," reprinted, revised, from *Goldmine* (April 29, 1994), and "In the Studio: 1991" by permission of the author.

Tam Fiofori, "Rapping with the King" from *Changes,* by permission of the publisher.

Barret Hansen: "The Influence of B.B. King (1968)," reprinted by permission of the author.

Scott Jordan: "It's Good to Be the King," reprinted from *Offbeat* (May 1995) by permission of the author.

Jim Kerekes and Dennis O'Neill: "Discography," reprinted from their web site, http://www.worldblues.com, with some alterations. Copyright © 1996 by Jim Kerekes and Dennis O'Neill, used by permission.

B.B. King: "My Ten Favorites," reprinted from Jim Ferguson's *The Guitar Player Book* (Grove, 1983) by permission of the publisher.

Michael Lydon: "B.B. King," reprinted from *Rock Folk* (1971) by permission of the author. Copyright © 1971 by Michael Lydon.

Richard Middleton: "The Sophisticated Tradition," reprinted from *Pop Music and the Blues* (1972) by permission of the author. Copyright © 1972 by Richard Middleton.

Jas Obrecht: "B.B. King & John Lee Hooker," reprinted from *Blues Guitar* (Miller Freeman, 1993) by permission of the publisher.

Jerry Richardson: "Analysis of B.B. King's Guitar Style," reprinted from his 1987 doctoral dissertation, by permission of the author. Copyright © 1987 by Jerry Richardson.

Jerry Richardson and Rob Bowman: "Conversation with B.B. King," reprinted from *Black Perspectives in Music* (1989) by permission of Jerry Richardson.

Jim Roberts, "From Itta Bena to Fame," reprinted from *The Tri-State Defender*, March 29, 1952, with permission of the publisher.

Gene Santoro: "E Pluribus Bluesman," reprinted from *down beat* by permission of the author. Copyright © 1990 by Gene Santoro.

Charles Sawyer: "Remembering My 1980 Biography" and "The Legacy: Keep the Hammer Down," reprinted from *B.B. King Der Legendare Konig Des Blues* (Hannibal Verlag, 1995), by permission of the author. Copyright © 1995 by Charles Sawyer.

Harold Steinblatt: "Blues is King," reprinted from *Guitar World* (July 1991) by permission of the publisher.

Tom Wheeler and Jas Obrecht: "B.B. King," reprinted from *Blues Guitar* (Miller Freeman, 1993) by permission of the publisher.

Otherwise, every effort has been made to identify the sources of original publication of these essays and make full acknowledgments of their use. If any error or omission has occurred, it will be rectified in future editions, provided that appropriate notification is submitted in writing to the publisher or editor (P.O. Box 444, Prince St., New York, NY USA 10012-0008).

Index

About the Editors

Richard Kostelanetz has written and edited many books about contemporary music, including, as author, *Fillmore East: Recollections of Rock Theater* (Schirmer, 1995) and *John Cage (Ex)plain(ed)* (Schirmer, 1996) and as editor, *Nicholas Slonimsky* (Schirmer Books, 1994), *The Portable Baker's Biographical Dictionary of Musicians* (Schirmer, 1995), *Writings on Glass* (Schirmer, 1997), *The Frank Zappa Companion* (Schirmer, 1997), and *Classic Essays on Modern Music* (Schirmer, 1997).

Anson J. Pope is currently a student at Rutgers University, Newark, New Jersey, and plans to work in the music industry. He works as a dj at WRNU.